THE PRICE OF DEATH

HIKARU SUZUKI

The Price of Death

THE FUNERAL INDUSTRY IN
CONTEMPORARY JAPAN

STANFORD UNIVERSITY PRESS
STANFORD, CALIFORNIA

Stanford University Press
Stanford, California

© 2000 by the Board of Trustees of the
Leland Stanford Junior University

Printed in the United States of America
On acid-free, archival-quality paper

Library of Congress Cataloging-in-Publication Data

Suzuki, Hikaru.
    The price of death : the funeral industry in contemporary
Japan / Hikaru Suzuki.
        p.   cm.
    Includes bibliographical references and index.
    ISBN 0-8047-3561-1 (alk. paper)
        1. Undertakers and untertaking—Japan.   2. Funeral rites and
    ceremonies—Japan.   I. Title.

    HD9999.U53 J37 2001
    338.4'736375'0952—dc21   00-058336

Typeset by BookMatters in 11/14 Adobe Garamond

Original Printing 2000

Last figure below indicates year of this printing:
09   08   07   06   05   04   03   02   01   00

ACKNOWLEDGMENTS

I was very fortunate to meet many brilliant professors and colleagues during my undergraduate and graduate years at Beijing
University and Harvard. But above all others, James L. Watson
and Rubies S. Watson provided me with the support, motivation,
and encouragement that I needed to complete this book. Even to
this day I consider them my supervisors, mentors, and *senpai*
(person I look up to); without their guidance the book would not
have been published and my personality may not have been what
it is today.

I owe much to the president, Mr. Sakuma Susumu, and vice
president, Mr. Sakuma Tsunekazu, of Moon Rise Corporation,
who made my research possible. Their generous support and
interest were pivotal to my understanding of the funeral industry. I would like to thank all the Moon Rise staff members who
opened their minds to work with me: Higuchi-san, Kanzaki-
san, Momosaki-san, Kamatani-san, Nakamura-san, Ohshima-
san, Uchiumi-san, Imamura-san, Katoh-san, Euchidani-san,
Kobayashi-san, Araki-san, and Kajiwara-san patiently trained me
for the job and treated me as a daughter or sister. I also thank the

Toyoshima and Mitsutake families for making my stay in Kita-Kyushu so enjoyable. They, as well as the deceased and their families, are discussed in this book under pseudonyms.

I received much scholarly assistance outside of my department. Dr. Robert Smith generously answered my inquiries and shared ideas throughout the creation of the manuscript. Dr. Theodore Bestor was most altruistic in reading my manuscript with great thoroughness; his detailed critiques provided significant turning points in the structuring of this book. When I visited Japan, Dr. Akata Mitsuo showed me recent research on graves and funerals by Japanese folklorists, and kindly introduced me to other Japanese scholars.

Many writers and editors have helped me in checking grammar, structure, wording, and framing. Pam Summa revised the very first version, and Judy Holt later proofread and corrected the writing to turn it into a manuscript. It was further revised and rearranged through the effort and patience of Anna E. Friedlander and Muriel Bell at Stanford; without their interest the manuscript would not have been transformed into a book.

I would like to thank Timothy Grinsteiner, whose academic achievements have had tremendous impact not only on this book but also on my professional career goals. He gave me unlimited inspiration from the first day of my graduate studies. His boundless passion for learning and his tireless encouragement have kept up my enthusiasm and my belief in myself.

TABLE OF CONTENTS

Photographs follow page 120. Unless otherwise credited, all photographs are by the author.

FIGURES AND TABLES

Figures

Tables

To my father,
who taught me the value of life,
as part of my return gift for that which
I can never fully repay.

THE PRICE OF DEATH

INTRODUCTION:
COMMERCIAL FUNERALS
FOR CONTEMPORARY JAPANESE

One's afterlife is designed freely during one's life. Each person's death presents an
art crafted by its owner while alive. Thus, a "beautiful death" is nothing but a
reflection of a "beautiful life."

—Ichijō Shinya, *Romantic Death*

It was an early spring morning, and I was listening through an
open window to the sounds of chirping birds when a phone rang
at the Moon Rise Funeral Hall. The caller, a young man, told
Hayashi that a woman had passed away at her home. Because the
caller said that he was her relative, Hayashi asked for the deceased's name, address, and religious affiliation and the family's
choice of coffin. Hayashi and Kita then loaded a new coffin into a
company van and immediately departed for the deceased's house.
As they approached the residence, however, they sensed that
something was wrong—an elegant wreath of colorful flowers
decorated the door of the house. Confused, Kita asked Hayashi,
"Did the guy on the phone say that the deceased was 100 years
old?"[1] "No, he said the deceased was a young woman," replied
Hayashi. "It seems odd, but let's ask them," Kita said and rang the
doorbell. A woman in her fifties greeted them with a bright smile.
"We are from Moon Rise Funeral Hall. Your relative told us there
was a death in your family," explained Hayashi. The woman was
openly surprised and said quickly, "You must have made a mis-
take." "Is that true?" asked Hayashi. "We were told that a woman

named Kobayashi Midori had passed away," he said apologetically. By this time the woman had become upset; "That's my daughter, but she is not dead!" A young woman, apparently the "deceased" herself, came running and joined the conversation. "What's going on? Who is dead?" she asked. Hayashi described the phone call he had received. As soon as she heard that the caller had been a young man, she exclaimed, "That bastard!"

An hour later, Hayashi and Kita returned with an empty coffin but with their hands full of sweets. "What's all this?" their colleagues asked when Hayashi and Kita distributed the sweets. "Our so-called deceased wasn't dead," explained Mr. Hayashi. "She's alive and kicking, and she's getting married tomorrow. Her rejected ex-boyfriend was the caller," Kita explained. "The mother of the bride was so embarrassed she gave us these sweets." As they were eating, the curious funeral staff asked, "What happened to the bride?" and Kita continued, "She was furious and cursing that guy." The office was full of smiles by then. "So after all, it was an April Fool's joke!" one said. "That ex-boyfriend was pretty smart to think of such a thing," remarked another.

Although the prank played on the daughter had been appalling, I found it interesting that the incident neither devastated the bride nor frustrated the funeral staff. However, when I related the episode to a woman in her eighties she was flabbergasted. Not only was she astonished that someone would dare to commit such an affront, but in particular she was deeply puzzled that the family did nothing about it afterward. "In my time, such an incident would not be settled until the boy's parents had apologized," she explained to me.

How can the different reactions of the younger and older generations to this episode be explained? It is not unknown for such pranks (*iyagarase*) to take place. Perpetrators have ordered numerous dishes from a sushi restaurant or an expensive item from a department store to be delivered to the house of a victim, who is then obligated to pay the bill. Though such hoaxes have long taken place, the funeral venue is new. Certainly lying about deaths and funerals is rarely acknowledged as humorous even today. As the grandmother told me, such a prank would not have occurred when she was young. However, although the prank was socially unacceptable, its use of death and funerals is undeniably significant because none involved took the practical joke very seriously. The funeral staff who visited the house and unintentionally helped perpetrate the joke dealt with the episode patiently. Despite the distasteful nature of the ex-boyfriend's revenge on the daughter, neither she nor her mother considered taking informal or formal action against him. Their reactions indicate a dramatic shift in the attitude toward funerals and death in Japan—they are no longer negatively associated with impurity, pollution, and superstition. It is these changes in views about death and in funerary practices that this book examines.

Research on the Commercialization and Consumption of Funerals

Earlier studies of death rituals have focused on communities and on the observed practices of the community members—household, lineage, and clan (see Chapter 2). Another area of Japanese scholarship has focused on mortuary rites and on memorial services such as household rites, ancestor worship, and grave-site ceremonies. In contrast, few studies have investigated contemporary funerals and providers of commercial funeral services in Japan. One of the few scholarly publications on the Japanese funeral industry is *Discussion of Funeral Culture* (*Sōsōbunkaron*), a volume edited by the Funerary Research Association (*Sōsōbunka Kenkyūkai*) and published in 1993.[2] The book provides a general description of the funeral industry and funeral practices but does not analyze the changes in funeral practices and their implications.

What is still missing in the overall picture is a "processual analysis" (Moore 1986), namely, an examination of the changes between funeral practices in a community-based society and funeral practices in today's more capitalistic society. This lacuna is the reason for my study, in which I attempt to bridge the gap between the research on community rituals and studies of commercialized ceremonies; to accomplish this I have examined funerary practices through the lens of a funeral company. I analyze how Japanese funerary customs have been changed by the funeral industry and the funeral industry's role in shaping Japanese cultural practices. Subsequently, I suggest implications for the production and consumption of funeral services in contemporary Japan.

Central to the endeavor is the distinction between two key terms, "funeral rituals" (*sōshiki*) and "funeral ceremonies" (*sōgi* or *osōshiki*). I use the former to mean "community-based funerals" (or later, community funerals), and the latter to refer to the "commercial funerals" marketed by the industry. "Funeral rituals" was the only term used for funerals in Japan before World War II. Today, however, they are commonly referred to as funeral "ceremonies" because, according to some, "funeral rituals" is considered in bad taste, even vulgar. This shift in terminology reflects changes not only in the image but, more important, in the structure of funerals and the values surrounding death. Community funerals reflected the participants' fear of death, which they believed caused the release of malevolent spirits. The decomposition of the physical remains was another source of fear. The ritual's purpose was to usher the deceased's spirit safely to the other world and to strengthen family ties as well as the relationship between the deceased's family and community members. In contemporary funeral ceremonies, the widespread use of cremation and the comprehensive services that the funeral industry provides have virtually erased the concept of the impurity of death. Professionals prepare, arrange, and conduct commercial funeral ceremonies, leaving the bereaved only the fees to pay. Deprived of the common ground on which funeral rituals united communities, funeral ceremonies cement the "system of different and special functions united by definite relationships" generated by the development of job specialization (Durkheim 1984, 83); they solidify the ties between the bereaved and the members of groups to which they belong, including the colleagues of the deceased.

The shift from community funeral rituals to commercial funeral ceremonies is manifested in the commoditization, commercialization, mass consumption, and professionalization of funerals. Because "commoditization lies at the complex intersection of temporal, cultural, and social factors" (Appadurai 1986, 15), various elements such as the migration of families into cities, the increase of nuclear families over households of extended kin, and the progress of work specialization have contributed to the transition. I believe, however, that the all-inclusive handling of the corpse was pivotal to the change. The commercialization of the treatment of physical remains—removal of the deceased, encoffining, transporting the body to a crematorium—contributed to funeral professionalization and the formalization of ceremonies into a commodity (a totalized service). Inasmuch as the treatment of the corpse functioned to unite cultural values, by taking over this responsibility the funeral industry further weakened the basis of the already attenuated community solidarity.

This investigation of contemporary funerals and the role of the funeral industry in Japan is separated into three thematic inquiries: the representation and reproduction of cultural values and practices, the objectification of values and cultural change, and differences in cultural homogeneity. After introducing previous research on funerals and the history of Japanese funerals in Chapters 1 and 2, I explore these themes in Chapters 3–7 and the Conclusion. First, in Chapters 3 and 4, I describe the mass production and mass consumption of commercial funerals. They reveal the influence of the funeral industry in conventionalizing cultural practices by creating a funerary system similar to what Bourdieu calls the structure of habitus (Bourdieu 1977). In Chapters 5 and 6, I examine how specialization in funerary performances serves to represent and regenerate cultural values and practices. In Chapter 7, I explain how a marketing process medi-

ates changing cultural values and how the commoditization of a
funeral ceremony serves to objectify the changing concepts of
dying, death, and the deceased in contemporary Japan. The last
chapter addresses the implications of the shift from community
funeral rituals to the mass consumption of commercial ceremonies; I conclude that the transition has produced a cultural homogeneity comprising individual differences in contemporary
Japan.

The aforementioned themes correspond to the interactions
taking place among three components: cultural values, industries
(commodity or services), and consumers, all within a culture.
Similarly, the funeral industry, consumers of funeral services, and
Japanese values related to death are mutually dependent and responsible for supporting and representing cultural practices as
well as changing them. Figure 1 illustrates the relationships and
interactions among these three components.

The argument of the model is that the interactions among
consumers, values, and industries are all responsible for the
change, reproduction, and continuation of cultural values and
practices. People's satisfaction with products and services and
their consumption patterns demonstrate current cultural values
and practices. These values and the repetition of these practices
lead to mass production and mass consumption, which in turn
help generate ranges of heterogeneous forms and shapes within an
overall homogeneous cultural structure. Finally, the commoditization of a product serves as an opportunity to mediate changes
in culture. The commoditization process, however, does not always reach its end; a new product turns into a "commodity" only
when it has embodied a value through exchanges. Thus, marketing success depends on a product's capacities and chances (with
financial, promotional, and other assistance) to objectify a value
internally. Moreover, the successful commoditization and the
objectification of values are parallel processes that represent
changes in cultural values, and as a consequence bring forth a new
cultural practice. I consider exchanges and the circular interac-

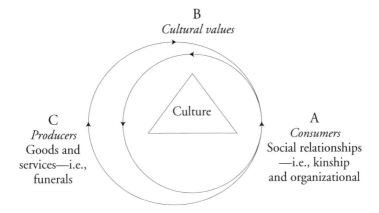

FIGURE I.   Tripartite interactions

tions A→B→C→A and A→C→B→A to be the mechanisms that produce both the continuation of cultural practices and the transition of cultural values.

Research Setting

"I wish to beautify death." So begins Ichijō Shinya's book *Romantic Death.*[3] Ichijō is the vice president of the Moon Rise funeral company, where I conducted my field research. He asks: "Are beautiful, fulfilling, peaceful, enjoyable, and happy funerals designed in our society today?" and goes on to say, "For a long time the Japanese vision of death has been of the underground (*chika eno manazashi*) and not of the celestial (*tenjō eno manazashi*). Now is the time to change the image of death by transforming funerals" (Ichijō 1991, 4, 7). He believes it is the duty of the funeral industry to introduce the poetics of death (9–10).

Ichijō sees the task of ushering the spirits of the deceased to the moon as the ultimate romantic ceremony. He goes so far as to suggest that a monument should be raised on the moon so that all humankind can look up and commune with the dead. While his celestial vision may be unrealistic now, I was intrigued by his determination to reconstitute a unique poetics of death within the formal services offered by the contemporary funeral industry.

At the end of *Romantic Death*, Ichijō mentions that his father, the president of Moon Rise, Inc., had majored in Japanese folklore during his undergraduate years at Kokugakuin University. By the time I turned to the last pages of his book, I was determined to conduct my fieldwork at his company. I knew nothing about Moon Rise and had no contacts among executives in the funeral industry. I simply called Ichijō the next morning. When he answered the phone, I said, "I was inspired by your book and would like to conduct my field research at your company for at least six months." I explained to him my desire to research the transformation of Japanese death rituals as my Ph.D. project at a university in the United States. Whatever I said seems to have aroused his curiosity. Within a week, I met Ichijō, the president of the company, Sakuma, and other top executives. I gave them the letter of recommendation that my academic adviser had prepared for me, and then, after answering numerous questions regarding my research, I was told that I could begin anytime and could conduct my research for as long as I needed to.

Moon Rise, Inc., is located in the city of Kita-Kyūshū in Fukuoka Prefecture, in the northernmost part of the Island of Kyūshū, facing Kan-Mon Channel. The city is composed of five subdivisions and as of 1992 had a population of about a million (1,020,877). Moon Rise, Inc. was built in 1966, and its total sales in 1993 were approximately 26 billion yen. Moon Rise's business includes the marketing of funeral and wedding services and the managing of hotels, brokers, and tourist agencies. The locations of these activities are dispersed from Hokkaido to Okinawa; however, its funeral business is concentrated in the Kyūshū region. My dissertation was based on nine months of fieldwork in Japan (October 1994–June 1995), including seven months at Moon Rise and two months of library research.

Moon Rise's president and founder, Sakuma Susumu, is responsible for establishing both the wedding and funeral businesses. I was amazed by the breadth of his interests, but what impressed me most was his attitude toward business. In one corner of his traditional Japanese house is a huge library filled with books, journals, and magazines from the fields of folklore, anthropology, and sociology. He appeared to have all the books available on Japanese death rituals, and his collection of contemporary funeral studies was especially impressive. He said to me in his library one day: "In order to design funerals, I have to study them. It is our mission to seek what is best for the Japanese and attempt to combine knowledge and practice." His point was a powerful reminder to me that business today cannot stand solely on profit-making, but must also nurture creativity based on a deep understanding of the culture.

To conduct my fieldwork, I worked for several months as a typical employee of Moon Rise. Wearing the company uniform, I attended funerals, wakes, and bathing ceremonies at the Kokura Moon Rise funeral auditorium. I occasionally visited other Moon Rise funeral halls in Kita-Kyūshū as well as a city crematorium. While working as a member of the funeral staff, I also had the advantage of talking regularly with the president and the vice president about business and what I thought about my experiences. I was lucky that Sakuma and his son were tremendously generous in their support of my research, allowing me to cross boundaries between task specializations, between genders, and between hierarchical distinctions, boundaries that are closed to other employees. I hope these interactions have provided me with a well-synthesized picture of commercial funeral processes, the professional workers who conduct them, and the executives who direct and market them.

Before turning to my study of the contemporary Japanese funeral industry and its professionals, in Chapter 1 I describe anthropological discourse and Japanese folklore studies of death rituals discussed in Chapter 2. Anthropological studies of death rituals examine the structure of cultural values and social relationships and the pattern of cultural cohesion by analyzing the symbolic meanings of exchanged goods and rituals. Folklorists and scholars who focus their research on Japanese death rituals concentrate on ancestor worship and mortuary rituals linked to the household system, deities, and Japanese cosmology.

In order to make clear the scope of changes from the community ritual to the commercial ceremony, Chapter 2 introduces the process of community funerals, describes the structure of Japanese death rituals before World War II, and provides a brief history of the funeral business from the emergence of funeral parlors to the development of the funeral industry. Community death rituals were structured from four ritual processes: the rites of attempted resuscitation, the rites of breaking bonds, the rites of ascendance to Buddhahood, and the rites of memorial services (Akata 1980, 125–45; 1986, 35–120). Fundamental to these ritual phases was the perception of the impurity of the spirit and the corpse. In community funerals, community members were responsible for placating the spirit and cleansing the impurity, actions that were key factors in maintaining solidarity among the community's members.

Funeral parlors emerged along with the expansion of a wealthy class that wished to demonstrate its social status with elaborate funerals, whereas the emergence of the funeral company is closely connected with poverty in the postwar era. The development and dissemination of commercial funerals, however, paralleled the processes of modernization, commercialization, and "individuation" (Dore 1958). Chapter 2 shows how funeral companies began to take over the responsibility of death rituals by expanding the tasks of handling the corpse and acquiring knowledge of community funerals.

Chapters 3 and 4 describe present-day funeral ceremonies as conducted by funeral professionals. First, Chapter 3 examines how funeral professionals treat the deceased and interact with the bereaved from the announcement of death to the wake. The time before the funeral ceremony is characterized by the negation of death, during which the deceased is "alive" in the minds of the bereaved. By treating the corpse as a living body, funeral professionals actively support the bereaved's perceptions.

Chapter 4 follows the process from the funeral ceremony to the seventh-day memorial service, which corresponds to the rites of separation, transition, and incorporation. The major distinction between community and commercial funerals is the disappearance of the impurity concept in contemporary funerals. Examination of commercial funerals reveals that, except for a vestigial presence during cremation, the impurity concept has disappeared. Unlike community funerals, commercial funerals are highly compressed formal ceremonies that depend heavily on funeral professionals. This chapter also describes variations in funerals according to the age, gender, occupation, religious beliefs, conditions of death, and ethnicity of the deceased.

Chapters 5 and 6 examine the representation and regeneration of cultural values and practices by focusing on funeral professionals. Funeral professionals include employees inside and outside of Moon Rise. Funeral staff, part-timers, assistants, and funeral conductors are Moon Rise employees, while bathing service staff, cremators, ash collectors, and priests are not. The division of work and interactions among the staff not only express current cultural values associated with commercial funeral ceremonies, but also reflect the professional boundaries and hierarchical differences among them. Specifically, handling the corpse and assisting the bereaved are important tasks determined by rank. What is significant about the power structure is that hierarchical position is not based on impurity but on the responsibilities of the individual tasks. Although cremation is still attached to the concept of impurity, other funerary tasks are considered virtually free of pollution. With this assumption, I believe that the rigid boundary distinctions and specialized tasks among funeral professionals function to support the continuation of commercial funeral practices.

Chapter 7 highlights the objectification of values and the

process of commoditization. I postulate that contemporary funeral services mediate and help cultural values take form by introducing new products and services. Marketing of a new product,
or the commoditization process, is carried out through tripartite
interactions among the value system, industry, and consumers.
During this period, customers question a product's meaning,
benefits, and worth, while company salesmen communicate and
translate the expectations and experiences of customers. A successful product, however, is one on which a value is bestowed and
objectified in a visible form. I discuss the complexity of the commoditization process by using the example of the bathing ceremony, a new service launched by Moon Rise during my
fieldwork. By describing its progression from design, production,
and marketing to commodity, I show how a product remains
merely a product until someone is willing to exchange something
of value for it. Following Georg Simmel's claim that "value is determined by exchange just as the converse is true" (Simmel 1971,
47), I argue that the key to the transition from product to commodity lies in obtaining cultural value through the interaction
and exchange of ideas that occurs between producer and consumers. This marketing process provides opportunities for a new
product, in its physical form, to be evaluated against existing and
changing cultural values. The marketing of the bathing ceremony
reveals a process in which the new service emerged as a channel
for Japanese consumers to express their feelings about death,
dying, and the deceased.

The Conclusion addresses the theoretical approach to cultural
homogeneity and differences discussed earlier. I examine how the
shift from community funerals to funeral ceremonies corresponds
to the generation of new cultural values and the patterns of social
relationships, and illustrate how the funeral industry serves to
maintain these changes. In this analysis I place the meaning of funeral services within the discourse of the commercialization and
mass consumption of commodities. Some nineteenth-century
theorists (notably Marx) considered the capitalist mode of pro-

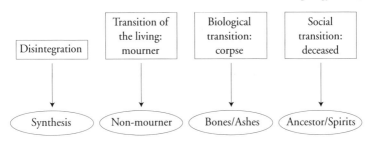

FIGURE 3. Hertz's scheme of disintegration to synthesis

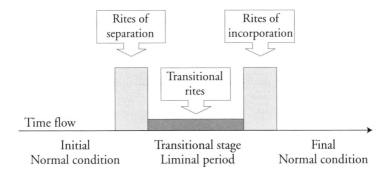

FIGURE 4. Van Gennep's rites of passage. *Source*: Data from Edmund Leach's "Rites of Transition," in *Culture and Communication* (New York: Cambridge University Press, 1976), 78; Loring M. Danforth, *The Death Rituals of Rural Greece* (Princeton, N.J.: Princeton University Press, 1982), 36.

vided the rituals, which otherwise seem undifferentiated and naturally continuous, into three components: the rites of separation, transitional rites,[1] and the rites of incorporation (Van Gennep).

Like Hertz's, the basis of Van Gennep's differentiation of these stages is the idea that the transition of the dead corresponds to the mourning stages of the living.[2] Van Gennep also applies his theory of the rites of passage universally: he postulates that in all cultures, whether technologically advanced or not, death rituals are composed of a structure of separation, liminality/margin, and incorporation/aggregation. For example, death rituals in rural Greece start with the funeral as a rite of separation and continue with the liminal period, spanning the time from the end of the funeral to the burial rites and rites of exhumation (see Danforth, 43). The liminal or mourning period is lifted when the decomposed remains of the dead are exhumed. The rites of incorporation take place when the deceased's remains are confined in their final resting place, the village ossuary (55–56).

Van Gennep's scheme of rites of passage, moreover, is important in defining the term "death ritual." A death ritual is composed of sets of rites—prewake rites, wake, vigil, funeral, and mortuary rites (e.g., burial, cremation, exhumation, secondary burial, double burial, reburial, and ancestor worship). Thus I define a death ritual as *the protracted process of accumulative rites that takes the living through various mourning phases according to the way the living perceive the condition of the deceased.* What Hertz and Van Gennep have delineated are the dynamics of death rituals engendered in different cultures by a single biological phenomenon—death.

Further studies on death rituals can be crudely categorized by their focus on three major questions: (1) What do symbolic meanings expressed in death rituals imply about cultural values? (2) What do exchanges and presentations in death rituals reveal about personal relations among the deceased, kin, wife-givers, and wife-takers? (Wife-givers are members of a family, clan, lineage or kin group from which a bride comes; wife-takers are members of those same groups whose groom receives a bride.) (3) What effect do death rituals have on the social collective (lineage, clan, or community)? These questions not only reveal the function of death rituals but also highlight the nexus—values, personal relationships, and order—around which a society is structured.

VALUES AND SYMBOLISM IN DEATH RITUALS

Death rituals are the crystallization of cultural values and symbolism. The rituals, as well as the food and objects associated with them, provide manifestations of multiple encoded symbols. In Chinese death rituals, for instance, the social role of the living corresponds to the different transitional stages of the deceased, following their categorization as yin/negative and yang/positive elements. For the Cantonese, the decaying flesh (yin in essence) and the release of the spirit from the body are the source of death pollution (Watson, J. 1982, 158–59).[3] The burden of pollution is shared by community members but is mostly absorbed by the chief mourner and the women mourners (155–86): "Male mourners (i.e., direct descendants of the deceased) take on pollution in descending order of seniority. The most polluted of all is the chief mourner—the senior son or designated heir" (170). Next to the chief mourner the women are the most contaminated. Married daughters and daughters-in-law must be present at all funerals and are expected to rub their unbound hair against the coffin in order to absorb death pollution (172–73). Women also attend funerals as their husbands' representatives in order to absorb their pollution (178). Thus, during the decomposition of the physical corpse, Cantonese men subject themselves to death pollution only when obligated by specific, usually filial, ties, whereas women are the designated recipients of death pollution, irrespective of their particular bonds to the deceased. Once the flesh has completely decayed, after burial and exhumation, the deceased's remains produce reverse effects. At this time, the flesh-free bones, being yang in essence (as opposed to the yin of the flesh) constitute, exclusively, the male being and realm; instead of pollution, the bones bring benefits and good auspices to the living descendants (112–15).

The opposition of flesh and bone, death, and fertility in Chinese funerals is elaborated by Stuart E. Thompson and Emily Martin Ahern. Thompson analyzes the opposing elements by deciphering the code of food presentations, namely rice and pork. Rice, Thomson explains, is associated with ancestors because it is grown on the land inherited from them. Similarly "bones are ancestral stuff" and are retained because they are "connected directly to your ancestors through your father's semen" (Thompson, 93). In turn, semen is considered to be produced by the consumption of rice; thus the three substances—rice, bones, and semen—are all interconnected aspects of a single unity.

The other central presentation in the Chinese funeral is pork. In the Yun-lin region in Taiwan, it is taboo for the surviving agnatic descendants to consume pork during a funeral because it is associated with the deceased's flesh and "would be like eating the dead person's flesh" (96). In much the same way that the male, rice, bones, and semen are linked, so are women, pork, and fertility (100). The dichotomy can be summarized as the purity of men versus the pollution of women. According to Ahern, the source of women's pollution is linked to childbirth and menstrual fluids; her proposition explains why women are associated with the corpse and death and are pushed into the role of absorbing pollution for men (Ahern 1988, 164–66). At the same time, the very substances that emanate from women's reproductive organs and that relegate women to a lower status than men are the capital of women's unveiled power (168–73).

The Merina funerals of Madagascar are similar to the Chinese in that they present a conceptual link between women, sexuality, and pollution (Bloch 1981, 1982). It is the women who are expected to weep, and are obliged to have contact with the corpse and carry the dead to the tomb (Bloch 1982, 215–17). Huntington explains that the values of the Bara, an ethnic group in Madagascar, are based on two oppositional categories—"absolute order" and "absolute vitality" (Huntington; Metcalf and Huntington). For them, death is a temporary imbalance of absolute order, composed of concepts such as maleness, fatherhood, semen, bone, death, sterility, and the tomb (Huntington, 76–77; Metcalf and Huntington 1991, 114–15). Central to the Bara funerals are erotic songs and dances that provide an opportunity to initiate sexual relationships, even to the extent of inviting incestuous behavior (Metcalf and Huntington, 116–30). The consequence is total chaos and disorder "in opposition to the fundamental Bara principle of morality and social order" (127). So the question remains, what is the meaning of this conceptual dualism?

The cosmological dualism expressed in funerals connotes fertility and celebrates the cycle of male dominion. Bara funerals, for instance, portray male control over female vitality as a means of regaining order and overcoming the disorder caused by death (Metcalf and Huntington, 122). Sexual songs, dances, and contests that induce fertility counteract the loss entailed in biological death. The burial also "takes the form of a double metaphor of sexual intercourse and birth" (129). During the transfer of the coffin to the tomb, men, who carry the coffin, break through a "blockade" of women.

As in the Bara culture, in Cantonese funerals the symbol of fertility is prominent. Notably, only daughters-in-law wear a green cloth on the belt of their mourning gown on the day of the funeral (Watson, J. 1982, 174). The color green represents spring, growth, and fertility. the same green cloth appears as the centerpiece in the back-strap harnesses used for carrying infants; this symbolizes that a component of death pollution is "essential for the biological reproduction of the agnatic line" (ibid.). Thus, funerals in certain cultures represent the dualisms that compose the culture's cosmological perspective of life and demonstrate primacy over one side of the dualism—fertility, women, and pollution—only to regenerate and fortify its opposite realm.

PERSONAL RELATIONSHIPS REFLECTED IN DEATH RITUALS

The performances in death rituals, especially the exchanges of presentations, play a pivotal role in reaffirming solidarity within a group and in continuing, recreating, and readjusting alliances between two groups. Property inheritance is of particular importance in the exchanges between the living and the dead. The transfer of property from the dead to the heir is precipitated by the heir's offerings to the deceased in the form of ancestral rites (Goody 1962; Ahern 1973; Freedman; Watson, J. 1982). Property can be divided into two categories, "partible," the property transmitted individually, and "impartible," which is the property pre-served in a single unity by a corporate group (Goody 1962, 321). The designated heir has the obligation to perform specific rites that indicate his position. According to Jack Goody, among the LoDagaa in northwestern Ghana, the heir is assigned to find money that has been hidden by the deceased and distribute part of it to other bereaved family members and to the grave diggers and musicians so as to display the wealth and the worthiness of the deceased (50). Among the Cantonese, the chief mourner does not wear a prophylactic red patch on his garb in order to ensure that he absorbs the maximum death pollution, and he does not avert his eyes during the dangerous moments in the funeral (Watson, J. 1982, 170). Once the heir has demonstrated his obli-gations through ritual performances, he is given the privileged re-sponsibility to worship his ancestors.[4]

While ancestor worship is the province of individual heirs, an-cestral rites operate as a centripetal force for the corporate group that shares an impartible inheritance or estate. Cantonese lineages are composed of exclusively male agnates who participate in the collective ancestral rites of their founding ancestor at their ances-tral hall or gravesites (Goody 1962; Ahern 1973; Freedman; Watson, J. 1982; Watson, R.). The limitations and boundaries of the lineage are revealed in the division of pork (Watson, R., 222; Watson, J. 1989). The pork is considered a gift from the ancestors themselves, because it is paid for from the estate they bequeathed. The pork is divided equally among male lineage members with exacting precision. This equal division of pork both identifies each member within the lineage and reaffirms and rejuvenates the lineage as a corporate unit (Watson, R., 222).

In the case of the LoDagaa, the presentation of a cow to the dead differentiates the kinship and descent organizations in the two groups of LoDagaa, the LoDagaba and the LoWiili,[5] and functions to solidify the link between the clans (Goody 1962, 156–82). For the LoDagaba, the provision of the cow is a responsibility of the matriclan in general, whereas among the LoWiili it comes from the deceased's agnates (ibid.). Thus, the disparity in the role of funeral obligations to the matriline or the patriline "provides descent and local groupings with a means of cohesion" (157).

The gifts exchanged between the living during death rituals are also significant for reaffirming, recreating, and readjusting alliances between two or more groups. For example, in Melanesian societies, pigs are frequently killed to pay the kinfolk of the maternal clan of the dead (Strathern, 209). The provision of pork, which is meant to compensate for the loss of the deceased, is also connected to the system of bridewealth (ibid.). The pork is received by the mother's local lineage, the mother's mother's local lineage, and so on. Thus, a death releases exchanges and compensation payments among the living and serves to solidify alliances between wider subclans (209–20). The death rituals of the Makasse of eastern Indonesia also illustrate the effectiveness of life-giving exchanges (part of all Makasse funeral and mortuary rituals) in bringing together the wife-taker and wife-giver groups (Forman, 163–77). Among the deceased's descent groups, the wife-givers demand a buffalo from the wife-takers, who also feed the wife-givers rice and pork that the wife-givers have given to the wife-takers (165).

The reciprocity and commensality among the living provide opportunities not only to reaffirm alliances but also to terminate, negotiate, or readjust existing relationships. Pork again can symbolize the termination or the continuation of affinal relations in Cantonese culture. It is a custom in Cantonese funerals for a married-out daughter of the deceased (a daughter who has married into a different lineage or community) to make an offering of the head and tail of a pig (Thompson, 96; Watson, J. 1982, 177). One interpretation of this is that the pig's head and tail are repayment by the affines, balancing the exchange between the wife-giving and wife-taking families; the presentation terminates the relationship by paying off the debt (Watson, J. 1982, 177).[6]

In the "black rituals," or funerals, of the Mambai of East Timor, gifts are central to the adjustments between wife-givers and wife-takers. The presentations made by the wife-takers to the deceased's family are elaborate: "During a series of intense, often acrimonious confrontations with their wife-givers, [wife-takers] agree to make specific payments, calculated in breast-disks, goats, and money" (Traube, 210). Over the course of the black performances (*maeta*), all the hosts confront a number of different wife-giving and wife-taking groups, and in their transactions "tempo and verbal dexterity are considered essential" (211).

The confrontation between the Cantonese lineage members is expressed in the division of pork (Watson, R.). The dispute over the division of pork between descent groups is an attempt to create a new boundary that fixes the rights of members. In other words, the pork negotiations and resulting distribution parallel the changes in status within a lineage (Watson, R., 227). Thus, performances in death rituals, such as commensality and the exchanges of presentations are, as Rubie Watson states, not only passive but also active; they are "part of the process in which new order, new status, and power arrangements are created" (204).

DEATH RITUALS AS A MEANS TO SOCIAL ORDER

Earlier anthropologists such as James G. Frazer, Edward Tylor, and Emile Durkheim analyzed death rituals in order to evaluate cultural progress in an evolutionary framework. The fear of death was the focal point of their analysis. The differences between the "civilized" and the "primitive," Frazer asserted, derived from the latter's fear of the spirits of the dead (Frazer, 3–96). Tylor also posits that the primitives performed death rituals because of their fear of the unknown (Tylor, 113). Culturally different attitudes toward death were viewed as proof of inferior intelligence.

Although their explanations differ, Durkheim, Alfred Radcliffe-Brown, and Bronislaw Malinowski all agree that individual deaths can contribute to the solidarity of the social collective. For Durkheim, death rituals are the collective's unconscious reaction to the death of their members, a reaction resulting in intense psychological and emotional sentiments (Durkheim 1965). Gathering to mourn the dead becomes a means of reproducing the group's collective sentiments or the "collective consciousness"—the essential source for the unity of a group (ibid.). Radcliffe-Brown, in contrast, postulated that the purpose of death rituals is to "show the continued existence of the social bond when it is being weakened" (Radcliffe-Brown, 245). He argued that it is the reaffirming of the sense of grief and the customary obligations toward the deceased that bind members together. Malinowski's view is an incorporation of the two; he reasons that because the disturbed emotions of individuals afflict the stability of a group, death rituals become necessary and the "most powerful means of reintegration of the group's shaken solidarity" (Malinowski, 53).

Later anthropologists analyzed the effect of death rituals on social integration from other perspectives. For instance, Maurice Bloch looked at the significance of tombs among the Merina of Madagascar. For the Merina, the link between the people and their land takes a concrete and material form in the tomb (Bloch 1981, 139). Land is cultivated individually, but its ownership remains within the group. As I mentioned earlier, the Merina funerals emphasize the negative symbols of dualism—namely women, pollution, sorrow, and individuality (Bloch 1982, 218). Bloch argued that the very order of society is created by the dramatic antithetical negative symbolism of the ritual. As a corpse is buried in the tomb, the death of an individual is encompassed by the whole through the land that is shared collectively (Bloch 1981, 139). Thus the unity of the social order is "achieved through victory over individuals, women, and death itself" (Bloch 1982, 217).

Jonathan Parry examines how social and cosmological continuity are expressed by the treatment of the physical remains (Parry 1982). In Hindu death rituals, hierarchical distinction is fundamental in the Hindu caste structure, and pollution and impurity are the backbone of the maintenance of boundaries between different castes. Parry, however, states that "death pollution springs from the act of cremation rather than from the corpse or its physiological remains" (79). Once a body has been disinte-

grated by cremation, the basis of the class boundary itself is eliminated: "dualities are abolished, polarities are recombined" (100).
The act of cremation, then, dissolves the separate units of society
into an undifferentiated universe, through which the spirit attains
a timeless unity (Bloch and Parry 1982, 38).

Last, the pattern of property inheritance can control individuals, thus maintaining the social order. In Jack Goody's research,
the two groups of LoDagaa, the LoDagaba and the LoWiili, practice distinctive forms of inheritance (Goody 1962). In both cases,
sons' claims to property derive from a pattern of labor services
and their interpersonal ties to their close kin (426). A son of the
LoDagaba is expected to work for his mother's brother and tends
to establish his own fields, whereas a son of the LoWiili farms
with his father until the father dies. As a result, the LoWiili sons
inherit all property patrilineally. The LoDagaba sons inherit immovable property from their father (with no claim upon the father's other accumulated wealth), while they also inherit movable
property matrilineally. The performances and exchanges displayed in the death rituals of the two LoDagaa groups demonstrate "a public reformulation of social norms that itself serves as a
sanction on behavior" (30). "Without some (such) system of inheritance and succession of intergenerational transmission of
these exclusive rights, social life would be marked by disorganiza-
tion rather than by relative continuity" (ibid.).

In sum, anthropological studies on death rituals have concentrated on the value structure, the composition of dualisms, and
the ritual's effect in overcoming individual deaths through fertility, rebirth, renewal, recreation, continuation, and adjustments of
personal relations and the social order.

Research on Japanese Death Rituals

Yanagita Kunio's article "About Our Ancestors," originally published in 1946, drew scholars' attention to Japanese death rituals
(Yanagita 1975b), a topic that had become a central focus of

Japanese folklorists as well as Western scholars who specialized on Japan. Only a limited selection of this scholarship is discussed here, because my focus is on just the key issues. For this purpose, I divide the research into the three themes of impurity and cosmology, ancestors and ancestor worship, and graves and the afterlife.

IMPURITY AND COSMOLOGY IN JAPANESE DEATH RITUALS

Maurice Bloch states that "some funerary rituals only consist of the first of the two sides . . . pollution and [the] sad aspect of the funeral; the second half, the ideological creation of timelessness and fertility, is largely absent" (Bloch 1982, 229). Bloch's first statement on pollution applies to the Japanese case. The emphasis of Japanese death rituals is *not* on the negativity of female essence and the power of fertility. Japanese death rituals stress impurity, *kegare* (Mogami 1959, 1963; Gorai 1992; Inoguchi 1954, 1965; Saito; Shintani 1991, 1992; Smith, R. 1974; Yanagita 1975a). Folklorist Gorai Shigeru explains that the source of death pollution derives from the deceased's body and the spirit/soul, the *ki* (or *ch'i* in Chinese).

The corpse's impurity can inflict harm on the living if one either touches the decomposing body or draws near the raging and undisciplined spirit that the body has released (Gorai 1992, 1046). The classification of Japanese impurity as elaborated by Shintani is shown in Figure 5.

Since death impurity is contagious, it is important for those who come into contact with it to perform a purification rite (*harai* or *misogi)* by using neutralizers such as water, fire, and salt (Inoguchi 1965; Gorai 1992; Saito; Shintani 1992). For example, the bereaved who have conducted a bathing ritual for the deceased bathe themselves at the seaside; if they bathe at home, they sprinkle salt on their bodies before they wash (Saito, 106–7). It is also a custom for participants to wash their hands with water and scrub them with salt after returning from a cremation or a burial (Gorai 1992, 675; Saito, 100). Throughout the funeral process, incense, candles, or torches burn, because fire is considered a pow-

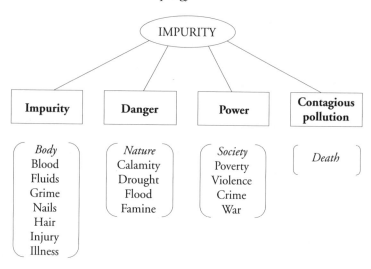

FIGURE 5.   The classification of impurity. *Source*: Data from Shintani.

erful means of casting out impurities (Saito, 167–68; Shintani 1992, 65). The other materials used in funerals are also intended to prevent impurities from entering the corpse as well as the bodies of the living. For example, sake—rice wine—is drunk before and after touching the deceased. Similarly, there is a custom of blowing sake on the deceased to get rid of impurities emanating from the body (Saito, 107–9). The sword and broom that are placed near the deceased, and the ropes worn by the bereaved, are intended to prevent contamination (ibid., 29–37, 103–5; Gorai 1992, 712–99, 342–44, 1010).

Regarding his statement about the nature of funerary rituals, Bloch suggests that some funerals consist of only one of two sides; that is, while pollution and the sad aspect of the funeral are present, the ideological creation of timelessness and fertility is absent (Bloch 1982, 229). Although fertility is not directly present in Japanese death rituals, both pollution and timelessness are prevalent and the interconnections between the two illuminate the dynamic operation of regeneration or reproduction in Japanese cosmology.

The term *kegare,* which I have so far translated as impurity or pollution, has an essential position in Japanese cosmology regarding regeneration. Japanese linear time is punctuated by phases that are vital (*hare*), normal (*ke*), and enervated (*kegare*). The meanings of these concepts have long been debated among Japanese scholars, but in this analysis they can best be interpreted as a tricyclic circulation of an increase in vitality or energy and a depletion of energy in the order of *hare, ke,* and *kegare* (Ito; Ohnuki-Tierney; Sakurai 1981).[7] *Ke* is identified with *ki,* implying the envelopment of spiritual energy (Sakurai 1981, 222; Miyata, 98). *Kegare,* in turn, is the exhaustion of *ke* or the condition in which *ke* is depleted (Sakurai 1981, 224; Miyata, 97–99). What eliminates *kegare* and fortifies *ke* is *hare* (Sakurai 1981, 224; Miyata, 101); here is the source of energy that "functions as a pump" (Sakurai 1981, 224) and reenergizes *ke.* In other words, the vitality of *hare* is absorbed by *ke*—a seed or a container, so to speak—which in turn facilitates the growth of life. Without the supply of *hare,* the seed gradually degenerates into the state of *kegare* (222). This circulation or triangulation is similar to Durkheim's model, not in its literal meaning but in the assumption that the alternation between the vitality of life and daily life is drawn from the power of the sacred and transferred to the profane phase (Durkheim 1965). Likewise, Japanese rituals, both funerals and festivals, proceed from the condition of *hare,* the opportunity to emanate energy.

Bloch suggests that the differences in funerary presentations "can probably be explained in terms of the different ways in which the source of creativity and the continuity is represented" (Bloch 1982, 229). The chief source of creativity and continuity in Japanese culture is rice (Tsuboi; Ohnuki-Tierney; Yanagita 1962). It is rice that is consumed in rituals on extraordinary days (*hinichijō* or *hare*), thereby becoming the source of vitality. It is crucial to note that the rituals of extraordinary days include both the positive/auspicious/peaceful/pure rituals of *hare* (i.e., marriages or harvest rituals), as well as the negative/inauspicious/fearful/impure rituals of *kegare* (i.e., funerals) (Sakurai 1981, 227; Namihira 1974, 237). This is because, despite the disparities, both the positive and the negative rituals generate vitality through the act of consuming rice. In contrast to the extraordinary days, daily life is considered to be a state of *ke*— that is, plain, ordinary, and without extra energy (Wakamori 1981, 245; Ishigaki 1983, 528; Tsuboi 1982, 419). In the past, the consumption of rice also differentiated the extraordinary from the ordinary (Miyata; Tsuboi; Ohnuki-Tierney).[8] It is not surprising that rice has been depicted as a life force for centuries since it has been "the food for commensality between humans and deities, on the one hand, and among humans, on the other" (Ohnuki-Tierney, 58). Therefore, the consumption of rice during Japanese death rituals propels and regenerates social life and the cosmic cycle (53–57).

ANCESTORS AND ANCESTOR WORSHIP

Ancestors and ancestor worship have received the most attention in Japanese death ritual research because they have a direct relation to the household, *ie*, the elementary structure on which Japanese society was based. Researchers have focused on two major questions: who are ancestors, and what are the characteristics of Japanese ancestor worship?

The Japanese concept of ancestorship is rooted in the structure of the household and ensures the continuity of the household (Akata 1986; Brown; Hozumi; Idota; Kirby; Ooms 1967, 1976; Smith, R. 1974, 1976; Takeda C. 1957, 1979; Tamamuro; Yanagita 1975b).[9] In the civil code before the postwar period, venerating one's household ancestors was decreed a national ethic (Hozumi). According to Yanagita Kunio, there are two ways one can become an ancestor (Yanagita 1975a, 170–74). One is through primogeniture, by leaving a legitimate heir to ensure the succession of the household. Another is to found a new household either by establishing it oneself or with the help of the main household (*honke*), thereby becoming a branch household (*bunke*). Yanagita's view of Japanese ancestors became the precedent, and hence most discussions on ancestors emphasized the lineal kin, the direct-descent line of households.

Further community studies, however, show that the range of ancestors varies regionally according to differences in the patterns of community social relations (e.g., Akata 1988; Embree; Beardsley, Hall, and Ward; Cornell and Smith; Dore 1958, 1978; Nakane 1967; Norbeck 1954, 1978; Smith, R. 1974, 1978). Akata Mitsuo documents the ways in which *dōzoku* households dominate in the eastern region of Japan, while in the western region linkage based on the community corporation prevails.[10] In each case, the differences in ancestor veneration parallel communal structures (Akata 1988, 56–57).

Robert Smith's detailed analysis of memorial tablets in the household Buddhist altar has demonstrated this variation in the concept of ancestors (Smith, R. 1974, 1976). Buddhist altars, which became more commonly used under the parochial system (*danka-seido*), were sites for memorial tablets that were the dwelling place or residence of ancestral spirits and therefore the object of ancestor worship (Takeda C. 1979, 25–26).[11] Smith's survey, conducted during the 1950s and 1960s, investigates the people represented by the tablets in the household Buddhist altar (Smith, R. 1976, 33–60). His results illustrate the differences in household ancestors according to various localities. None of the agricultural households of Takane in Iwata prefecture, which are based on the *dōzoku* structure, possessed tablets of the nonlineal or non-kin, who are "persons entirely unrelated in any way to any past or present member of the household either lineally or non-lineally" (44). In contrast, Sone in Mie prefecture, Yasuhara in Kagawa prefecture, and other urban areas like Tokyo, Osaka, and Kyoto, kept between 20 and 30 percent of nonlineal kin tablets on the household altar. Also, Yasuhara, a village based on *kō* or the community corporation, had the lowest percentage, 38.4, of lineal tablets for progenitors (45, 47). This research underscores not only the differences in the scope of ancestors by region, but also the distinctive characteristics of Japanese ancestor worship.

In general, Japanese ancestor worship is a socioreligious practice devoted to the continuation of the household system; priority is given to the maintenance of the household as a whole and not to the individuals who constitute it (see Akata 1986, 1988; Hozumi; Ooms 1967, 1976; Takeda C. 1957, 1979; Tamamuro; Yanagita 1975a). However, what is notable and particular about Japanese ancestor worship is that it venerates three categories of spirits: the lineal kin, the nonlineal kin, and the non-kin (who are wandering spirits or *muenbotoke*) (Ariga 1979; Kirby; Mogami 1979; Ooms 1976; Plath; Smith, R. 1976; Takeda C. 1979; Yanagita 1975b).[12]

The *muenbotoke*, or wandering souls, include three kinds of spirits: non-kin who died while traveling, from a natural catastrophe or through violence, such as in war; nonlineal kin members who had no offspring or spouse, as well as lineal kin, including mothers who died in childbirth, stillborn children, children, unmarried daughters, and divorced/returned daughters; and the family members' siblings or one's own siblings who married out (Takeda C. 1979, 35–36; Ooms 1967, 252, 283; 1976, 63–69; Smith, R. 1974, 49–54; 1976, 60). Whether or not wandering souls are malevolent is a topic debated among scholars (Ariga 1979; Kirby; Mogami 1979; Ooms 1976; Plath; Smith, R. 1976; Takeda C. 1979; Yanagita 1975a). Wandering souls in the first category, non-kin who have died by violence away from home, are always considered harmful and dangerous. They linger in the place where they die, bringing misfortune to the living unless they are cared for and placated. The second and third categories, however, are not inherently harmful ghosts; they wander only because they did not follow or live out the normal course of life (Ooms 1967, 254; Smith, R. 1974, 50), and are venerated with the household ancestors because they are pitied.

Wandering souls are worshipped along with ancestral household spirits both during the Festival of the Dead and on the New Year. One of the explanations suggested for venerating wandering souls "derives from compassion and fear" (Ooms 1976, 69). "The living venerate them together with the ancestral spirits for the purpose of placating their negativity for the good of the household" (Mogami 1979, 391). This practice of venerating wandering souls is significant not simply for understanding the household structure, but for grasping the nature of Japanese ancestor worship.

The diversity of spirits that are worshipped demonstrates the dual characteristics of Japanese ancestor worship: offerings to the spirits (*senzo-kuyō*) and veneration of the spirits (*sosen-sūhai*) (Smith, R. 1974, 1976). Robert Smith states that "the distinction between *sosen-kuyō*, where the spirits are prayed for, and *sosen-sūhai*, where they are prayed to, is that the major ancestors are more often prayed to and the minor ones more often prayed for (Smith, R. 1974, 128). *Sosen-kuyō* is the act of memorializing, consoling, and comforting the individual spirit, while *sosen-sūhai* is the veneration and worship of the collective ancestral spirits of the household (Smith, R. 1976, 61). "The nature of the prayers addressed to the ancestral spirits is without a doubt a function of the identity of those spirits" (Smith, R. 1974, 145). Descendants do not pray *for* ancestors who had authority and responsibilities in the household in life in contrast to other minor ancestors, but they pray *to* them, "for their spirits both exercise direct tutelary functions by virtue of positions held in life and have a claim on their descendants for comfort and support" (ibid.). By corollary, Japanese ancestors and the meaning of ancestor worship are distinguished by age and gender differences, the social status of the deceased, and the position of the deceased in his or her household.

GRAVES AND THE AFTERLIFE

Among Japanese folklorists, the double-grave system (*ryōbosei*) in mortuary practice has received much attention because it is closely connected with the transition of an impure corpse to a pure beneficial ancestor (Akata 1980, 1984, 1986, 1988; Haga; Harada; Inoguchi 1965; Mogami 1963; Shintani 1985, 1991; Takeda C. 1957; Tamamuro).

Unlike the single-grave system (*tanbosei*), the double-grave system utilizes two locations. The first site is the burial grave where the corpse is physically interred. The second site is the ceremonial grave where a monument is built (Akata 1980, 146; 1984, 102; Haga, 151; Inoguchi 1965, 190; Smith, R. 1974, 75; Takeda 1957, 100–103; Tamamuro, 144). In the single-grave system, the cremated bones or the corpse of the deceased is buried in the same location where the tombstone is erected (Akata 1980, 146–47; 1984, 102; Haga, 154). Although today the double-grave system is rare, it used to be widespread in the Kinki and Kantō areas (near Osaka and Tokyo), while in the northern and the western parts of Japan single graves were predominant (Akata 1980, 148; 1984, 102; Haga, 151; Inoguchi 1965, 190; Takeda C. 1957, 100–103; Tamamuro 1964, 144).[13]

The debate among Japanese folklorists about the double-grave system focuses on its historical origin and the reasons behind its evolution; scholars have not come to a consensus in four decades. Their main discussion concerns the functional separation between the location of the burial grave and the ceremonial grave. They have four major arguments.

The first is that the construction of a monument at a ceremonial grave derives from the tradition of a second burial (*kaisō-ikotsu*) of the bones at another site. It is thought that the construction of the stone monuments, which was influenced by Buddhist tradition, came to replace the ceremonial grave and the second burial. In other words, adherents of this theory claim that the double-grave system is an abbreviation of the older practice of second burial (Yanagita 1975a).

An alternative explanation is that the ceremonial grave comes from the concept of death impurity. Since a corpse is considered the source of impurity and believed to attract evil spirits and ghosts, burial graves were feared by the living. Visits to burial graves were limited to funerals and the 49-day mourning period, after which the living abandoned them (Mogami 1959, 1963). The site of the memorial grave, in contrast, was considered pure, benevolent, and auspicious for the living because it did not contain an impure physical body. The ceremonial grave, then, became the main location for ancestor veneration. Many scholars argue that the Japanese fear of death impurity is the reason for ceremonial graves, which are free of the deceased's remains (Inoguchi 1965, 190; Haga, 154; Mogami 1963, 170; Shintani 1991, 232; Takeda C. 1957, 101).

A third argument emphasizes the Japanese perception of the dead and the spirit's transition from newly dead to ancestor. Although the proponents of this theory agree that impurity and purity are linked to double-grave practices, they do not acknowledge this as the direct cause. Harada, for instance, claims that the ceremonial grave was established for the purpose of strengthening the veneration of the ancestral spirit (Harada, 247–48). Takeda Chōshū further believes that the burial grave is used exclusively for offerings to recently dead spirits, while the ceremonial grave is for the ancestors and ancestor worship (Takeda C. 1957, 102–5). This explanation of the double-grave system accounts for the Japanese perspective on the process of death—that over time the deceased's spirit is transformed into an ancestor.

A final view, proposed by Akata Mitsuo, links the double-grave system with the dissemination of stone monuments. He explains that the double-grave system is a relatively new phenomenon (it began in the Meiji period, 1868–1911) and derives from the Japanese custom of erecting memorial towers (*kuyōtō*) (Akata 1980, 154–55). He suggests that the second grave developed as a place for the construction of a stone monument as a miniature substitute for the memorial tower, but at a different location; similarly, the single grave is also the site of a stone monument like the memorial tower, but at the actual burial site (ibid.). This theory focuses on the way each community came to construct stone monuments at different locations. It views the double-grave system as a reflection of the power structure and social relations in a community.

Graves provide a key to understanding the Japanese perception of the afterlife, and also their perception of the ideal social ordering of communities. Impurity or pollution and the Japanese view of the dead and their transformation into ancestors are associated with the regeneration of life. In the Japanese cosmology, it is crucial for the living to provide offerings for the deceased of a household so that the spirit of the dead can be transformed from a benevolent spirit into an ancestral spirit, an ancestor, and finally an agricultural deity (Akata 1988; Matsudaira; Nakamura; Ohnuki-Tierney 1993; Yanagita 1975b; Orikuchi 1955a; Takeda C. 1979; Smith, R. 1974). The importance of the ceremonial grave is that the living benefit by speeding up the process of transforming newly dead spirits into pure ancestral spirits.

After 30 to 50 years, the ancestral spirits join the collective of household ancestors, thereby losing individual characteristics and becoming deified (Matsudaira). It is thought that they become the rice deities who secure the rice harvest as well as the harmony of the household (Akata 1988; Nakamura; Ohnuki-Tierney; Yanagita 1975c; Orikuchi 1955a; Takeda C. 1979). The process, however, does not stop there. The deity of the rice grain is supposed to attach spirits to the rice crop (Ito, 50). "The soul of [the] rice grain is not simply equivalent to deities but is identified more specifically as the *nigitama*, the positive power of divine purity" (Ohnuki-Tierney, 55). Therefore, eating rice at funerals or other festivities contributes to the "harnessing of the energy of the deities to rejuvenate their own lives, which otherwise would wither into a state of impurity" (54). Hence the flow of life and death is perpetuated through ancestor worship and rice consumption. The construction of the ceremonial grave is significant because it shortens the time in which a spirit is in a state of impurity, nurtures the deceased's spirit, and quickly transforms it into a deity that will regenerate life.

The attention given to the double-grave system overlaps with research on the social structure of communities. Akata Mitsuo, who regards the double-grave system as an alternative form of the tradition of erecting a memorial tower, has collected data on the historical development of double graves and their relationship to social structure in Osaka, Nara, Kyoto, Okinawa, and all the prefectures in Shikoku, to name only a few of his sites (Akata 1980,

1986, 1988). His research reveals that the pattern of graves not only relates to the ordering of communities but is also actively manipulated by community members.

The point is clearly demonstrated with two examples from his work. The village of Tochihara in Kyoto is a community based on a cooperation group called *mura-gumi*. In 1777 the village constructed a memorial tower inscribed with "*namuamidabutsu*" (We believe in merciful Buddha) on its cooperatively owned burial site. No stone monuments were built during the Edo period (1600–1867), implying that the community members differed little in their social and economic status. It was not until the year 1900 that some households began to erect gravestones individually, but household grave monuments were not common until 1931 (Akata 1986, 133). Thus, until 1900, the village followed the single-grave system (for individual graves), and during that time the temple dedicated to *kannon* (or *kannondo*), shared by the community members, functioned as the fundamental institution for ancestral and spiritual worship (134). In other words, the strength of the village cooperative group maintained the single-grave system until the turn of the century; but when Westernization generated a new wealthy class, those who were successful demonstrated their wealth by building individual household graves.

The Yanagizawa community in Akita prefecture is another case that shows the complexity of the emergence of the double-grave system. This community comprises the *dōzoku* group, and until 1917 all households shared a single graveyard. In short, it used the single-grave system: the place of burials and graves coincided. In 1917 the branch households began to build their deceased's monuments on a nearby mountain while continuing to bury the corpse in the communal graveyard. Thereafter, when the head of a main household passed away, his descendants buried him at the new site instead of in the communal graveyard. Thus, the double-grave system emerged in this community as a result of conflict between households due to economic and social changes and developments (Akata 1988, 64–65). The decision of the branch house-holds to use the new site has two implications. On the one hand, they were contesting the power of the main household by forcing it to relinquish exclusive use of the new gravesite; on the other hand, their acceptance of the new site suggested subordination to the main household.

Summary

In general, anthropologists' research reveals that values, personal and social relationships, and the pattern of cultural cohesion are symbolically expressed in death rituals. Folklorists' and scholars' research on Japanese death rituals has focused on mortuary ritu-als, the processes of achieving ancestorhood and of ancestor wor-ship that illuminated the Japanese cosmology, and significant re-lationships between the living and the dead in the household system.

The notable differences between the earlier death rituals and contemporary Japanese funerals are: the more recent emphasis on memories and an evaluation of the deceased's life and personality (e.g., appreciation, praise, sympathy, and pity), with less emphasis on the deceased's contribution to a household; a shift in the rela-tionship between the living and the dead from a balanced ex-change to an asymmetric one; and the attenuation of the notion that death, corpses, and the deceased are connected with impurity and pollution.

THE HISTORY OF JAPANESE
FUNERAL TRADITIONS

Rituals must be routinized and conventionalized before they can be accepted as part of the standard repertoire at a Chinese funeral. But this does not mean that they are immutable. . . . These changes are always made, however, within a recognizable framework of cultural convention; modifications are never arbitrary, given that they must conform to general notions of "Chineseness."

—James L. Watson, *Death Ritual in Late Imperial and Modern China*

Until the end of World War II, family and community members knew exactly what needed to be done when a person died. "Look at young people today in the presence of death," said an 84-year-old elder from Michihara. "The first thing they do is call a funeral company. They act like helpless children. Such an embarrassing situation never arose in the past," he claimed. "Amazingly, young people today don't seem to be embarrassed about it either," his wife added. When asked what is most different about today's funerals from those before World War II, he answered. "People were superstitious [*meishin bukai*] in those days. When a woman was pregnant she wasn't allowed to go near the deceased. It was said that if a cat jumped over the deceased's head, the evil spirit of the animal would go into the corpse and make the body rise up. The cat was kept away from the dead when there had been death in the family. My granddaughter—she goes to a medical school and dissects corpses—makes fun of me when I say such a thing to her," he ended with a laugh.

Community Funeral Rituals

Community funeral rituals, which predominated during the first half of Shōwa (1925–89), comprised four types of rites for the deceased: the rites of attempted resuscitation, *soshō* or usually called *sosei*; the rites of breaking bonds, *zetsuen*; the rites of achieving Buddhahood, *jōbutsu*; and the rites of memorial services, *tsuizen* (see Figure 6) (Akata 1980, 125–45; 1986, 35–120).[1] The *soshō* rituals attempted to resuscitate the deceased by bringing the spirit (*tamashii*), which was considered to have escaped from its owner upon cessation of breathing, back into the deceased's physical body. After it was realized that the resuscitation attempts had ended in vain, the *zetsuen* rituals were performed to break the bonds between the deceased's spirit and its physical body so that the liberated spirit could safely depart for the world of the dead. The rituals of *jōbutsu* helped the deceased's spirit achieve Buddhahood, and the *tsuizen* rituals were memorial services performed until the deceased's spirit was fully transformed into an ancestral spirit guarding the household (ibid.). These four rituals were based on the belief in Japanese cosmology that the spirit of the dead lived on even after it had separated from the physical body (Akata 1986, 35–75), and that the spirit was dangerous even to the immediate family members if it was not well cared for by the living (Gorai 1992, 731). Traditional funerals had two distinctive features: they were executed through the cooperation of community members, and the goals of community funerals were to usher the deceased's spirit to the other world and protect the living against the danger of a spirit and the impurity of a corpse. Community funerals therefore were cooperative efforts to process the impurity (*kegare*) and pollution (*fujō*) of death.[2]

THE RITES OF ATTEMPTED RESUSCITATION AND BREAKING BONDS

The rite of attempted resuscitation took place when a person was dying; the family member who sat closest would dip a bamboo chopstick wrapped with cotton on one end into water and wet the dying person's lips. Sometimes birds' feathers were used instead of chopsticks and cotton, but the purpose was the same—to give last water (*matsugo no mizu*) to the dying, in a final attempt to resurrect the person.[3] At the last moment of life, the family would also call out the deceased's name (*tama-yobai*). In Sarugai, Moji (west of Kita-Kyūshū city), someone on the roof, from which tiles had been removed to make a hole for the spirit to pass through, called the deceased's name (*yobimodoshi*) so that the spirit would return to its body (Kita-Kyūshū Education Committee [later KEC] 1988, 48). These rites reflected the belief that the embodiment of the soul or the detachment of the spirit from a body defined life and death.

Villagers called a doctor only after the family was certain of a person's death. His task was not to treat the living but to verify death and provide a death certificate so the family could acquire burial permission from the local government.[4]

After the failed resuscitation attempt, the family closed the deceased's eyes by gently stroking the eyelids and folded the deceased's hands in the posture of prayer (*gasshō*). The deceased's face was turned upright or toward the west and covered with a white cloth. The mattress was turned so that the deceased's head faced north. A razor (*kamisori*) was placed on or beside the mattress. In Kokura and Dairi-Honmachi, a sword was used instead of a razor. In Kokura, Saruhami, Tanoura, and Kurosaki (communities in Kita-Kyūshū), the golden folded screen (*kin byōbu*) owned by each community was erected upside down at the bedside. The purpose of maneuvering these objects was twofold: to ward off malevolent spirits that might enter the body of the deceased and to differentiate the period of time from ordinary days (Saitō, 29–81). A small table (*kyōzukue*, literally, a sutra table), was placed in front of the deceased, and on it family members arranged a bowl of rice (*makurameshi* or *oppan*), a plate of sticky-rice balls (*dango*), a glass of death water (*shinimizu*), a candle, and incense. The rice was placed in the deceased's rice bowl, with a single set of chopsticks erect in it. Gorai explains that rice and rice balls were offered to pacify the deceased's spirit (Gorai 1992, 743).

Death was referred to as the "black shadow" (*kurobi-gakari*) or "black pollution" (*koku-fujō*), and was considered dangerous not only to the living but also to deities. The family placed a message, "in mourning" (*ki-chū* or *mo-chū*), on the house gate to inform others of the danger. They also covered their shrine altar (*kami-dana*, literally, "god shelf") with white paper in order to protect the deities from death pollution. In Saruhami, Nuki, Ohma, Ideura, and Michihara, the folding fan (*sensu*) was erected to shield the shrine altar (KEC 1988: 49–50). Dried rice stalks were placed on top of a shrine altar in an X form in Saruhami. The bereaved also avoided visiting any shrines for a year after the death of a family member, to avoid polluting the deities there.

The community cooperative or mutual-aid group (*kumi* or *kōgumi*) consisted of five to seven households that took full responsibility for providing rituals for the deceased and his or her family.[5] This group helped with funeral rituals as well as with transplanting rice crops, building houses, repairing roofs, and conducting weddings and other annual festivities.

After a doctor had pronounced the person dead, a family member notified the head of the community organization. The community head (*kumi-chō*), a role that was taken in turn by the household heads of a *kumi*, was responsible for assigning someone to fetch a priest, to inform relatives who lived far from the village, and to buy the materials necessary for the wake and funerals (which included decorative papers for ritual ornaments and food for before and after the funeral). The food included different kinds of tofu (bean curd), which was indispensable as the main ingredient of the dishes since no meat was allowed. Because vegetarian food was considered to be pure, it helped the living purify themselves from death pollution (Gorai 1992, 859–62). Last, the community head ordered a local handicraft shop to make a coffin.

On the evening of the wake, the *kumi-chō* gathered male *kumi* members to discuss the rest of the jobs. One of the most important was digging the grave. Other tasks were making all the necessary items—the death flower (*shikabana* or *shikanohana*),[6] a box (*ihaibako*) for a memorial tablet and death flower, dragons (*tatsuguchi* or *tatsugashira*),[7] a box roof (*akoya* or *tengai*),[8] and six candlestands (*hi* or *kōshō*).[9] Most of these objects had to be made by hand since they were used only once and were left at the burial site or burned after the funeral. And last, men were assigned to arrange the funeral altar, to bring from the temple the objects that the priests would use, and to lead the procession to the grave.

The deceased was left on his or her mattress until the priest arrived to read the first sutra chanting (*makura-gyō*). When the priest had finished the recitation and the sun was down, the bereaved performed a bathing ceremony (*yukan*) for the deceased; they shaved his or her head (the sign of a Buddhist disciple) and clipped his or her nails. (The bathing ceremony is described in detail in Chapter 3 and the Conclusion.) After the bathing ceremony, the deceased was dressed in a white death robe, which symbolized pilgrimage, a triangular headcloth (*zukin*), a pair of hand guards (*tekkō*), a robe (*kyō-katabira*), a pair of knee guards, and a pair of Japanese-style socks (*shiro-tabi*), all of which prepared the deceased for his or her journey to gain Buddhahood. Three women of the community followed strict rules in making the death robe. They measured the cloth by hand instead of with a ruler, tore the cloth instead of cutting it with scissors, sewed the seams so that the stitches were visible, left the ends of the threads unknotted, and made no collar. Making the garment different from the clothes worn by the living emphasized the contrast between life and death (Matsudaira, 189). The deceased, dressed in the death robe, was placed in a round, cask-like coffin (*maru-kan*), which forced the corpse into a sitting posture with the knees bent.

Then the *kumi* members built a funeral altar made from flat wooden boards to stand in front of the coffin and placed an incense pot, food offerings, and a vase of white chrysanthemums on the altar. (No photo of the deceased was placed on the altar until funeral companies introduced the practice.) Meanwhile, the bereaved brought out the deceased's kimono and hung it outside on a bamboo stick facing north. This *zetsuen* ritual continued until the seventh day of death. The kimono was doused at the hem in a pail of water and was kept moist for seven days and seven nights. A former elementary schoolteacher in Tenraiji explained to me that the kimono represented the deceased crossing the river located to the north, which lies at the boundary to the world of the afterlife (*sanzu-no-kawa*). The kimono was taken away on the eighth day to show that the deceased's spirit had crossed the river safely and had liberated itself from the world of the living (one of the rituals of *zetsuen*).

Family, friends, and neighbors gathered in the house of the deceased for a wake, which began after sunset with a priest chanting a sutra. After the chanting each person at the wake lit an incense stick in turn; the incense was kept burning all night. Then women helped the family serve tea and sweets. The priests stayed with the guests and joined in conversation about the deceased. The women might leave early, but most men remained until late, drinking sake and talking. The deceased's family stayed awake through the night. They took turns making sure the incense and candles continued to burn so that no evil spirits would enter the deceased's body (Saitō, 50–54). The community head allotted the funeral tasks to different men in the *kumi*, and it was his wife's job to organize the women's preparation of the many vegetarian dishes (*otoki*) for the funeral meal.[10] Although the menu itself was predetermined, the women had to decide who would cook each of the five to seven different vegetarian dishes. The food was served on a set of trays and plates and in bowls that the community owned in common.[11] It was the women's responsibility to wash them before and after the ritual. Since using fire and cooking were prohibited in the deceased's house, the food was prepared and eaten at a neighbor's home. Several women went to that house to help clean and to arrange the trays for the next day.

On the day of the funeral, members of the immediate family wore white robes (*shiro-moku*) with white Japanese-style socks (*shiro-tabi*), and clogs with white thongs (*shiro-hanao*). The women wore their long hair tied at the nape of the neck and donned white hats (*wata-bōshi*). More distant relatives and neighbors wore black kimonos. Different clothes distinguished kin with the closest relationships to the deceased from those with more distant relationships and indicated who was most contaminated.[12]

Around noon, the family and relatives, served by women in the community, ate a vegetarian meal in front of the coffin. The same meal, served exactly the same way, was also offered to the deceased. The dinner was called departure food (*detachi no zen*) and was the last commensal dinner with the deceased. All family members drank a cup of rice wine (sake) to purify themselves from death pollution.

Meanwhile, two community members stood at the doorway of the deceased's house to greet the guests and record the incense money or condolence gifts (*kōden*) in the gift book;[13] this practice was important to the maintenance of community cooperation because the giving of a gift must always be reciprocated on some other occasion (Kurata, 223). In Kita-Kyūshū, close family members brought one straw sack (*ippyō*, 60 kg) of rice, and neighbors and friends brought one bag (*isshō*, 1.5 kg) of rice, or they could both bring the money equivalent. One of my informants from Tashiro emphasized that a fixed amount was set so that all the gifts were the same among community members. The rice bags were piled in the open corridor of the living room with name tags to show who had given them. Relatives and friends also brought cloth flags at half mast (*chōki*) as gifts.

The funeral usually began in the late afternoon with the arrival of the priest. If the household was wealthy, two or three priests officiated. The priests sat directly behind the coffin. Behind the priests sat the deceased's family members, other relatives, friends, and neighbors in that order.[14] The funeral began with a priest's sutra recitation, followed by each person lighting an incense stick. The coffin was then opened to allow family members to view the deceased for the last time and to put in food (e.g., cooked rice balls and sweets), thread and needles for women or a razor for men, coins (*rokumonsen*), and other personal belongings. These items were placed in the coffin for the deceased to use on the journey to and in the afterlife.

The family used a stone as a hammer to nail the coffin shut; nails were considered effective to keep the deceased separate from the living. The chief mourner was first to hammer a nail into the coffin with a stone, followed by the other relatives, moving from closest to furthest in relationship. Two kinsmen then turned the coffin counterclockwise three times; it was then removed through a window instead of the door. If it was a round coffin, the side where the deceased's head was located had to emerge first; if it was a rectangular coffin, the exit had to be made feet first. As soon as the coffin was out of the house, the deceased's rice bowl was smashed on the ground. I was told that these bond-breaking (*zetsuen*) practices were performed to keep the deceased's spirit from returning home.

The procession was the highlight of the funeral ritual. All the *kumi*, except for the very old and the very young, walked in the procession to the burial site. Two *kumi* members had left earlier to place candlestands along the way. The procession was led by the men of the *kumi*, followed by the family members, relatives, friends, and *kumi* women. The sequence of the procession was as follows: a *kumi* member with the firebrand; a *kumi* member holding banners at half mast; two members carrying bamboo dragons; the priest(s); the chief mourner carrying the memorial tablet; the second chief mourner with the death flower; the remaining family members and relatives; a *kumi* member holding the heaven cover (*tengai*) over the coffin; two kinsmen carrying the coffin; and friends, neighbors, and *kumi* women. A long strip of cloth was tied around the coffin and extended behind it; from there it was held by a line of *kumi* women. (I was told that participants later cut up the cloth to keep.) In wealthy households, a carriage (*kago*) full of sweets followed the procession. The sweets were passed out to children on the way to the burial site with the aim of feeding the hungry spirits (*segaki*, literally, "providing for the evil spirits") that gather around a death. When the procession reached the gravesite, the coffin was again turned counterclockwise three times and then lowered into the grave with four ropes. The chief mourner was the first to shovel soil on top of the coffin. Other family members and relatives followed in turn. Each time a person finished shoveling, he or she laid the shovel (*kuwa*) on the ground instead of handing it to the next person (also part of the *zetsuen* rituals). Throughout, the priest recited. Finally the bereaved family took off their clogs and left them at the site. Those members responsible for filling in the grave remained, while the rest of the procession returned home without turning back. Upon reaching home, they sprinkled salt over their clothes and rubbed and washed their hands with it to cleanse themselves from death pollution before entering.

Meanwhile, the three men who had dug the grave buried the coffin. They filled in the hole and made a rounded mound. The box roof from the procession was put on top of the mound together with the death flowers and memorial tablet. All community members waited to eat dinner (*hone-kami*, literally "bone-biting") until the three men returned from the grave to take their place at the head of the table.[15] The *kumi* men ate first, waited on by the women, who fed themselves and the children later. At the end of the meal, offerings of food and sweets were distributed among all *kumi* members.

In the Kita-Kyūshū area, the mourning period was completed on the 49th day (*shijūkunichi*) after a death, when the spirit of the deceased was considered to have arrived at the world of the dead. The deceased's family invited priests and relatives for memorial services (i.e., sutra recitation and commensality) on the 7th day (*shonanoka*) and the 49th day (KEC 1988, 56). The rites of achieving Buddhahood and of the memorial services took place in the form of a sutra recitation by priests and worship by the deceased's family. The rites of achieving Buddhahood were performed from the time of the funeral procession to the 77th memorial service (*nanajū nanaki*) in the form of prayers at the household altar, whereas the rites of memorial services were conducted during the Festival of the Dead (*bon*), at the New Year (*Shōgatsu*), as part of the equinox (*higan*) celebrations, on the monthly anniversary (*gakki*) of death, as a periodic anniversary rite (*nenki*), and at the final memorial service (*tomurai-age*) by inviting a priest for a sutra recitation (Akata 1986, 89).

The four variations of rites for the deceased emphasize the progressive phases of the deceased's spirit and capture the nature of Japanese death rituals (Akata 1980, 1986). In the framework of the rites of passage, the rites of separation come first, but in the four variations of rites for the deceased, the rites of attempted resurrection (*soshō*) (or "the rites of attempted incorporation" if you will) precede the rites of separation. Then the rites of breaking bonds (*zetsuen*) follow the rites of achieving Buddhahood (*jōbutsu*) and the rites of memorial services (*tsuizen*); the first corresponds to the rites of separation, and the following two are analogous to the rites of incorporation.

The Japanese community ritual was unique in that it attempted to incorporate the deceased's spirit once again into the world of the living before sending it away. Second, the incorporation of the spirits into complete ancestors was a gradual process and required lengthy formal rituals. The rites of memorial services (*tsuizen*) in particular were rigidly scheduled rituals that continued until the final rites (*tomurai-age*), conducted on the 33d or 50th anniversary of death, when the deceased was considered to have finally been transformed into a household ancestor and a Buddha.[16] In sum, the additional rituals to verify the irreversible return of a spirit and the extended incorporation rituals demonstrate the importance community funerals put on distinctions between the impure and the purified spirit.

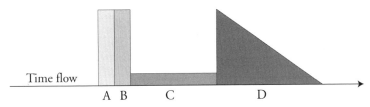

Time flow

A B   C   D

A. Attempted resurrection
B. Breaking bonds/rites of separation
C. Rites of transition
D. Rites of achieving Buddhahood and memorial services/rites of
   incorporation

FIGURE 6.   Rites of passage in Japanese community death rituals

Development of the Funeral Industry

The transition from death rituals to funerals is tied closely to the
process of modernization, urbanization, and commercialization
in Japanese society. The development of the funeral industry is
also closely intertwined with the historical vicissitudes of kinship,
social networks, and material objects.

In the Edo period (1600–1867) the conventionalization of
Buddhist death rituals was accomplished under the pressure of a
parochial system introduced by the Tokugawa government in 1640
(Smith 1974, 20–21). To extirpate Christianity, this regime decreed
that all commoners must become affiliated with a Buddhist temple. As a result of this edict, Buddhist priests gained the status of
leaders in their communities; they were responsible for birth, marriage, divorce, and death registrations (Kitagawa, 212). The edict
not only helped incorporate Buddhist death rituals into cultural
practice but also linked priests with individual households.
Subsequently, propitiating malevolent spirits, avoiding death pollution, practicing ancestor worship, and perpetuating households
were associated with Buddhist death rituals.

When the Meiji government eradicated the stratification of warriors, peasants, craftsmen, and merchants (*shi-nō-kō-shō*), these lower classes began to imitate the funerary customs of aristocrats (Inoue S. 1990, 76, 79). Funerals of the wealthy in Meiji were distinguished by the display of embellished decorations and the use of numerous ornaments (78–79). For example, large vases of flowers (both natural and artificial) decorated cages filled with pigeons and sparrows, and a stack of sweet-cakes (*kuyō-gashi* or *hikidemono*) was pulled in a cart during the funeral procession (67–69; Murakami 1991a, 76). Upon arriving at a temple, the birds were freed (*hōchō*) as part of a funerary show, and funeral cakes were passed out to onlookers, as well as to the funeral attendants afterward. The cakes outnumbered the attendants to emphasize the family's wealth and to avoid embarrassment. In his book *Roadside Stone* (*Robō no ishi*), Yamamoto Yūzō described a poor woman who made her living by disguising herself as a funeral participant in order to collect funeral cakes and other funeral gifts (Yamamoto, 304–10). This was a common practice around large funeral processions during Meiji (Inoue S., 67–70).

The aristocratic practice of using horizontal coffins (*shinkan*) and palanquins (*koshi*) to transport them replaced the cask-like vertical coffin (*zakan*) carried by a litter (*kago*) that peasants used (79). The importance of the coffin was not simply its shape, but that it was suited to be the focal point of an elaborate procession. Funerals for the wealthy began to incorporate a servants' parade (*yakko no gyōretsu*),[17] in imitation of the parade of feudal lords (*daimyō*) during the Edo period. Like the earlier parade specialists for the feudal lords, the performers in funeral parades in Meiji were trained entertainers who pranced with umbrellas, the traditional warrior's luggage box, banners, and spears (95–101). The mimicry of aristocratic funeral practices, and what Inoue Shōichi (81–89) called the "spectacularization of funerals," was a way for the growing rich to enhance and display their social status.

Accompanying the trend of funeral spectacularization was the rise of urban funeral parlors. The Tokyo Funeral Parlor (Tokyo

Sōgisha), established in 1887, was the first of its kind (91). A newspaper from that time reads:

> Recently, a couple of entrepreneurs formed the Tokyo Funeral Parlor in Kanda. It is equipped with complete ornaments for both Buddhist and Shintō funerals, and it provides all funeral needs at an affordable price. It opened its branch shop at Nihonbashi three days ago with the purpose of reforming [the situation created by] litter shops that are gorging on profits. (Mori S. 1969, 132)

As the article indicates, the idea of funeral parlors sprang from the need of urbanites to rent ornaments and transport the deceased. Most funeral parlors began as litter, coffin, cooper (*oke-ya*), and craft or furniture shops (Inoue S., 91; *Sōgi* 1991, 87; *Sōgi* 1993a, 86; *Sōgi* 1993b, 81). Craftsmen who had the skills to create funeral objects changed professions at the prospect of higher earnings. For example, Ichiyanagi-Sōgu-Sōhonten, one of the earliest funeral parlors established at Nagoya in 1877, was founded by a craftsman who left his village to open a funeral ornament shop in the city (*Sōgi* 1991, 86–89). Early in his career he made decorations and later took over the recruitment of parade servants, undertakers, and pallbearers (87–88). Nakamura-gumi, established in Kita-Kyūshū in 1896, began as a carrier cooperative (*ben-riya*) that delivered coffins and other funeral ornaments to the deceased's household. A decade later, the carrier cooperative had become the Nakamura-gumi Funeral Parlor (Nakmura-gumi-Sōgisha) by incorporating the rental of funeral ornaments and the transportation of the dead to a burial site.[18]

The death rituals during Taishō were not as lavish as those of the Meiji period. The wealthy class ceased their midday funeral extravaganzas, returning to the practice of holding plain processions in the evenings or no procession at all (Inoue S., 109). Inoue gives three reasons for the change: the development of transportation systems, the distance of crematories from residential areas, and the rationalization of funerals by the elite (114–30).

Rickshaws (*jinriki-sha*), stagecoaches (*noriai-basha*), and horse cars (*tetsudō-basha*) were flooding city streets, and they made it impossible for the people in funeral processions and parades to stride with dignity. The awareness of infectious disease[19] also popularized the practice of cremation among city dwellers (Asaka and Yagisawa, 58);[20] and population growth forced crematories farther from residential areas, making the prospect of a long procession unattractive. Soon city dwellers were making their way to funeral sites by rail (Inoue S., 121–23).

But most important, the change in funeral practices was influenced by the Taishō Democracy and its introduction of Western rationality.[21] The atmosphere of the time is conveyed in the writings of Sakai Toshihiko, a socialist intellectual, who commented on the meaning of the procession as follows: "I do not believe that today's processions are based on the traditional spirit of sanctity. The majority of funerals nowadays are merely displays of fallacy and ostentation. . . . A man of honor should not allow himself to be deceived into such foppery. The society also should not permit this mummery to claim right-of-way on the streets" (Sakai, 314).[22]

With all of these modernizations, elaborate funeral processions disappeared. As a corollary, the ceremony of bidding farewell (*kokubetsu-shiki*) was a response to the desire to perform frugal funerals (Murakami 1992b, 104). The main focus of bidding farewell was the presentation of memorial addresses and valedictions by participants. The ceremony of bidding farewell can also be seen as the consequence of city dwellers' estrangement from temples (Murakami 1991b, 106). People who migrated to cities lost their ties with the temples of their natal households, and at the end of the Edo period (1867) they were no longer required by law to join a temple in their new neighborhood. Hence, while Buddhist funerals remained the standard, the priests' power over funerals declined (discussed in Chapter 7), leading to an emphasis on practices of bidding farewell that have continued to the present.

City funerals at the beginning of Shōwa were the first to use the hearse. The first hearse appeared in Japan in 1917 (the sixth year of

Taishō); it was owned by Gayu, one of the oldest funeral parlors in Osaka (Inoue S., 132). In 1922, Ichiyanagi Wholesale Funeral Ornaments (Ichiyanagi-Sōgu-Sōhonten) imported a hearse from the United States (and even gave it an English name, "Vim") (*Sōgi* 1991, 88). Nakamura-gumi Sōgisha, the oldest funeral parlor in Kita-Kyūshū, also imported a hearse in 1931. Kakuda, the current vice president, told me that his father, the founder of the funeral parlor, was the first civilian to receive an automobile license in Kita-Kyūshū. By the beginning of Shōwa (the late 1920s), the hearse had become a necessary part of urban funerals because of the distance of crematories from the city proper (Inoue S., 135). The adoption of the hearse parallels Westernization, faster-paced lifestyles, and the growing rationality of urban dwellers (133–34). The extravagantly embellished Japanese hearses are hard to over-look. A typical hearse (see photo section) is a vehicle with a shrine-like roof decorated with dragons, phoenixes, lanterns, and other gold-painted ornaments.[23] Its outward appearance suggests the lav-ish Meiji processions; in fact, it seems that the entire ornamenta-tion of Meiji processions was transferred to the hearse (147–49).

The invention of the Japanese hearse and the disappearance of the procession, however, reduced the need for special funerary ob-jects and labor and resulted in a decline in the number of funeral parlors. Funeral parlors were also less important around World War II, when the average Japanese household could not afford os-tentatious funerals (Murakami 1992b, 104).

In the overall picture, the surge of funeral parlors in the mod-ern period was concomitant with the growing wealthy class in cities, who adopted the earlier aristocratic funeral practices to in-crease their social standing. The development of funeral parlors was also due to urbanization. The weakened community integra-tion in cities made funeral parlors more convenient and reliable than neighbors one did not know well.

A decade into the postwar period, the funeral industry began to flourish, aided by the formation of Mutual-Aid Cooperatives (*Gojokai*).[24] The first Funeral and Wedding Mutual-Aid Cooperative was founded in Yokosuga in 1948 by Nishimura Kamahiko (Zenkoku Kankon Sōsai Gojokai Renmei 1974, 34). The name of his company, Yokosuga City Wedding and Funeral Mutual-Aid Cooperative (Yokosugashi Kankon Sōsai Gojokai), reflected his objective of taking over the community members' role in funerals and weddings in urban settings where community ties had become weak. Furthermore, Nishimura envisioned a great business opportunity in marketing funerals and weddings on the installment plan. Most Japanese faced economic difficulty after the war and had trouble affording a lump-sum funeral payment. He based his business on a management principle called the Mutual-Aid System (*Gojokai-seido*), which forms the backbone of today's funeral and wedding ceremonies (Edwards, 42–43). The Mutual-Aid Cooperative relied on its depositors, the Mutual-Aid members (*Gojokai-kaiin*), who became prospective customers when they purchased a membership (ibid.). The cooperative at the time offered two programs: a twenty-yen monthly fee for ten years (¥2,400) or eighteen yen monthly for ten years (¥2,160) (Zenkoku Kankon Sōsai Gojokai Renmei 1974, 37). After making payments for six months, members could have either a wedding or a funeral within the range of their plan and continue paying in installments after the ceremony. If a member wanted a ceremony before the six-month period was up, he or she had to pay the remainder immediately (ibid.).

The Mutual-Aid System (MAS) spread rapidly among the lower class in cities. Entrepreneurs who saw future opportunity in the system sought assistance from Nishimura, who shared his management philosophy with newcomers. As their numbers grew, cooperative managers established Zenkoku Kankon Sōsai Gojokai Renmei (ZGR) (the National Wedding and Funeral Mutual-Aid Association, later NMAA) in 1959. The NMAA has effectively controlled the quality of companies that adopted the system; only upon receiving the committee's permission were start-up companies provided with management assistance within the Mutual-Aid System (ZGR 1974, 159–60).[25] In this way, the

NMAA controlled not only the quality of the MAS but also the number of companies involved.

The years between 1976 and 1982 were the peak growth period of funeral companies based on the MAS. By 1973 the NMAA had increased to 347 companies, and the number of Mutual-Aid members had risen to 4,267,000. This wave of success was due to the authorization of the NMAA as a licensed business in 1973, which was brought about by the efforts of President Sakuma of Moon Rise, Inc. He discussed the issue with Minister Nakasone, the former minister of international trade and industry, and this move was critical in gaining both political and economic status for funeral companies. Ministry authorization obliged its members to become corporations and required each enterprise to warranty insurance coverage by contracting with a bank or with the Mutual-Aid Association Insurance Corporation (ZGR 1974, 59). These rigid requirements have reformed the management of funeral companies and improved their status in the business world.

What accounts for the success of funeral companies today? The vice president of the Nakamura-gumi Funeral Parlor gave me this reply: "Although the present status of the funeral profession is not the highest, it is nothing like before World War II. I have to admit, our position today owes much to the development of the Mutual-Aid System and those companies that incorporated it." Many funeral parlors like the Nakamura-gumi Funeral Parlor incorporated comprehensive services and transformed themselves into funeral companies. Although they may not have joined the National Mutual-Aid Association, they had to provide the same kind and level of services to survive. The incorporation of three elements was pivotal: corpse handling, standardized programs, and comprehensive services. By specializing in these tasks and appropriating ritual knowledge, funeral companies became professional businesses.

Funeral parlors before and immediately after World War II simply delivered a coffin and other ornaments to the deceased's household and later transported bodies to temples, gravesites, or crematories; their service centered on providing necessary funerary equipment (Bestor, 199). The Mutual-Aid Cooperatives and the professionals of funeral companies, however, took over the funeral tasks that were previously the responsibility of family and community members. Funeral professionals collected and encoffined the deceased and provided transportation to burial sites. The MAC freed the bereaved from contact with the deceased from the moment death occurred.

The standardization of programs was another key element in the MAS. All funeral companies offered similar preplanned programs for a similar fee. For example, in 1967, Moon Rise's first Mutual-Aid membership (with installment payments of ¥300 per month for 60 months) offered a set of comprehensive services and materials: all handling of the corpse; funeral materials (coffin, funeral altar with five platforms, and two artificial lotus flowers, or *renka*); hearse rental; other decorations and ornaments (two memorial tablets, an ashpot, a death robe); and administrative services to acquire a cremation certificate and official notification of death. Since 1977, Moon Rise has also employed ceremony conductors (*shikaisha*) to act as ceremonial cantors.

As the nation's GNP increased, funeral companies offered more elaborate ceremonies at their funeral halls than the standard Mutual-Aid membership programs. Fees have increased over the years, as have the number and the cost of more elaborate ceremonies. In the late 1990s Moon Rise offered 21 options to its customers, and the price of its Mutual-Aid membership program was ¥240,000 (¥3,000 over 80 months). Although funeral companies may offer different options, the basic Mutual-Aid membership plans are similar in price and offer virtually identical services. In fact, if a Mutual-Aid member who has paid installment fees for ten months moves to a different locale, Moon Rise (or any other company belonging to the NMAA) will transfer the person's Mutual-Aid membership to a funeral company in that area.

Finally, the superiority of the MAS lies in its provision of comprehensive services.[26] Moon Rise, for example, offers and provides access to every commodity needed for a funeral: it prints notification cards for funerals (*gokaisō-oreijō*); rents mourning suits and kimonos; supplies gifts for wakes, funeral ceremonies, and postfuneral services; provides vegetarian dinners (*shōjin-ryōri*) and banquet dinners after ceremonies; arranges fresh- and dried-flower bouquets; and offers Buddhist altars.

The growth of funeral companies has also been furthered by the establishment of funeral halls. Just as the use of wedding halls has increased (Edwards, 44), funerals at company funeral halls increased significantly in the 1970s and 1980s. According to funeral professionals at Moon Rise, the shift of ceremonies from homes to halls has changed funerals into more formal and elegant ceremonies. At the same time, however, the shift to funeral halls explicitly displays differences in the scale (and price) of funerals. The size of funeral altars and halls is a factor in the stratification of funeral ceremonies (discussed in Chapter 5).

After the war, funeral parlors' business was fragmented; it included the provision of funeral accessories, the transportation of the deceased at the end of funeral rituals, and the recruitment of undertakers, pallbearers, and parade servants. Because the extent and quality of their services varied greatly, so did their prices. Funeral parlors and their workers were also stigmatized by a low (if not the lowest) social status. Their lack of unified services and the perception of impurity contributed additionally to their inferior reputation. However, their low status was also due to deficiencies in language and manners. The founders of funeral parlors, who were mostly craftsmen, had little education, and the workers they employed had less. Parade servants, undertakers, and pallbearers were notorious for their unruly behavior and were even despised by the funeral parlor owners who hired them. It was said that they were rascals who spent their money on drinking and gambling; once the money was gone, they returned to the streets (Inoue S., 104).

In contrast, funeral companies established themselves as corporate enterprises and their employees as professional businessmen. With the development of the MAS, funeral companies took over the majority of tasks involving the deceased, including all handling of the corpse. It was this element that contributed to the professionalization, and higher status, of funeral companies. Inasmuch as the treatment of the corpse functioned to unite cultural values in communities, the funeral industry, by taking over this responsibility, replaced this basis for community solidarity. Hence, not only did funeral staff acquire dominant roles by totalizing funeral programs, they also came to be respected as professionals for their knowledge about death ceremonies and their polished manners. President Sakuma said to me proudly, "When I started this job, people called us '*sōgiya*' [undertaker], but today people call us 'Moon Rise-*san*' [a person working at Moon Rise] or '*sōgiya-san*' ['Mr. Undertaker,' with a polite connotation]." As a corollary, the commercialization of funerals based on the MAS led to the standardization of ceremonies and prices, which in turn has contributed to the homogenizing of funeral practices in Japan.

Today's funeral parlors (*sōgi-ya*) have become funeral homes (*sōgi-sha*) by adopting the management principles of funeral companies, namely the comprehensive services and corporate structure. Therefore, the distinction between funeral homes and companies is slight nowadays. The only differences are that funeral companies belong to the NMAA, recruit Mutual-Aid members, often possess branch halls elsewhere (franchises), and also market wedding services, whereas funeral homes are independent enterprises (often family owned) that operate solely on the open market. But the profits that funeral companies earn from non–Mutual-Aid members has been increasing since the mid-1980s. This phenomenon reflects the stability of the Japanese economy and people's ability to pay funeral costs in a lump sum.

The blossoming of the funeral industry in the contemporary era must be considered together with modernization, urbanization, and commercialization in Japan. The MAC, which initially began as a low-cost alternative for the urban lower class, has expanded to the middle and upper classes in both cities and villages. This saturation was possible only through industrialization, the migration of families to the cities, the attenuation of communal ties, the specialization of occupational tasks, and the development of commercialization.

My father-in-law was a retired vice president of one of the largest companies in Tokyo. Our family wanted to have a simple funeral [for him], but when the funeral company, which had conducted our mother's funeral three years earlier, arrived to discuss it, we were told that it is not proper to have a smaller funeral for our father than for our mother. The Buddhist temple priests nodded in agreement with the funeral professionals. As a result, we purchased a 2 million yen coffin for our father, a million yen more expensive than that of our mother, and had three priests instead of two. One can imagine [what funeral professionals will say] when our turn comes; they will explain [to our children], "for your grandfather's funeral your father purchased the most expensive coffin."

— "The Halt of the Salt-Purification Rite in Funeral Ceremonies,"
Asahi Shimbun

Before the Rites of Separation

The handling of the deceased, whether transporting, dressing, or bathing, is the most important responsibility of funeral professionals. Near the end of my fieldwork at Moon Rise, a colleague told me about a funeral professional who had failed in this responsibility and was subsequently fired. My colleague told me that, while this funeral professional was transporting the deceased and his family from a hospital to the Moon Rise funeral hall, the back door of the company van had opened and the coffin had slid onto the street and fallen open; the deceased had landed face down on the pavement with an upturned coffin beside him. (Apparently the back door of the van had not been securely locked.) The family members were furious; enraged, they shouted at the professional that he had injured (*kizu wo tsuketa*) the deceased, who was almost hit (*hikareru tokoro datta*) by a car behind the van. The funeral professional knelt on the pavement, touching his forehead to the ground, and apologized to the family in a continuous kowtow. The family's ire did not dissipate, however, until the managers had apologized and offered to pay for the entire funeral.

What was manifested in this episode was the perception of the continued life of the deceased in the eyes of the family. Although dead in the medical or physical sense, the deceased was not yet acknowledged to be dead. Japanese believe that a person experiences death twice, once at the hospital and again at cremation. The pronouncement of death by a doctor does not complete the deceased's death; it is only after cremation that the finality of death is attained. As Ebersole points out in reference to the Izanami and Izanagi in Nihonshoki myth (where "Izanami's entry into Yomi and her 'death' are not viewed permanent until Izanagi breaks the taboo of entering the burial hall and view[ing] the corpse"), "the finality of death is a result of the actions of the living" (Ebersole, 88).

Contemporary Japanese funeral ceremonies normally take two to three days. Several events occur before the funeral ceremony, starting with the announcement of death, followed by the transportation of the deceased, the consultation (*uchiawase*), the bathing ceremony (*yukan*), and the wake (*tsuya*). These performances of commercial funerals, however, have different meanings from those of community funerals. In community funerals, rituals of *soshō* (attempted resuscitation) were executed immediately after death. In contemporary funerals the period from death at a hospital to the end of a funeral ceremony can also be called a phase of *sosei* or "resurrection," but for a different reason. In community funerals the bereaved conducted a series of rituals to resuscitate the deceased by attempting to call back the spirit that had escaped from the body; in today's ceremony the living neither consider death a result of spirit ascendance nor attempt ritual resuscitation. The deceased is treated as if still alive, and death is delayed until the end of the funeral.

On the morning of November 29, 1994, the Moon Rise telephone rang at 10:00 A.M. The receptionist answered it. "It has happened" (*hassei desu*), she announced to the funeral staff in the room. At Moon Rise, the term "happen" (*hassei*) indicates that someone has died. She looked around to see who could take the call. It was another busy morning; recent deaths and funeral ceremonies in progress were all vying for attention. Most of the funeral staff were out of the office, at hospitals, at the homes of the deceased, and in the different rooms or halls of the auditorium. She put the call through to Tomi, who had been organizing another ceremony schedule.

Tomi reached for a notepad and a pencil. He opened his conversation with a sympathetic phrase that is used when hearing news of a death in a family. "I am very sorry for the loss of your family member" (*konotabiwa makotoni goshūshō sama deshita*). I noticed that the funeral staff spoke this sympathetic phrase only once during the initial conversation with the deceased's family. Tomi quickly switched to a businesslike manner and said, "I am sorry, but I need to ask you several questions concerning the deceased." He asked the person's name, gender, and age; the name of the chief mourner; the place where the person had died; the time of death; and the address and phone number of the person's home. Then he asked if the deceased was a Mutual-Aid Cooperative member (*gojokai-kaiin*); what religion and which sect the deceased belonged to; and what price of coffin the family desired. If the deceased had purchased a Mutual-Aid Cooperative (MAC) membership, there was a specific set of funeral materials provided according to the price of the MAC membership fee. If the deceased was a MAC member, the family could simply ask for the prepaid coffin. However, the items provided on the membership installment plan are usually the inexpensive ones, and it is common for the funeral staff to provide information about a higher-priced range of coffins. Funeral staff always end the conversation by reassuring the family that they are on their way. "Please feel at ease; we will be seeing you as soon as we can get ready," Tomi said and hung up the phone.

As soon as the phone call was completed, Tomi and Mitake, an assistant, began packing the necessary materials. First, they put the ¥100,000 coffin that the deceased's family had chosen into a company hearse. Because the deceased was a Buddhist belonging to a Jodoshinshū sect, they packed a Jodoshinshū coffin cover (*kan-ooi*) and the braided-string decoration that goes with the cover (*sutachi*). It is important to know what religion and sect the deceased belonged to; this determines the type of coffin cover and other funeral materials. Whether a sword (*morigatana*) is necessary or not also depends on the specific Buddhist sect. For instance, the Nichirenshōshū and Jodoshinshū sects do not require the sword. Also, for the Buddhist sects of Jodoshinshū, Shingonshū, Jōdoshū, Zenshū (Sōtō, Ohbaku, or Rinzaishū), Nichirenshū, and Tendaishū, coffin covers are made of thick silk in bright colors such as red, purple, or orange with gold and have large flower designs on them. In contrast, the Nichirenshoshū sect and Shintō use white and silver with diagonally striped designs. For Christians, the coffin cover is black velvet with a silver cross stitched on the front. Death garments differ for Buddhist and Shintō members as well.

Other objects that are packed include: dry ice cut into rectangular shapes; a box of stationery (*tebunko*), necessary during a wake and funeral ceremony; a pair of coffin stands (*kandai*); deodorants (*bōshūzai*); a chrysanthemum; a death robe (*shinishōzoku*); candles; a candle stand (*rōsokutate*); a vase; and incense (*senkō*). For Nichirenshoshū, Shintō, and Christians, the chrysanthemum is not necessary. Without much talk, the two men loaded these items quickly into the van. Moon Rise has three types of hearses. The one used most often is an ordinary white van that has been altered to leave room for a coffin and two passenger seats in the back. The minibus is larger than the van and has eight passenger seats as well as space for a coffin. The stretcher hearse is a black Cadillac that has been modified with a stretcher on the left and two passenger seats on the rear right. This hearse is used when the family members cannot decide on the price of the coffin at the time of the initial phone call, or when a family member specifically states that they do not want to put the deceased in a coffin until he or she is taken home, in which case the body is laid on the stretcher. All of these hearses have black lace curtains so that they can be immediately distinguished from other vans on the street. They are used specifically for transporting the dead from hospitals to their homes or to the funeral auditorium. Although these hearses could be used for transporting the body to the crematorium after the funeral, they are unpopular for that purpose. In fact, MAC members can use these hearses free of charge but rarely choose to do so, preferring the lavishly decorated golden hearse for the trip to the crematorium (see Chapter 4).

I joined Tomi in the van as soon as the coffin and other materials were loaded. Mitake led the way in another van. In most cases two funeral staff members work together at the initial stages of greeting the family of the deceased. Working in pairs speeds the encoffining; having two vans is convenient if the bereaved need a ride home or to the auditorium from the hospital. As usual, Mitake raced past other cars, speeding along, and we followed closely in the second van. It is customary for funeral staff to rush to hospitals whatever the traffic conditions; I noticed that police never stop them for speeding.

The hospital we went to that day was a modern, beautifully designed structure. From the outside it looked almost like a hotel. There was even a small gift shop on the first floor, unusual in Japan.[1] The hospital, Tomi told me, had been built recently by the city government and accepted only city officials and their family members. Tomi remarked that just by knowing the name of a hospital he could guess the approximate social status of the patients and their family. Companies often built hospitals for their workers, although private hospitals for the general public are also stratified by cost. Passing the entrance and parking spaces in front, we drove into the basement to the back door of the hospital, unloaded the coffin onto a hospital gurney, and headed to the room for the soul.[2] The room for the soul (*reianshitsu*, literally, the peaceful room for the soul) was on the top floor. In general, those who die are segregated immediately from other patients. In most hospitals, the room for the soul is located at the back or in the basement. Tomi explained that modern hospitals have relocated the room nearer to the sky than to the ground, in an attempt to change the common dark image of death. On our way there, we passed spacious tatami rooms where family and relatives could wait for the funeral staff. Pretty pastel-colored sofas and small tables lined the corridor. Sunlight and fresh air entered through tall windows. This hospital was distinctly different from most others, where the rooms of the deceased have few or no windows and smell of antiseptic.

TRANSPORTING THE DECEASED

The deceased had been laid on a bed across from the door. The body was covered with a comforter and the face with a white cloth. I could only see the long braided black hair. A young woman and a middle-aged man were standing in front of the body. (Later we learned that the man was the father and the woman the sister of the deceased.) A narrow piece of stained glass resembling a church window hung on the wall where the deceased lay. In one corner of the room on a table was a set of materials for burning incense sticks (*shōkō*). After bowing and introducing themselves, Tomi and Mitake confirmed that the man was the Mr. Yamaha who had called Moon Rise. The funeral staff explained that they would begin preparing for the departure. They rolled the table with the incense to the bed. Tomi lit a candle on the table and asked Yamaha and his daughter Sanae to burn incense. The father chose an incense stick, lit it with the candle flame, and placed it in the incense pot (*kōro*). He then pressed his hands together in front of his chest and bowed to the deceased. Sanae and each funeral staff member followed and offered incense. Since the medical staff had not already offered incense to the deceased, we waited for them to do so.

While waiting, Tomi asked the relatives if they would like to have a bathing ceremony for the deceased. He explained that although the body is wiped clean with antiseptics by nurses, a bathing ceremony provides a true bath for the deceased. "We use a real bathtub. Wouldn't you like to have her bathed for the last time in this life?" asked Tomi. Yamaha and Sanae looked at each other. "Will I be able to put makeup on Yoshiko one last time with my own hands?" Sanae asked. "Certainly," Tomi answered. When Sanae was assured that she could, the father said, "Please go ahead with that [bathing ceremony]" (*sōshite kudasai*). Tomi then asked if the father planned to have a wake at home or at the auditorium. The father said that he wanted to have both the wake and the funeral at the funeral auditorium, but wished to take Yoshiko home first. "My daughter Yoshiko was very sick for half a year and [during that time] she couldn't even come back home once," he explained. "I am sorry to hear that," Tomi said in a sympathetic tone. Their conversation stopped; the medical staff had finally arrived.

The medical staff burned incense for the deceased in the hierarchical order of doctors first, then senior nurses, and finally the younger nurses. When all the people who had cared for the dead woman had offered her incense, Tomi extinguished the candle and moved the table to its original position. Nurses and doctors bowed to Yamaha and left; there was no conversation between the medical staff and the family.

When they were alone again, Tomi asked the father's permission to begin the preparation of the body. "Yes, please," the father answered with a nod. Sometimes the family wants to help, but most of the time, as in the case of Yamaha and his daughter, they chose to watch the funeral staff perform their tasks.

The Buddhist death garments are laid out first; they are completely white and consist of a triangular head cloth (*zukin*), a pair of hand guards (*tekkō*), a robe (*kyō-katabira*), a pair of knee guards, a pair of Japanese-style socks (*shiro-tabi*), and beads (*juzu*). The comforter was removed from the corpse (the face cloth was not taken away at this time), revealing the body of Yoshiko in her *yukata* (Japanese gown, a thin kimono).

Tomi and Mitake shared the task of putting on the death garments. The hand guards and knee guards were easily placed, but putting on Japanese socks can be time-consuming because the big toes must fit into the division for them. Anchoring the beads between the fingers is often the most difficult part of the process. When the deceased has just passed away and rigor mortis has not set in, the hands laid on the chest easily fall apart. Sometimes hospital nurses have already tied the hands together with a cord, but in this case they had not. The funeral staff had to struggle to keep the hands and beads in place.[3] When all of death garments were in place, except for the head cloth,[4] Tomi gently removed the white cloth covering the face of Yoshiko, and she was ready to be encoffined.

The coffin, which had been left outside of the room on the stretcher, was brought in. The coffin stands were set on the floor, the coffin placed on them, and the lid removed. Tomi supported Yoshiko's neck and head while Mitake lifted her feet. Yoshiko was so light they were able to carry her easily to the coffin without any help. (The funeral staff sometimes ask family members or nurses for help if the body is particularly heavy.) When the deceased was encoffined, the funeral staff opened a fresh packet of a deodorant set, which contains four fragrance bags and a small perfume spray. The fragrance bags were placed at the top, left, and right and beneath the deceased, and the perfume was sprayed directly onto the interior of the coffin. The perfume is sufficiently powerful to be effective for the rest of the day. Next, the four rectangular dry ice blocks were placed directly on the deceased's body—one on the chest, two on the stomach, and one on the feet. Last, Yoshiko was covered with two blankets and the lid of the coffin was closed. When the bright orange coffin cover and the braided purple string were in place on the coffin, it was ready to leave.

The funeral staff lifted the coffin onto the gurney and rolled it to the elevator door while the rest of us followed. We all entered the elevator and got out at the basement where our van was parked; Tomi and Mitake loaded the coffin into the van. Sanae decided to come with us so she could remain with Yoshiko. Sanae sat in the back of the van beside the coffin. The father said he would drive his car and lead us to his house. With nurses sending us off at the back gate, we left the hospital.[5]

In more than half of the cases in which a person has died in a hospital, the funeral staff are asked to take the body home first. Often the deceased had expressed feelings of homesickness while hospitalized, or the family has missed the deceased and wants all the family members to be united one last time. While we were taking the body home, Sanae continued to sob with her arm on the coffin. The silence at the red traffic light emphasized the sound of her weeping. Tomi called to her and said, "Cheer up, Miss Yamaha, we will be home very soon." Sanae answered "Yes" (*hai*), quietly.

We arrived at the deceased's home, an apartment on the third floor of a newly built condominium. Tomi and Mitake helped Sanae out of the van. They then checked the width of the elevator and stairs. The elevator was too small to carry the coffin horizontally—a problem because the deceased must always be transported in a lying posture—so they could not use the elevator. Although the stairs were very narrow and steep, they were the only choice. "Customers are deities" (*okyakusama wa kamisama desu*), Tomi later told me. I responded, "You mean, the deceased are deities." "You got me on this one" (*ippon yarareta*) was his reply.

The coffin was carried with extreme care since striking the coffin in any way would be considered rude, inconsiderate, and immoral behavior on the part of the funeral staff. It was the beginning of winter, but perspiration was rolling down both the men's faces. After ten minutes of struggle on the stairs, they were able to safely negotiate the coffin into the apartment. The apartment was very clean. I noticed Tomi surveying the rooms while he was working.

Yoshiko was welcomed by family members and relatives who were waiting inside. "You are finally back," the women in the house sobbed as the coffin was set down in the room beside the kitchen. Mitake brought materials for burning incense from his van and prepared them for the family. One by one, each family member and relative burned a stick of incense. The window of the coffin was opened and the family began telling Yoshiko how much they missed her.

The family wanted to keep the deceased at home until other family members arrived. They said they would call us when they were ready to transport the deceased to the auditorium. We headed back to the auditorium to wait for their call. On the way back, Tomi told me that he once had to carry a deceased all the way up to the twentieth floor. "Japanese elevators in these condominiums are too narrow," he complained. "Do Americans have the custom of taking the deceased back to their home?" he asked me. When I said I hadn't heard of such a case, he commented with a little envy, "American funeral professionals must have an easier time than we do." The father called two hours later and was requested to prepare a photo of the deceased as well as his own seal (*inkan*).[6] The funeral staff returned to the family's home and collected the coffin to take to the auditorium; the family followed them in their car.

Moon Rise's Kokura Funeral Auditorium has five funeral halls (equipped with chairs) and six tatami rooms. Each hall and room has a name instead of a number to make it easy to find and avoid confusion. The Yamaha family was taken to the tatami room called the Moon Room (*tsuki-no-ma*) on the first floor. On the left-hand side of the room there was a funeral altar. Yoshiko's coffin was placed on a coffin stand in front of the altar, and the coffin cover was folded down so that the family could see Yoshiko's face through the coffin window.[7] When the family arrived, I added flowers to the vase in front of the altar. Yamaha was sitting alone near Yoshiko. It seemed that the rest of the family had left for a while to do errands. This was my first chance to talk to him. "I am so sorry about your daughter's death," I began. He nodded and told me that Yoshiko had become ill in June and within six months was much worse. "She passed away when none of us had time enough to care for her. It is often said that children who die earlier than their parents are bringing unhappiness to parents [*oyafukō-mono*], but I don't blame her. It really was not her fault." "Sickness is not a crime," I agreed. He continued telling me how much he regretted that he had not taken enough care of her; he seemed to feel that Yoshiko's death was his fault. I served him green tea, which he accepted with his head down. I left quietly.

Thirty minutes later I took freshly cooked rice and rice balls to the Yamaha family's room. This time Sanae was sitting alone near the coffin, looking at her dead sister and sobbing. She stopped crying when I entered the room. I set the rice bowl and rice balls on the small table. The room, saturated with mourning, was to-tally silent. Not knowing what exactly should be said, I told her that the auditorium prepares these foods for the deceased but that she was welcome to bring other items or food for her sister if she wished. She nodded and said, "Anything?" I said nothing made out of metal but anything that could be burned.[8] I asked her how old Yoshiko was. Sanae told me that Yoshiko was only 29. "She went so quickly, without enjoying her life," Sanae sobbed. There is a Japanese saying that those who are pretty and well liked die young (*bijin-hakumei*); I told Sanae that Yoshiko must have been such a person. "Yes, she was a good-natured person," Sanae replied. "She suffered so much at the end, but after she died her face became peaceful at last. Don't you think so?" She was looking at her sister through the coffin window. I agreed that Yoshiko looked peaceful. This was my first encounter with the death of someone around my age; the experience made me think about my own life, and the grief of the Yamaha family left a deep mark in my memory.

CONSULTING WITH THE BEREAVED

The size and cost of the wake and funeral ceremony are decided during the consultation (*uchiawase*). Tomi and I went into the consultation room with a heavy black briefcase packed with pamphlets and sample photographs. Yamaha, Sanae, and an aunt, Mariko (in the absence of the deceased's mother), were present.[9]

The father, who was the chief mourner, made most of the decisions during the consultation. The consultation process requires making a series of decisions that determine how much is spent on each funeral item. Tomi began by asking the father if Yoshiko had been a MAC member. She had not, but the father had completed his payments for the course of ¥420,000. Upon hearing this, Tomi told him that although the membership was in his name, it could be used for a family member. The father agreed to do so. Meanwhile Tomi had taken out the order form (*chūmon-seisho*). At the top of the form is space to write the name of the deceased, the family's surname, address, and telephone number, the time of the wake, ceremony, and departure for the crematorium (*shukkan*), and the place where the wake and ceremony will be held. Directly below it, the price and the name of the wake and funeral altars are indicated; the price ranges from ¥60,000 for the altar named Bright-Light (*Kōmyō*) to 3 million, 5 million, 7 million, or 10 million yen for a custom-made altar.[10] Under the altar prices, the order form is divided into two columns, where all items as well as the number of staff members needed for the wake and funeral ceremony are listed.

Tomi explained all the benefits included in the membership course of ¥420,000. A member in this category receives a funeral altar worth ¥420,000, a ¥30,000 coffin, the use of a hearse worth ¥10,000, one chairman during the wake and funeral, and the food (*kumotsu*) for the deceased all free of charge. This membership also provides a basic white porcelain ashpot, a postceremony altar made out of cardboard, free photo enlargements of the deceased for the wake and the funeral ceremony, photographs of the family members in front of the deceased's coffin, ¥3,200 worth of dry ice, ¥3,200 worth of deodorants, a credit of ¥12,000 for the use of a room for the wake, and a credit of ¥24,000 for the wake altar rental. These prices were listed on the sheet, which Tomi showed Yamaha. Then Tomi showed pictures of altars that cost more than the covered price of ¥420,000. He began with the photo of an altar costing 1 million yen and slowly turned the pages to show cheaper altars for ¥800,000 and ¥700,000. The funeral staff members' strategy is to show an altar that he considers appropriate to the status of the chief mourner; this standard is the staff's assessment of different customers (and is not the average cost of altars from the total sales at the funeral company).

It was obvious that Tomi had already calculated Yamaha's social standing well before this consultation. In this case he knew that the deceased had been hospitalized in a modern facility, that the family lived in a beautiful condominium, that the other daughter was also an adult with a job, and that the father worked for a successful company. He told Yamaha that if he decided to rent a more expensive altar than the one provided by the MAC course, the price of the MAC altar would be deducted. The father was looking at photos trying to decide. At this point Tomi said, "Father, this is your only chance to do something for your young daughter. There is no other chance after this one." Under this pressure, the father made up his mind. He said he would take the 1 million yen altar. The price was duly noted on the chart, ¥580,000 after the price of the standard altar had been subtracted.

Tomi continued, "Would you like to have the ceremony in a tatami room or in a hall with chairs? It depends on how many guests you will have. Tatami rooms are too small for more than 50 guests." The father looked at Mariko and Sanae for the first time and was trying to think how many guests would attend. "We will have nearly 100 guests," the father said. "In that case," Tomi replied, "you should have it in the hall. It is more convenient for elders to sit on chairs than on tatami." He looked at Mariko, who seemed to prefer the idea. "I don't think many people can sit in a Japanese style for a long time," she agreed. They settled on using a hall for the funeral ceremony. Now the Yamaha family had to choose an altar and a room for the wake. Since fewer people were expected at the wake and the tatami room was cheaper than the hall, they decided to have the wake in a tatami room. They still had to decide on an altar for the wake. This time, Tomi showed the altars that cost ¥180,000 and ¥120,000. The father chose the latter.

From the perspective of funeral staff members, selection of the altars constituted 70 percent of the cost decisions, and the rest of the decisions had to do with a multitude of small items. The appreciation or notification cards (*reijō*) are often chosen by the chief mourner, who will have the most guests. Cards are distributed not only to guests at the wake and funeral but also to people who cannot attend. Tomi brought out sample cards in various styles. What is written on these cards is similar; the price differences reflect the paper quality. Yamaha settled on a card costing ¥250 (the middle of the range) and ordered 150. After the cards, the catalogue of return gifts (*reihin*) was passed around. Mariko and Sanae chose the return gifts (which are offered to guests in return for the gifts they have brought) for the wake and ceremony. Women often have much more say about these gift items, since they know what would be appreciated and what would not, while the men, whose guests are in the majority, decide on the number of gifts. For the wake, most people choose small packs of sugar or green tea, which are about ¥250 to ¥300. For the funeral ceremony, a larger pack of green tea, seaweed, a handkerchief, rice seasoning (*furikake*), or a stationery set is preferred. The price range for the return gifts is between ¥1,000 and ¥2,000. The women from the Yamaha family chose sugar for the wake and green tea for the ceremony; both are the most popular items purchased.

While Mariko and Sanae selected gift items, the father was writing down information for the appreciation card. He put his name as the chief mourner and his brother-in-law's as the relative's representative. "Could we write the aunt's name?" the father asked. "Usually people only use men's names for these cards," Tomi answered. He then moved on to the next item, a pamphlet showing fresh-flower arrangements and dried-flower wreaths for decoration. Since flowers are considered a necessity for funerals, the family ordered a bouquet that comes in a tall standing pot in the name of family and relatives. The flower bouquets cost ¥15,000 for one and ¥30,000 to ¥40,000 for a pair; they have wooden plaques attached to them on which the word "family" or "relatives" is written in calligraphy, indicating who presented the gift to the deceased.[11] The Yamaha family did not purchase dried-flower wreaths. They believed that the Yoshiko would prefer real flowers.[12]

One bureaucratic service that most funeral companies perform for their customers is taking the death certificate and notification of death forms to the city office to receive a cremation certificate (*kasō-kyokasho*), a permit for cremation.[13] Tomi asked Yamaha for the death certificate (*shibōshindansho*), helped him finish filling it out, and asked him for his seal. Then Tomi turned to the family and asked if they had brought a recent photo of the deceased that could be enlarged for the wake and the funeral. They brought out a professionally photographed picture that had been taken on Yoshiko's coming-of-age celebration (*seijin-shiki*). It was a beautiful picture of Yoshiko wearing a bright kimono; although the photo would be in color as the family wished, Tomi reminded them that the photographers would have to make the kimono black for the funeral picture.[14] They nodded.

"Did you decide on the time of the wake?" Tomi asked them before closing his order form. The father said that the priest of his temple had requested 7:00 P.M. "Seven o'clock today then," said Tomi. He also reconfirmed that they would have the bathing ceremony and added this to the order form. Taking out his calculator, he estimated the approximate total (about ¥1,800,000), and handed the form to Yamaha for his signature. Yamaha signed without even glancing at the figure. Tomi completed the consultation by stating, "I am sorry to have taken so much of your time. The professionals who will perform the bathing ceremony will be right with you." Tomi and I then bowed flat on the tatami and left the room.

The consultation had taken one hour, less than the average

time of 90 minutes. The amount of time spent on the consultation depends on the number of people present; the more people, the longer it takes to come to an agreement. Naturally it is easier for the funeral staff when fewer people make the decisions.

As soon as the consultation was over and no one was in sight, I asked Tomi how he knew which size altar to show to the family. Tomi smiled proudly and said, "Hospital, house, bathroom, kitchen, and company." He explained that the hospital in which a deceased has stayed, the size and the location of the house, the modernity and cleanliness of the bathroom and kitchen, and the deceased or the chief mourner's occupation are the main factors on which he bases his assumption about the family's social status. I then recalled that while we had been at the deceased's house, Tomi, who had been carefully observing the kitchen, suddenly disappeared. He whispered to me that he had been using and inspecting the bathroom. Accompanying Tomi that day, I noted that there is one commonality shared by funeral staff members and anthropologists; we are both careful observers.

The Bathing Ceremony

Traditionally, the bathing ceremony (*yukan*) was performed to cleanse the impurity of the deceased and further safeguard both the deceased and the living from death pollution. The ritual was performed by close family members at home.[15] The bathing ritual ceased after World War II, in part because of a decrease in deaths occurring in the home and an increase in hospital deaths, where nurses wipe the body with antiseptic.[16] Having introduced a commercialized bathing service in November 1994, Moon Rise now has a contract with a Bathing Service Company called CSC, and CSC reinstated the old custom as part of the contemporary funeral ceremony, for an additional charge of ¥50,000.[17]

Hirata and Oka, who work for CSC and Moon Rise, met the Yamaha family after Tomi had finished his consultation. They bowed first and asked immediately who the chief mourner was.

They both knelt in front of the deceased's father, and Oka sincerely stated the words of condolence (*okuyami no kotoba*) and followed them with a deep bow. She then apologized to the family members in advance that the bathing staff would be moving around the room constantly during the ceremony. She also asked which religion the deceased had belonged to so that she would not use the wrong type of death garments.

A clean fluffy futon was brought in and placed near the body. (All the necessary accoutrements are brought in the CSC vans.) A nylon sheet was laid in the middle of the tatami room and the tub was brought in. Next, the coffin was opened. A big bath towel was slipped beneath the body; Hirata grasped both sides of the towel and twisted the towel over the deceased's body to make a handle to lift the deceased. Hirata and Oka took hold of the towel and the deceased's neck and legs, lifted her, and laid her gently on the futon. This method of lifting the deceased was used throughout the ceremony.

The nightgown and some parts of the death garments that Tomi and Mitake had put on her at the hospital were removed. When Yoshiko was completely naked, a large white towel was laid on top of her, covering her body. Her hands and fingers were taken out of the pressed-together position. The bathing staff then began to massage the deceased's joints; by this time rigor mortis had begun to set in. The staff bent her arms, wrists, and hands into different positions to loosen the stiffness. Then they carried her to the bathtub in the towel. The body of the deceased is laid on a stretcher-cum-hammock that hangs inside the tub; this design allows water and soap to drain through while the deceased is being washed. On one side of the tub there are three rubber hoses connected to the van; two hoses provide hot and cold water, and the third vacuums out the used water after the ceremony is completed.

When Yoshiko was on the stretcher, Hirata explained that the traditional bathing ceremony was meant to cleanse the deceased of the impurities of this world before her soul's departure to Buddhahood. Then he brought out a wooden bucket (*oke*) and a wooden ladle (*shaku*) with a long handle. Following the custom of the traditional bathing ceremony, he added cold water to the hot water in the bucket to make the water warm (which is the opposite of the usual way to make warm water). Hirata explained that the initial stage of the ceremony, "the splashing of water," would be performed by the family members, and he described to them how to do it. The person should stand in front of the deceased and hold the wooden bucket in the right hand and the wooden ladle in the left. Then the person should scoop the warm water out of the bucket in one movement and pour it on the deceased, beginning with the lower part of the body and working up to the heart. Hirata warned the Yamahas not to add more water to the ladle before emptying it completely. Returning a partially full ladle to the bucket is like calling back the soul to this life and would confuse the deceased (whose soul should travel toward Buddhahood, not back toward life). The Yamahas rose and took turns performing as they had been instructed.

The splashing of water (particularly the way the water was mixed, the use of wooden bucket and ladle, and the prohibition against refilling the ladle before it was emptied) is closely connected to the concept of impurity in traditional funeral rituals. Everything, from preparing the warm water to the materials used, was performed contrary to usual everyday practices. Hirata explained that non-ordinary behavior by the living indicated the irreversibility of the deceased's death so that the person would depart from this world. The performance of pouring water, during which a family member is not allowed to add water in the midst of the ritual act, also denotes that the deceased is forbidden from returning to or staying longer with the living. The bathing ritual was intended to make clear to the deceased the distinction and the boundary between this world and the world after. What lay behind this performance during community funerals had been fear that the malevolent spirit (*onryō*) would harm the living. However, in the commercialized bathing ceremony, the staff members put little emphasis on the concept of impurity, and the performance of the rituals is designed to bring the family members together and let them be part of the ceremony.

The remainder of the bathing service was very different from the traditional bathing ritual; there was no mention of impurity again by the bathing staff. After the family had taken turns wetting the body, Hirata asked them to sit down while the staff performed the rest of the ceremony. Oka began washing Yoshiko's toes with body soap and a fluffy bath sponge. During this time, Yoshiko's torso was kept covered with a white towel. Oka soaped her from her toes, up her legs and arms. Hirata shampooed her hair, and when that was finished, he helped Oka wash the chest, stomach, and abdomen. The front part of the body is uncovered by lifting the towel up toward the family. While Oka was soaping the body, Hirata kept his back toward the family, effectively blocking their view. The two worked in a coordinated rhythm, assisting each other in washing every part of Yoshiko's body. Hirata lifted the torso forward so that Oka could sponge her back.[18] When all of the body had been soaped, they rinsed off the lather with warm water from a shower head. Then they dried her with many bath towels. Yoshiko was lifted so that thick cotton could be put between the buttocks and legs. The towel covering her was exchanged for a fresh large white one. Then Hirata asked Yamaha and Sanae to come forward to dry Yoshiko's face. Hirata handed a fresh towel to the father. This was for the sake of performance because the deceased had been dried completely by the bathing staff.

The deceased was carried back to the futon by means of the wrapped and twisted towel. The death robe had been spread neatly on the futon earlier; it was a simple matter to place the deceased on top of it. Yoshiko was then dressed in a new set of death garments: a white gown (*kyō-katabira*), knee guards, and Japanese-style socks (*shiro-tabi*). Those that had been used at the hospital were discarded. When the deceased was dressed, her hands were pressed together and a pair of hand guards (*tekkō*) and beads (*juzu*) were carefully attached.

Oka knelt on the tatami near Yoshiko's face. She removed the cotton from inside the nose, ears, and mouth where the hospital nurses had placed it. She used long, narrow pieces of fresh cotton for the nose and ears, and thicker, wider cotton for the mouth; this helps form aesthetically shaped cheeks and lips. Then Oka asked Sanae if she would like to apply the makeup. (Usually Oka applies the makeup, but in this case Tomi had passed on the information that the sister had requested to do so.) Sanae brought out her own makeup kit. While she applied foundation to the deceased, the aunt, Mariko, approached to observe the process. Sanae and Mariko began talking to the deceased: "You are so clean. I'm so glad you had a chance to take a bath; you couldn't take a bath for a long time, could you?" Their conversation drew everyone near. Soon family and relatives all commented to each other how fresh Yoshiko looked after her bath. Meanwhile, Sanae was asking the deceased her color preferences. "Yoshiko, do you prefer brown eye shadow? Is red lipstick O.K.?" As if Yoshiko had replied, Sanae went on, "Yes, I know you always liked bright red." As soon as Sanae completed the makeup, Mariko murmured, "You look so beautiful, as if you were a bride." The statement triggered the emotions of the entire family; they broke into sobs. The deceased had died young and never married.

Meanwhile, Hirata had been cleaning the tub and putting it back into the van. When he returned, he asked the father to help him lay Yoshiko in the coffin. When she was settled in the coffin, he began the last stage of the bathing ceremony—the decoration around the deceased's face with white cotton and cloth. One pack of cotton, about the size of a big cushion, was used to make a frame for the face. Oka cut a flat rectangular sheet of cotton into four narrow rectangular pieces and handed them to Hirata, who carefully laid each piece around the deceased's face like a picture frame. The cotton was added in many layers to give depth. A triangular head cloth (*zukin*) was arranged on top of the deceased's head. Oka handed blocks of dry ice wrapped in white flannel cloth to Hirata, who placed them on the stomach. Two comforters, one white and gold and one pure white, were used to cover Yoshiko's body. At this point, the finale of the bathing ceremony, Hirata called the family members for the last performance: all family members held the coffin lid and shut the coffin. Hirata laid the coffin cover and the decoration string on the coffin but kept the window open for viewing. The small incense table that had been moved out of the way was put back in front of the coffin. The candle and incense were lit again. Hirata knelt down facing family and relatives and said, "We have concluded the bathing ceremony. I am sure the next few days are going to be very difficult for you. I hope you will all take care of your health. Thank you for your patience today." We bowed to the family while kneeling on the tatami floor. The family bowed back to us and said, "Thank you for all you have done." We bowed once again at the door. The whole bathing ceremony had taken about an hour and a half.

The reactions of the deceased's family during bathing ceremonies varied according to the age and gender of the deceased, as well as the cause of death. The atmosphere of the bathing ceremony described above was very emotional because Yoshiko was a young unmarried woman. She had much unfinished business and was pitied for the unfortunate illness that had struck her down so quickly.

In contrast, the bathing ceremony of Mori Rei, a woman in her nineties, was almost joyous. When we entered the room, the male family members stood up to go to the coffee shop in the auditorium. The son, Mori Teruo, a man in his late sixties who was the chief mourner, said to me with a smile, "I don't think I want to see my mother take a bath, and mother would be embarrassed, too," and left with the other male relatives. The women family members stayed and watched us with much curiosity. They chatted with each other and spoke to Rei from the beginning. One woman commented, "How lucky you are to have a bath for the last time." The other woman added, "How nice to be washed by such a young man and young women. I didn't think that young people did such things these days." No aspect of the bathing ceremony passed without comment from the women. When the bathtub was carried in and the shower was used to wash the deceased, the women came to admire the Western bathtub. "This is such a convenient thing, isn't it?" one woman said to the others, who all nodded in agreement. Before Hirata had a chance to announce the completion of the ceremony, the women were complimenting the deceased. "You look so fresh and young." "Rei looks so nice; now she is ready to meet her husband in heaven." The family seemed not only satisfied but pleased as well. The women told me during the ceremony that Rei had died quietly in her sleep. The reaction of the living naturally corresponded to the peaceful nature of this woman's death. Everyone was celebrating her death and her life.

One bathing ceremony that I remember clearly was for Tano Genzō, a man in his sixties. It took place at his home on a morning in early spring; the weather was still so cold that the boiler in the van took some time to heat the water. From the beginning, Hirata, Oka, and I all felt something was distinctly different about the reaction of this family. The atmosphere of the room was very heavy. It was not the silence that made me uneasy, but the way the family either stared at us or avoided our eyes while inspecting each other's faces as if they were trying to read each other's thoughts. As soon as we unclothed Tano Genzō, we saw a blue line on his neck, which looked like a scar. I assumed that the deceased had had an operation on his throat. While we were washing the deceased, the family did not speak to us, to each other, or to the deceased. There was an atmosphere of intense silence, ambivalence, and seriousness. When Oka and I went outside to the van for fresh towels, she commented that the atmosphere was extraordinary. "I don't understand this family," she whispered. "All families react in some way, but these people are completely silent, as if they've been turned to stone" (*ishimitaini kataku natteru*).

When the bathing was completed, male members of the family helped Hirata place the deceased into the coffin; so far no one had said a word. Then, as the bathing staff prepared to frame the deceased's face with cotton, the son, who was the chief mourner, approached and said something in a low voice that no one else in the room could hear. Hirata nodded and replied, "I will do so." After we had left, Hirata told us that the son had said, "Could you hide that scar?" Hirata had arranged the cotton around the face, and later the comforter, up to Tano's chin to hide his scar.

The second time the son spoke he asked if it was all right to put objects in the coffin. Interestingly, the first object they brought out was a Buddhist sutra. Often family members bring clothes, eyeglasses, and other objects that were used by the deceased in daily life or that were valuable to the deceased. But in this case many Buddhist objects were placed in the coffin. Hirata announced the end of the ceremony, and we bowed to the family and moved toward the door. At this point the family surprised me again: all of them came out of the house. The three of us got into the van and Hirata started the engine, then the van started to move. They were still standing in the cold rain. From inside the van we bowed at them while the car was moving forward. Then I saw the Tano family members bowing to us with their heads down low. I had never seen the bereaved bowing so low. I looked back from the moving van; they were still standing there.

"What is all this appreciation about? Weren't they bowing a bit too deeply?" I asked Hirata, who had been doing this job for three years. Hirata said that the deceased had committed suicide. According to him, when people hang themselves, they often bite their tongues. Their lips cannot be opened easily. That was exactly how Tano was that day. Oka had tried to put cotton in the mouth, but it had been shut tight. "The rigor mortis of the suicide victim occurs more rapidly than it does for people who die from other causes," Hirata added. The scar on Tano Genzō's neck was a mark from hanging. Hirata's explanation unraveled the mystery of the family's unusual behavior. "A suicide is still considered a very bad death in Japan," he said. "They must have been worried that we would treat the deceased with fear or refuse to perform the ceremony if the fact was revealed. The deep bows were the expression of their appreciation to us, that we did the job without causing the family to lose face."[19]

Although the size of the funeral is determined by deceased's social status, age, and gender, the atmosphere of the funeral corresponds to the cause of death and the deceased's personality. It was not difficult to tell if a death had been a "good death" or a "bad death" by the way families and relatives interacted with the funeral staff. The death of a young person is always traumatic, as are violent deaths whatever the age of the deceased, whereas anticipated deaths are more peaceful. Deceased who were well liked called forth strong feelings of grief. Such distinctions were amplified in the vigils and funerals.

The Wake at the Funeral Auditorium

The wake for the Yamaha family was scheduled for 7:00 P.M. on the same day the deceased was transported to the funeral auditorium. A few hours before the wake, Doi, the conductor hired by Moon Rise, arrived to meet the bereaved. He began by explaining the sequence of events and details about the wake and the funeral, such as where the bereaved would sit and what they would be expected to do. He finished by asking the family if they had any questions or problems so far. Yamaha and Mariko asked how large the monetary donation (*ofuse*) for the priest should be.[20] "That varies according to different temples, the rank of the deceased's posthumous name (*kaimyō*), and the number of attending priests," Doi replied. "In the case of my temple, which is Jōdoshū, I would enclose ¥100,000 for one priest." The higher the rank and the number of the priests, and the higher the rank of the posthumous name given, the larger the donation. Doi drew a picture of a donation envelope and wrote "contribution" on the upper portion and the name of the chief mourner below the ribbon. The father, who was also worried about his funeral speech as the chief mourner, asked what he was expected to say. Opening his file, Doi took out copies of sample speeches and told Yamaha that he need only say a few words and thank the guests for coming in spite of their busy schedules. This meeting, which was a basic lesson on Japanese funerals, took about 40 minutes.

The Buddhist priest, from a Jōdoshinshū sect temple, arrived about fifteen minutes before seven. He was a young man in his late thirties. We bowed to him, and he lightly bowed back to the funeral professionals. A woman funeral assistant was there to take him to his waiting room, but instead he went directly to the tatami room where family and relatives had gathered for the wake. The family greeted the priest with a bow and began to talk to him about the deceased. Priests often do not have any knowledge of the deceased; the wake is the first time a priest is told about the cause of death and the deceased's life in general. Sometimes this may even be the first time the priest meets the family.[21] While the family was talking to the priest, Doi went into the room and introduced himself to the priest.

The guests arrived gradually. The first and most important obligation of a guest is to offer incense money to the deceased's family. In community rituals, incense money, or condolence money (*kōden*), was predominantly offered on the day of the funeral, but today those who cannot attend the funeral ceremony present their gifts at the wake. Incense money is enclosed in a special envelope with one's name on the lower portion in front and the amount of money on the back. The amount of money varies according to the giver's relationship to the deceased or to the bereaved (see Table 1).

The gift of incense money necessitates a return gift (*kōden-gaeshi*). The exchange is a formal performance during which both sides present their gifts and then bow deeply. These exchanges are made even more solemn by elders who present their envelopes with both hands and use traditional incense money wrappers (*fukusa*) made out of dark-colored silk. This custom is fading,

TABLE I

Incense Money Donations (in yen)

Donor's relationship to the deceased or the bereaved	AGE OF DONOR			
	20s	30s	40s	50s
Boss	¥ 5,000*	¥ 5,000	¥ 10,000	¥ 10,000
	6,100	7,000	8,600	7,760
Family member	3,000	3,000	5,000	5,000
of boss	3,800	3,900	5,200	5,000
Business	3,000	5,000	5,000	5,000
colleague	5,700	62,00	7,300	7,300
Family member	3,000	3,000	5,000	5,000
of business	3,400	3,500	4,200	4,400
colleague				
Younger	3,000	5,000	5,000	5,000
business	4,600	6,000	7,700	6,500
colleague				
Family member	3,000	3,000	5,000	5,000
of younger	3,600	3,200	4,200	8,000
business colleague				
Friend or	5,000	5,000	5,000	5,000
acquaintance	6,300	6,000	7,300	8,000
Brother or sister	10,000	10,000	50,000	50,000
	29,500	35,800	37,400	59,600
Grandparent	10,000	10,000	30,000	50,000
	21,000	26,300	32,300	40,100
Uncle or aunt	10,000	10,000	10,000	30,000
	13,000	17,600	18,600	29,400
Nephew or niece	10,000	10,000	10,000	30,000
	13,000	17,600	18,600	29,400

* The first figure is the amount cited most frequently by survey respondents; the second figure is the average of the figures cited by respondents. 110 yen = approximately one U.S. dollar.

SOURCE: Survey by Shizuoka Newspapers in Shizuoka Prefecture, in *Shizuoka Ken no Kankon Sōsai* (*Weddings and funerals in Shizuoka*) (Shizuoka: Shizuoka Newspapers Press, 1995), 172.

however. The younger generations, including people in their fifties and sixties, hand an unwrapped envelope of incense money directly to relatives or helpers who represent the bereaved family. I occasionally saw embarrassed guests, who had forgotten to inscribe their name on the envelope, quickly writing their names on the spot.

It is not unusual for the funeral staff to help the deceased's families prepare a money offering to the priests, and also to assist guests with their incense envelopes. The coffee shop at the Moon Rise auditorium sells such basic funeral items as envelopes for incense money, rosaries (*juzu*), black neckties, black socks, and black stockings, because guests quite often forget to bring these items or wear inappropriate attire.

While representatives from Yamaha's family at the front desk were keeping track of incense money and giving return gifts, funeral assistants guided those guests who had finished the exchange to the tatami room. The room was becoming crowded, and an assistant had to ask people to move forward and add more cushions (*zabuton*). The guests were all seated neatly in two rows facing the coffin and the wake altar at the front of the room. The priest sat at the very front of the altar, and the family was seated in the front row on the right. Finally the wave of arriving guests subsided. It was time to begin.

Doi took a seat near the priest. He straightened his back and announced the beginning of the wake. He gave the deceased's name and age, the time of death, and the priest's rank and temple. Then he asked the priest to begin his sutra chanting. The priest began with the rhythmic "*nam-mu-a-mi-da-bu-tsu*" (Lord have mercy upon him/her), loudly at first, then more quietly at the end. After repeating the verse, he chanted the sutra text for twenty minutes. Unless one is a specialist in religion, it is difficult to understand even a word of what is being chanted. Many guests closed their eyes and lowered their heads until it was time for the incense offering (*shōkō*). It is not uncommon for people to fall asleep during the sutra chanting, and even to snore. Another participant quickly wakes the person.

When the priest had completed the major portion of the text, Doi announced the offering of incense. The offering began with the closest family members and continued until all of the guests had offered incense at the alter while the priest, sitting to the right, continued to chant. By 8:10 p.m. everyone had offered incense. The priest, who had been facing the altar, turned around to the family and guests. He announced that the prayers for the wake (*otsutome*) had been completed. He began to tell Buddhist stories (*hōwa*):

> There are two kinds of life in person. One is a physical life, and the other is the spiritual life. The world is alternating [*mu-jō-jissō*]; nothing stays the same and everything changes. All things change with a certain aim, namely, to achieve Buddhahood. Why do flowers bloom? Why do flowers fade away? Why do fruits ripen and fall? All lives exist for the sole purpose to become and to reach Buddhahood. The life of the physical body may stop at an early stage. But the spiritual life grows and develops without any limitations or bounds. The end of the physical life is not the final end. There is a life beyond in the world of Buddha [*jōbutsu*].

Unfortunately, the guests did not seem overly impressed with the priest's story; at least I did not notice anyone nodding in agreement. The message of the preaching was difficult to accept, even contradicting the emotions felt by a family that had lost a daughter so young. When the priest had completed his Buddhist exhortation, a funeral assistant served him a cup of tea. The priest pressed his hands together (*gasshō*), bowed, and drank a sip. Then he chatted with the chief mourner while sipping tea. Ten minutes later, the priest bowed once more to the family and left the room.

The priest's departure was the cue for other guests to leave. The vigil was about to begin. Family and relatives gathered around the table that had been prepared by a funeral assistant while guests were leaving. The Yamaha family asked Doi to join the vigil, but he courteously declined for the reason that he had to prepare for the funeral the following day. The funeral assistant helped the family arrange two large plates of vegetarian sushi, nuts, other food items, plates, and cups. The assistant and the women of the family began serving sake and beer to the male family members and relatives. By 9:15 P.M., observing that the gathering was proceeding on its own, the funeral assistant also left.

The family spent a few more hours drinking and talking. At community funerals, wakes commonly served only vegetarian food (*shōjin*), no meat or alcohol. However, almost all the wakes I observed during my fieldwork served alcohol. Men drank, but few women did so. Drinking patterns at wakes and funerals varied according to the circumstances of the deceased's death and reflected a pattern in society at large. In the case of the Yamaha family, sipping sake was a way to share the sadness of losing a young daughter. For those who had lost an old grandmother, drinking was a way to celebrate her long life and peaceful death. For those who had lost loved ones in an accident or by suicide, gulping beer helped temporarily dull their grief. Drinking is not taboo at contemporary wakes or at funerals. On the contrary, it is an appropriate or even necessary gesture to demonstrate one's sympathy, pain, and sorrow over a particular death. Moon Rise's funeral auditorium has refrigerators stocked with beer beside each tatami room because drinking during a wake goes on until midnight and sometimes throughout the night.

The women in the Yamaha family retired before midnight, leaving the men drinking. After emptying a dozen large beer bottles and a dozen small sake bottles, male participants asked the funeral staff to call them cabs for the ride home. By midnight everyone had left except the two relatives who were staying overnight with Yoshiko in the tatami room.[22] Their bedding (futon, pillows, and blankets) was rented for this purpose.

Quite a few families do not have anyone stay with the deceased for the vigil. Elder funeral staff lamented about this to me. "Some families leave their deceased all alone. It's shameful." But in fact, the feeling of shame for not attending the deceased during the vigil is weakening. In community funerals, sitting or lying near the deceased's coffin or bedside throughout the night was essential. The deceased was at that time in a transitional period and had to be protected from the evil spirits (*akuryō*). For this reason, the family took turns keeping incense burning to ward off evil spirits and prevent them from entering the body. Today, however, funeral staff and funeral conductors are often asked the same questions by family members: Is it really necessary to stay with the deceased at night? Will anyone be at the auditorium for the night shift? Funeral professionals commonly state that it is not compulsory to stay with the deceased during the vigil and that there are three funeral professionals on the overnight shift. Upon hearing this, most families conclude that they do not need to remain because, as they put it, "The deceased is taken care of by the funeral staff." The funeral staff make sure the family understands that that they will not be in the deceased's room itself but in the night-shift room downstairs. A typical response to this is: "It's okay [*sorede kekkōdesu*], as long as someone is in the building." The bereaved, however, should not be solely blamed for this change in practice; even the funeral professionals themselves put out all incense and candles at night to avoid the risk of fire.

Why then did families cease to stay up with the deceased through the night? The change in this practice demonstrates that both the family and funeral professionals do not consider the deceased to be in a state of impurity. In this chapter I have described funerary performances after the announcement of death and prior to a funeral ceremony. What is explicit during this period is the absence of the perception of impurity, death pollution, and evil spirits. These concepts are irrelevant not only to professionals of Moon Rise but also to the bereaved. The reason the Yamaha family left two relatives with Yoshiko was not because she was in a dangerous transitional state but because "she will be lonely" (*hi-*

toride kawaisō dakara). Similarly, the funeral staff complained about the bereaved who did not stay with the dead, saying, "They are not fully showing respect to the deceased." On the one hand, if the living perceive the deceased to be alive, there is no impurity or danger of evil spirits to be dealt with. On the other hand, if funeral professionals view the deceased as alive but in a state of unconsciousness, then a family member should stay to assist the person just as would be done during a hospitalization. Both of these two commonly expressed rationales by the living and professionals place the deceased, until the end of the funeral ceremonies, in a resuscitated state rather than in a biological or social transition phase. The belief in the "living-dead" explains why funeral professionals (who are engaged before cremation) display extreme respect and caution while treating the deceased's body.

4

THE FUNERAL CEREMONY:
RITES OF PASSAGE

A mother lost her twenty-year-old son in a traffic accident that he caused while riding the motorbike that she had bought for him. A year later, the mother was still grieving and regretting having purchased the motorcycle for her son. What was the meaning of his life? It is meaningless if he died just when a whole life was in front of him, she thought. She was depressed; sometimes she heard a noise and imagined that her son was there.

One day a friend encouraged her to write a memoir of her son's life. The mother began writing. She recalled many activities that her son had participated in and that had given joy to the family. Thus the mother recognized that her son had had a short but valuable life. Finally, when she was able to accept his death, she emerged from a tunnel of grief.

—Himonya, *Learning About the Funeral Ceremony*

One of the distinctive characteristics of a contemporary funeral ceremony is that it is highly compressed: the rites of separation, transition, and incorporation take place in a single day. In an abridged ceremony, the form of the deceased and the attitude of the living toward the deceased change dramatically over the course of the process. For example, when a coffin arrives at a crematorium, it is once more surrounded by the bereaved. When it finally disappears into an incinerator, the chief mourner and the second-chief mourner push a button. Many mourners hesitate to press this button because they perceive their action to be the final death sentence for the deceased. According to cremators there are occasions when none of the bereaved will push the button because "no one wants to be responsible for the deceased's death." On such occasions one of the cremators will press the button. But one time when a cremator did so, an outraged chief mourner yelled at him, "You are killing my mother!" (*Haha wo korosu kika*). "I had to apologize to the son for killing his mother," the cremator explained with a suppressed smile and added, "That was unpleasant" (*Are niwa ōjō shimashitayo*). When the remains are taken from an incinerator they are no more than a collection of brittle bones and a skull. At that time, in contrast to the earlier phase of the funeral ceremony, the deceased's skull is necessarily treated with violence. Using long metal chopsticks, a cremator pokes the skull at a right angle a couple of times, cracking it into several pieces.

As I described earlier, traditional community death rituals comprised four stages: the rites of attempted resuscitation, breaking bonds, achievement of Buddhahood, and memorial services. The categorization of four stages, however, cannot be applied to contemporary funeral ceremonies because it assumed a funeral process to be a transition of the deceased's spirit from malevolent (ara-mitama) to peaceful (nigi-mitama) or a shift from an impure to a pure state. Contemporary funeral ceremonies not only suppress the concept of impurity but also distance themselves from the very idea. It is wrong to state that death pollution or impurity is completely absent from today's funerals, but people perceive it only at the stage of cremation, and furthermore it does not last for an extended period because most cremations are completed within two hours (see Chapter 6). In addition, ceremonial performances are not performed to appease the deceased's spirit or to cleanse impurity. For example, in community funerals the performance of scattering purification salt (*kiyome-jio*) on one's body and washing one's hands with it after returning from a procession (*okiyome*) was essential to purify oneself. Today, funeral companies still prepare a cart with salt, water, and towels for their guests returning from the crematorium. However, if a professional is not present to help the bereaved, they often ignore the cart and go right back into their room; their behavior demonstrates that they do not consider death impure or that they do not understand the purpose of this performance. (If a funeral professional is present to assist the bereaved, they will use the purification materials accordingly.) There is a recent trend to discontinue using purification salt completely. In 1998, 63 funeral companies within Osaka City brought the salt-purification rite to a halt, and the Yokkaichi-City Buddhist Association in Mie prefecture, which includes 196 Buddhist temples, agreed to cease the practice by a unanimous vote (*Asahi Shimbun,* September 8, 1998). Temple priests and funeral companies stated that "The salt-purification practice is a superstition that perceives death to be impure. In Buddhism, death is not considered polluted because the deceased is regenerated into a Buddha. Thus, the practice must be eradicated not only because it contradicts Buddhist thought, but also because it gives a wrong impression of death. It interprets death as the emanation of pollution that must be eradicated quickly, rather than the opportunity for enlightenment that must be contemplated seriously" (ibid.).

In response to the waning belief in the impurity, pollution, and danger of death, the corpse, and the deceased in contemporary Japan, I apply the framework of the rites of passage—the rites of separation, transition, and incorporation—as a means to analyze the commercial funeral process. Unlike community funerals, the rites of passage do not prioritize the transition of the deceased, the corpse, or the spirit; instead they provide flexibility in selecting the target of focus. My intention is to illustrate funeral ceremonies from the perspective of the bereaved's social roles and the expected behavior and responsibilities of funeral professionals.

The end of the funeral ceremony and the beginning of cremation, which serve as the rites of separation, are the focus of this chapter. In order to demonstrate how they vary according to the age, gender, ethnicity, and religion of the deceased, I have included descriptions of a company funeral, the funeral of a devoted disciple of religion, the funerals of an ethnic Korean and an ethnic Chinese, and the funeral of Yamaha Yoshiko.

Cremation and the seventh-day memorial services, which correspond respectively to the rites of transition and the rites of incorporation, follow, and they complete the funeral ceremony. After the completion of a funeral, what remains tangible to confirm the death of the deceased are the ashpot (with cremated remains), group photos (taken immediately before the funeral), incense money, and the bill from the funeral company. These compressed ceremonies are notable in two respects: for the disappearance of the notion of death pollution, and for a shortened mourning and healing period for the bereaved. If there is no death pollution, then equally, there is little reason to have a mourning period (*mochū*), during which certain activities by the deceased's family members are forbidden (e.g., visiting a Shintō shrine) and during which the family receives sympathy and care from community members. Whereas "*imiake*" (the lifting of pollution) used to take place 49 days after a death, the official mourning period is now only one day, the day of the funeral (Kita-Kyūshūshi Kyōikuiinkai 1988, 56). Today Japanese people go back to work and proceed with their usual lives on the day after the funeral of a family member.

A reduced period of mourning, however, means that the bereaved spend less time healing from the loss of a loved one. Kübler-Ross identified the five stages of the grieving process as denial, anger, bargaining, depression, and acceptance. She believes that the sooner a person can accept the deceased's death as reality, the faster she or he can recover from the feeling of loss. Then how does a bereaved person come to terms with the loss of a loved one? I believe the answer lies in the quality of the healing occasions experienced by the bereaved.

Communicating with others about the death of a loved one helps the bereaved recover from the tragedy. Untangling one's emotions is a quest that helps one to understand not only the death of a loved one but also one's own life. Do commercial funeral ceremonies provide such opportunities? The answer is both yes and no. On the one hand, many funeral companies like Moon Rise emphasize the quality of their services in an effort to help the bereaved emotionally. On the other hand, funeral companies must make sound business decisions; they cannot, for example, indefinitely extend the allocated time for funerals. The ceremonies must be well planned in order to accommodate the schedules of priests, participants, hearse drivers, and cremators. The risk is that the more attention the funeral companies pay to punctuality, the less significant the funeral experience will be for participants. Achieving a balance between the length of the funeral and the quality of service is the constant battle faced by the funeral industry.

Contemporary Funerals

The funeral was scheduled for 1:00 P.M. At 9:30 that morning, two part-time female employees made fresh rice and sticky-rice balls for the deceased. They bowed and spoke words of condolence to the family when they entered the Moon Room and arranged the rice dishes on the table in front of the coffin. The rice and the sticky-rice balls from the day before were carefully wrapped in white paper and left behind on the corner of the table to be placed in the deceased's coffin at the end of the funeral. Doi, the funeral conductor, arrived at the auditorium at 10:00 A.M. and gathered all the telegrams that had arrived for the Yamaha family. With these telegrams in hand, he went to Yamaha and gave him the approximate schedule for the day. The conductor also conferred with him about telegrams to be read during the ceremony; the telegrams from higher executives in his company and important teachers from Yoshiko's schools were selected. By 10:30 A.M., all the close relatives had arrived at the auditorium. Male mourners wore black suits with black neckties. Women mourners began to change into black mourning kimonos, which most of them had rented from Moon Rise. In another room a funeral assistant was fitting kimonos on Sanae and Mariko, the sister and aunt of the deceased. The other women mourners were busy helping each other get dressed and applying makeup.

After helping the family with their kimonos, the funeral assistant set out vegetarian lunch boxes (*otoki*). The lunch boxes, ordered by the family for themselves, close relatives, and the deceased, had been prepared and brought in by the Shōhakuen Hotel, which was owned by Moon Rise. The deceased's lunch box was placed in front of the coffin with a pair of chopsticks. When the women were ready at around 11:00 A.M., everyone sat down to the farewell meal. The vegetarian lunch box contained rice, tofu, fried vegetables (*tempura*), cooked vegetables, seaweed, and fruits. While the family ate, the assistant served them tea. After the meal, funeral staff arrived to transfer the deceased to the funeral hall. The coffin was carried by four of the funeral staff into Hagoromo-no-ma, a funeral hall equipped with 150 chairs. The family followed the coffin and watched while it was set at the center of the funeral altar.

The one-million-yen altar was decorated with 200 chrysanthemums, 20 chrysanthemum flowerpots, 10 white nonnative flower arrangements (such as calla lilies, Chinese bellflowers, and carnations, which are not indigenous to Japan), and an artificial garden at both sides (see Table 2). The chairs were in two rows of 75 with an aisle up the center leading to the altar. Seventeen tall flower bouquets stood on pedestals on both sides of the room; they were colorful mixtures of native and nonnative flowers, including freesia, gladioli, asters, blue marguerites, snapdragons, and iris. Each bouquet included a card displaying the giver's name written in calligraphy. With the exception of two pairs of bouquets ordered by the family, the flowers were gifts from guests, mostly the chief mourner's company colleagues and bosses.

Doi guided the family into the hall and began to seat them on the right-hand side of the front row. Yamaha was seated on the aisle, and Sanae sat beside her father. (If the mother had been alive, she would have taken this seat and Sanae would have sat next to her.) Mariko sat next to Sanae. Then grandparents, aunts, uncles, and their spouses sat according to their closeness to the deceased. When the first row was filled, relatives sat in the second row, once again from the left to the right. When everybody was seated in the correct places, Doi began to explain the sequence of

TABLE 2

Size and Quality of Funeral Altars

		FLOWER ARRANGEMENTS		
Price of altar	Length (yards)	Size (cm²)	Number of each size	Gardens
¥60,000	1.9	1.75	two pairs	none
¥240,000	2.95	1.75 3.0	six pairs one pair	none
¥360,000	3.93	1.75 3.0	eight pairs one pair	two gardens of 2.15 sq. yds. each
¥600,000	6.88	1.75 2.5 4.0	four pairs twelve pairs one pair	two gardens of 4.3 sq. yds. each
¥1,300,000	8.85	all sizes	more than 50 (covers the whole altar)	two gardens of 8.6 sq. yds. each

SOURCE: Moon Rise Inc., 1995.

the funeral in detail. This was a rehearsal for the family members to prevent any embarrassment. He told people when to come up and which path to take at the rite of offering incense; where to stand for the speech; who was expected to greet the guests when guests had offered incense. He had the family practice their roles and then return to their seats. The Moon Rise photographer arrived to take a group photo of the Yamaha family as Doi and the family were finishing up the rehearsal. Doi turned the proceedings over to the photographer and left the hall.

The photographer arranged a row of ten chairs in front of the casket; she asked the closest family members to sit in the chairs and had the other relatives stand directly behind them. The father, sitting in the center, held a photo of the deceased. This is one of the rare times that people pose for a photo without any expression on their faces. I once asked a funeral staff member why a photo is taken on such a sad occasion. He replied, "These days family and relatives don't have time to see each other unless someone passes away or someone marries." Even a wedding may not be considered an event significant enough for busy people to take a day off work, whereas a funeral is an appropriate reason to miss work. Thus, a funeral provides a rare occasion for families and relatives who live in different locations to gather. Families also told me that the photo would console them after the funeral: "A photo is the only proof that we have conducted a nice funeral for the deceased." It was half past twelve when the photographer finished with the Yamaha family. They waited quietly for the next event.

Guests arrived gradually. The front desk became crowded with people writing names, giving incense money, and receiving return gifts. Since the deceased was a young woman, there were many women in attendance, probably from her school and her workplace. More than half of the guests, however, were her father's colleagues. Each guest was seated by part-time female employees who guided the guests to the chairs lined up on the left-hand side, across from the immediate family and relatives. When rows on the left were filled, guests were seated on the right, a couple of rows behind the family. The room became noisier. The chief mourner's colleagues talked among themselves, some guests left their seats when they spotted a friend, two male guests exchanged business cards, and some were introduced to others by friends. In the midst of all this, Yamaha, sitting with his head down and his back bent forward, looked small, sorrowful, and exhausted.

Five minutes before the funeral ceremony, Doi checked the stereo system, looked around the hall to see if there were enough chairs, and asked Yamaha if he had any last questions. At exactly 1:00 P.M. Doi asked the participants to be seated. The entire hall became silent. He announced the arrival of the Buddhist priests, their rank, and their sect. A member of the funeral staff led the two priests in, walking slowly in front of them. (The younger priest was the same priest who had come for the wake; the older priest was his father.) As the priests entered the hall, all the funeral professionals standing in the corridor and the room bowed deeply and maintained that posture until the priests had passed. When the priests were seated at the center of the front stage, closest to the coffin, Doi announced the beginning of the ceremony and asked all participants to fold their hands in prayer (gasshō) along with the priests. Then Doi announced the beginning of the priests' sutra chanting. For the next 30 minutes sutra chanting and the occasional ring of the priest's bell dominated the room. When the priests finished reciting the sutra, they stood and offered incense to the deceased. The conductor then announced the incense offering by the chief mourner. Yamaha stood up, bowed once to the guests, as in the rehearsal, burned some incense, and returned to his seat. The conductor then announced that he would read the telegrams. The first two telegrams, which were read in full, were from executives of the company where Yamaha worked. Many telegrams followed, but only the names of the senders were read.

Until the memorial address, the deceased's name was mentioned only at the opening of the ceremony, and the entire proceeding passed without raising much emotion. The participants, however, were extremely moved by the memorial address (chōji) read softly by one of Yoshiko's close female friends, who stood in front of the coffin and spoke to the deceased:

> Yoshiko-san, it is only two days ago that I heard of your
> sudden death from Sanae-san. I cannot believe you went
> so quickly. It was only a month ago that you told me that
> you would be out of the hospital soon. Despite your pale
> face and thin arms, your eyes were shining when you looked
> out of the window. You left without waiting for the spring
> that you have long been yearning for.
>
> I remember when we were classmates in high school. I
> remember you being tender and yet firm, standing up for
> the right things. All these years, I never heard you complain
> or trouble anyone. When we returned from the field trip in

our senior year, we were all exhausted. While everyone else was just sitting around or chatting, you left without a word and brought us tea. But this was just one of many occasions that showed your sisterly affection for your friends. You spoke few words but your actions impressed us.

I looked at your face yesterday at the wake. You were smiling; the smile that I remember from high school, the smile I am used to, the smile I adored. I don't want to say good-bye to you. This is not good-bye is it? Because you live within us.

Sleep in peace, Yoshiko-chan.

By the end of this memorial address women were sobbing into their handkerchiefs; men also had their heads down, and some were wiping away tears. All the family members were weeping. I saw that part-timers and funeral assistants who were standing at the back with me had red eyes from trying to suppress their tears. The funeral atmosphere was no longer rigid and formal; it was filled with sympathy and feelings for the young woman who had died. Doi, probably the only person in the room who was not affected, at least not visibly, announced in a professional tone that the appreciation speech would be given by the father. Yamaha faced the guests with tearful eyes and read his speech in a trembling voice. "My daughter, Yoshiko," he began, "was only 29. She has been hospitalized since this summer. We thought that she would get better after the operation. We were all looking forward to her return, but her illness became worse and metastasized. She never came back to us." He paused to wipe away his tears. "I appreciate your attendance at my daughter's funeral in spite of the cold weather today. I know she is happy to have you all here. Even though she is gone, I hope you will continue to feel the same friendship to our family. Thank you very much for taking time out of your day to come." He bowed to the guests and went back to his seat.

It was time for the rest of the participants to offer incense to the deceased. The priests began to chant the sutra again as the family members and relatives burned incense at the table close to the deceased (the same table where the priests had offered incense). Then the deceased's friends and acquaintances of the Yamaha family lined up in the center aisle, guided by part-timers. The guests offered incense at the second table, each bowing and pressing his or her hands together. The chief mourners, Yamaha and Sanae, stood on the left and greeted the guests who had finished their offering. Most guests passed them with a bow, but some people stopped to give a few words of condolence. When everyone was seated once again, Doi announced the departure of the two priests, who were again led by one of the funeral staff past the line of bowing funeral professionals. The end of the funeral was announced at five minutes before 2:00. "The family will now prepare for the coffin departure," Doi announced. "Anyone who would like to present flowers to the deceased, please stay in the room. Otherwise please help yourselves to a cup of tea in the second-floor lobby." Some of the deceased's friends remained in the room, while Yamaha's male acquaintances left, chatting to each other. Some headed for the coffee shop, also located on the second floor.

Preparation for the departure of the coffin (*shukkan*) is emotional because this is the first moment when the bereaved must say farewell to the deceased. At the Yamaha funeral only family members, relatives, and close friends remained. Funeral staff transferred the casket to the center of the room. The pots of flowers were also moved forward, closer to it. People gathered around and Doi opened the lid. Funeral professionals began cutting flowers and handing them to the participants. The family members were sobbing as they placed flowers in the coffin. "Yoshiko will like pink flowers," Mariko said, looking at her niece. In a few minutes Yoshiko was embowered in flowers. The rice and sticky-rice balls (served earlier) wrapped in white paper were placed in one corner of the coffin. Doi asked Yamaha and Sanae if they had any other objects for the deceased. Sanae had Yoshiko's kimono, a bright pink one, the *furisode* (a kimono with long sleeves worn only by young women) that she had worn for her coming-of-age celebration (*seijinshiki*). Some sweets, books, photos, and a teddy bear also joined Yoshiko in the coffin. Everyone was quiet.

It was 2:03; an hour had passed since the beginning of the ceremony. Doi announced that he must close the lid now. Two funeral staff approached with the lid, but were halted by Sanae, who stood in front of the coffin. Bending toward Yoshiko, Sanae looked as if she wanted to say something. Moments went by, punctuated by the sounds of sobbing. Women had handkerchiefs over their mouths while looking at the deceased. Men stared at the floor; their pain seemed so great that they could not even view the young woman. The funeral staff had to maneuver through the crowd, while Doi took Sanae's arms and gently moved her away. The lid was closed, and Yoshiko was separated from the living.

Three family members stood in line in the aisle between the chairs, while the part-timers and funeral staff handed them specific objects. The father held the Buddhist memorial tablet (*ihai*), which was placed in the death-flower container (*shikabana*).[1] Sanae carried the photo, and Mariko held an ashpot. The coffin, carried by the funeral staff and male relatives, followed the three family members. Relatives walked at the end of the procession. Meanwhile, the funeral assistant told the guests to wait to the left of the auditorium gate. A golden hearse with a dragon on its roof was parked in front of the gate. The procession snaked down the stairs to the entrance, where everyone stood and watched. When the casket was inside the hearse, Doi spoke into a microphone, saying that there would be a word from the chief mourner. Yamaha faced the guests and said simply, "Thank you all for coming today," and he bowed deeply toward the guests. A funeral assistant helped him into the hearse.[2] As the hearse began to leave for the crematorium, Doi urged everyone to fold their hands. The hearse moved away slowly while everyone bowed lightly. When the hearse left, Sanae, Mariko, and other close relatives were taken to the microbus that would convey them to the crematorium. Half of the relatives stayed behind at the auditorium. Doi, before leaving, had announced to the guests that they could take the flowers left in the hall room if they wished. Many women guests went back to the hall to pick up flowers while Yamaha's colleagues were leaving. When I passed them on my way to the crematorium, they had already changed from their black neckties into ordinary ones.

Variations in Funeral Ceremonies

Yamaha Yoshiko's funeral was not only one of the saddest funerals I attended but also one of the few that focused more attention on the dead than on the living. Not many funeral ceremonies affect the participants' emotions so strongly.

A COMPANY FUNERAL

Company funerals (*shasō*), sponsored entirely or predominantly by companies rather than by the bereaved, leave a feeling of emptiness. For this reason, the deceased's family often conducts a separate funeral attended only by family, relatives, and very close friends (*missō*, literally "secret funeral") before the company funeral takes place.[3]

One of the company funerals I attended (without a *missō*) was given for a president of the local tea company, Kyūshū Tea Company. The funeral was sponsored by Kyūshū Tea Company and its parent company, Tokyo Tea Company. For this company funeral, funeral committees from the company planned the ceremony schedule and presented themselves as chief mourners. The retired president of the Kyūshū Tea Company was selected as the head of the funeral committee, and the other seven committee members were high executives of both companies. The funeral was held at the Kokura auditorium, a hall that can hold 1,500 guests. There were repeated discussions between the committee members and the conductor, Doi, about how to carry out the ceremony. Details such as who should read the memorial addresses, who should sit where, and whose telegrams should be read were some of the decisions that occupied them because the company wanted to use this opportunity for strengthening business connections.

On the day of the funeral, four company executives stood at the front gate to welcome guests; they bowed each time a company guest passed them. The front desk, where incense money was received and gifts were exchanged, was divided into two sections, one for general guests and another for company guests; there were three times as many tables for the company guests. Inside the auditorium, white papers were attached to the backs of the seats and inscribed with the names of important guests from other companies. The funeral committee members waited at the front desk so that when these important guests arrived they could guide them to their seats on the left side of the aisle. At the extreme left of the first row on the right side, where the closest family member is usually seated, sat the head of the funeral committee. Beside him sat the deceased's wife. Giving the main seat to the head of the funeral committee indicated not only that the position of the chief mourner was shared by the wife and the former president of the company, but also that the former president was the most responsible person at the funeral. The deceased did not have children, so the deceased's parents sat beside the wife.

The company funeral was similar to other funerals, except for the special incense offering (*tokubetsu shōkō*). During the early part of the ceremony, incense is usually offered only by the Buddhist priests and the chief mourner; the rest of the participants, including family members and relatives, wait until later. However, at the company funeral, the head of the funeral committee and other important company guests offered incense after the wife had done so. Then Doi solemnly announced the names of the vice president and executives of the Tokyo Tea Company. One by one they stood up and went to the stage to offer incense. This special incense offering by executives had a back-stage story.

Doi told me later that there was a conflict between the priests and the company concerning this matter before the funeral. The head priest argued that the burning of incense was for the deceased's spirit and not for the living. The priest also objected to announcing important guests because the act demonstrated political ties between the companies, which ignored the true meaning of offering incense to the deceased. The priest criticized the company for attempting to use the funeral for business purposes rather than keep it a sacred ceremony for the deceased, who should be the center of attention. Doi conveyed the priest's complaints to the company committee members. In order to resolve the situation, two funeral committee members were sent to talk to the head priest. They pleaded with the priest to allow them to proceed with the special offering of incense; the three came to the agreement that only four men would be allowed to do so. "Despite what the priest agreed to," Doi stated, "my view is that the conflict was caused by the company's lack of respect to the priests because the company committee members were deciding the funeral process all by themselves. Everything was accepted as soon as the company sent representatives to bow to the priests." (The temple was one of the wealthiest and oldest Buddhist temples in Kita-Kyūshū.)

Although the company funeral was like ordinary funerals in most respects, each event in the company funeral was more elaborate. Instead of one memorial address, company guests and executives gave four addresses. The content of these speeches, however, was indistinguishable. They all honored the deceased for his leadership and talked about his role in the company. It was like listening to a long recitation of the deceased's résumé. About 50 telegrams, including those sent by a mayor, other government officials, and company representatives, were selected from the hundreds that had been sent, all of which were written in a formal, bureaucratic style. The names of people who had sent the 50 chosen telegrams were read one by one. When the participants offered incense, the process took almost fifteen minutes despite the use of twenty incense pots at the front of the altar. Many participants from the company went outside while the family and relatives surrounded the coffin for the last time. The sponsoring companies videotaped the ceremony, but the only time the deceased and his wife were filmed was when flowers were being arranged inside the coffin. This was also the only occasion when I saw the family and relatives in tears.

This company funeral had nearly 100 flower bouquets from other companies and their executives. It was conducted by five Buddhist priests, and the entire Kokura funeral staff was involved.[4] There were more than 1,200 guests. The price of the ceremony paid just to Moon Rise, and not including the priests' fees, was ten million yen. The funeral was, however, an empty ceremony. After the funeral, the company executives who were on the funeral committee came into the coffee shop loudly cheering, "We are finally done!" (*yatto owatta*). As soon as they sat down, one executive asked what was on the schedule for tomorrow. The women guests were busy taking the beautiful flowers that were left over from the ceremony. "Could you wrap these flowers for me?" one older woman asked me with a smile. Some men went back to the hall to see if their gifts of flower bouquets existed or had been properly placed at the front of the auditorium. As soon as the deceased's hearse departed for the crematorium, many of the people seemed to resume their ordinary lives with no further thought of the ceremony in which they had just participated.

THE FUNERAL OF A DEVOTED BELIEVER

Very few funeral ceremonies are religious in the sense of being attended by devoted believers. However, among the many Buddhist sects, the Nichirenshōshū sect and some groups from the New Religions have funeral ceremonies that emphasize their religious beliefs. In the funerals I observed, the Nichirenshōshū sect and Sōkagakkai (one of the New Religions that branched out from the Nichirenshōshū sect) stood out for the large number of believers.

One of the Nichirenshōshū funeral ceremonies I attended was for an elderly woman, Okada Kyōko, whose chief mourner was her son, Okada Ken. The ceremony was distinctive because the attendants participated fully. The use of white for most decorations and the absence of flowers made the funeral seem inexpensive: the funeral altar had only a few white chrysanthemums. The altar was mostly decorated with anise plants (*shikimi*). The cushion (*zabuton*) for the priest and his robe were also white. Ken ordered one of the least expensive funeral altars and used it for both the wake and the ceremony. In contrast to the starkness of the visual effect, however, was the believers' chanting, which filled the room and echoed throughout the halls of Kokura Auditorium.

About 60 believers attended the funeral. As usual, the funeral began with a hired conductor announcing the ceremony and a priest reciting the sutra. But at this point, all the believers joined in the chant. They were in no danger of falling asleep; most of them knew the long verses of the sutra by heart and only a few of them had to rely on the sutra text. To my further astonishment, they continued to recite for 57 minutes straight. All the believers held a rosary (*juzu*) between the middle fingers of both hands and rubbed this against their palms while they chanted. During this time, the incense pot was passed around from the front to the back, and people burned incense while sitting on the tatami floor; those who could not get into the room offered incense in the corridor. After the chant, the funeral conductor read the telegrams. Then Okada Ken gave his speech, saying, "My mother wanted to tell you, all the believers of this sect, that she is going to heaven [*gokuraku*] and that she deeply appreciates the teaching of Buddha. My mother is so lucky to have believers like all of you sending her on her way. I really appreciate it very much." The priest started to chant the verses and once again the believers joined in. They continued for another five minutes. While they chanted, they removed the scroll (*honzon*) from the top of the altar. When the conductor announced the end of the funeral, most of the believers remained in the room with the family and relatives to place anise plants (*shikimi*) into Kyōko's coffin. The deceased was covered up by the plants. When the coffin was closed and ready to be carried out, the participants chanted the sutra again. While the coffin was transferred to the hearse, the followers pressed their hands together and remained until the hearse was long out of sight.

In this religious funeral, the sutra chanting by participants dominated the entire ceremony, except for the short reading of telegrams sent by executives of the company Ken worked for and the speech given by Ken. Although no memorial address was read, the sutra chanting focused the funeral on one purpose—to send off the deceased peacefully. Even Ken's company colleagues seemed to have been struck by the followers' seriousness—so much so that they refrained from doing business.

A KOREAN FUNERAL

Many Chinese and Korean descendants reside in the Kita-Kyūshū area, and I observed some of their funeral ceremonies in the Kokura auditorium. Their ceremonies used the same materials and personnel as other contemporary Japanese funerals, such as funeral altars, Buddhist priests, and a hired conductor. What was distinctive about the Chinese and Korean ceremonies was their food, the mourners' behavior in front of guests, and the inclusion of Chinese or Korean funeral customs.

I attended one funeral for a young Korean mother, Ping Kim. The deceased and her husband, In-Soo Kim, were second-generation Korean. The deceased's parents spoke in Korean, but the other sons and daughters spoke Japanese most of the time. When I went to their tatami room in the morning, I noticed that they had many more food items than was usual at Japanese funerals. In front of the casket many plates of food were displayed on two small tables. Instead of the usual apples, pineapples, and oranges, there were melon, bananas, and pears. There was also a plate of cooked spinach, bean sprouts, and bracken (*warabi*), which made a nice combination of green, yellow, and brown on the plate. There were plates of three long dried fish, a cooked octopus, scallion pancakes, two plates of sticky-rice cakes, a glass of water, and a large bowl of bean-sprout soup. These items were also carried into the funeral hall and arranged by the female family members when the coffin was transferred there. At around the same time, the sisters-in-law were preparing food just outside the gate where the coffin would leave for the crematorium. They laid out newspapers on the floor and arranged three slippers; a plate of spinach, bracken, and bean sprouts; three rice bowls with three spoons erect in them; three glasses of water, and a plate of three dried fish.

Everything was analogous to Japanese funerals until the casket was filled with flowers. When it was closed, In-Soo Kim's father took charge. He ordered his family members to move it to the center of the passage, shift the two tables of food and fruit dishes before the coffin, and arrange the table with an incense pot in front of these food tables. Then a long and narrow mat (*goza*) was rolled out toward the coffin. The deceased's father-in-law called In-Soo, the chief mourner, and said something in Korean. (Probably he told him to take off his shoes and to perform the kowtow.) The son, now barefoot, walked on the mat that led to the incense pot and the coffin. When he reached the table he offered incense, then he knelt on the floor and kowtowed twice, his forehead touching the floor. Then Ping Kim's small children performed exactly as their father had, bringing sobs from the family and relatives. Then the deceased's father-in-law, brother-in-law, and sister-in-law, and next the deceased's parents, brothers, and sisters burned incense in the same way. I was told that this ceremony usually takes place in front of the hearse after the coffin is inside, but because of the rainy weather that day the family decided to perform the rite inside. When the coffin left for the crematorium, the food items that had been arranged at the gate were carried to the crematorium by sisters-in-law who followed in their car.

A CHINESE FUNERAL

A Chinese funeral ceremony was one of the largest funerals I observed during my fieldwork. The deceased was Wen Liang, a famous Chinese man in his seventies who had established his own company and dedicated his life to the improvement of the overseas Chinese community in Kita-Kyūshū. The deceased's wife and his son gave the ceremony in the name of his family and the company, which the son had inherited.

Two elements suggested that the funeral was for a Chinese family. One was the dominating number of participants who spoke only in Chinese; about 1,000 people attended the ceremony, and more than half were overseas Chinese. The other distinguishing element was the two large plates full of steamed buns (*mantou* in Chinese) arranged with fruits on the altar. Otherwise, the wake and the funeral ceremony followed the same procedures as the common Japanese ones. Chinese participants had brought incense money and received return gifts. Five Buddhist priests were in attendance and the deceased was given a Buddhist posthumous name. There were many telegrams from Chinese organizations as well as the Sino-Japanese Friendship Organization (Chūnichi-Yūkōkyōkai), but all were written in Japanese.

What distinguished this funeral from the Japanese or the Korean funerals I had witnessed was the behavior of the family and the guests. The chief mourner and other mourners stood at both sides of the altar while guests offered incense. Instead of simply stopping to give the words of condolence to the family members, Chinese guests took the hands of the chief mourner, Wen Liang's son, Jiayu Liang. Some hugged him to show their sympathy. Jiayu was sobbing out loud. Other family members were weeping as well.

At the last moment of farewell, the crying among the family grew in strength. While they put flowers into the casket, all the men and women wept with tears rolling down their cheeks; they did not wipe away their tears or try to hide them. Jiayu Liang stood beside his father's head and leaned his face toward him. He did not move from that position. The sound of grief filled the auditorium. The family surrounded the coffin and held on to it. The conductor told Jiayu that it was time to close the lid. Jiayu did not move, and neither did anyone else. The funeral staff brought out the coffin lid. The conductor forced people to back up by pulling steadily on the son's arm.

Putting flowers in the coffin and closing the lid are the most emotional moments in the funeral for all families, Japanese and others. However, Chinese family members showed much more emotion in front of funeral staff and guests than any Japanese I had observed. Weeping in public was not shameful; instead, there was a sense that mourners were honoring the deceased with the intensity of their grief.

I followed the deceased's family to the crematorium with the conductor. Immediately after pressing the incinerator switch, Jiayu Liang broke into tears again.

MEMORIAL ADDRESSES

Company funerals, funerals with a religious emphasis, and funerals for those of different ethnicities can leave intense memories. Often the most emotional parts of the funeral are the informal memorial addresses (*chōji*) given by the deceased's close friends and the speeches given by chief mourners (*moshu aisatsu*), which reveal personal aspects of the speaker's relationship with the deceased. Within the highly structured funeral ceremonies, the memorial address personalizes and makes unique the otherwise mass-produced ceremony. Here are two examples.

The majority of the attendees at the funeral of a grandmother, Murata Mie, in her late seventies, were colleagues of the deceased's son, Murata Ryō. The atmosphere of the funeral was very superficial because most of the attendees had never met the deceased. But when Rika-chan, the seven-year-old granddaughter, stood up and began reading her memorial address to her grandmother, the whole audience was seized by the child's images of the deceased. It was as if a drama, which until then had been observed from a distance, had shifted into a play that the attendees themselves were participating in. Rika-chan began:

> Grandma [*obā-chan*], why are you leaving me? Where are you going? Papa told me that you are going to meet Grandpa. Is it true? I will miss you, though. I will always remember that I have to wash my hands before eating and finish my home-

work before dinner. But without you, I don't know if I will be able to get up in the morning. I liked it so much when you woke me up. I was happy to come back home and know that you would be there. . . . Obā-chan, we will all miss you.

The granddaughter's gentle memorial address seemed to help the participants understand the meaningful life of the deceased through Rika-chan's eyes and make them understand the mutually dependent relationship between the little girl and the deceased that had been severed. Perhaps the address overcame the guests' superficial and distant attitudes and transformed them into participants in a real sense of the word.

Another funeral I attended was for a man in his mid-forties. The deceased, Kanda Tarō, did not have a stable job, he had quarreled with everyone in his family except his sister, Fumiko, and her family, and he lacked close friends or colleagues. Thus the main attendants were not his family but Fumiko and her in-laws. Fumiko's husband, Kishi Tadashi, acted as the chief mourner at the funeral and read a memorial address:

Tarō, we all know what a tough life you had. You attempted many things [jobs] but it never turned out well. Sometimes you were rough, you drank, and you were depressed. You had conflicts with the Kanda family, and they abandoned you. They did not even come today to say farewell to you. But you are my brother-in-law and you are part of the Kishi family. We never gave up on you. Fumiko thought and worried about you every day. I know how disappointing life was for you. But we know that you tried hard at least; whatever the outcome, we honor your efforts. You also taught us the importance of family in difficult times. Although the Kanda family abandoned you [*misuteta*], I assure you that the Kishi family will remember you. Finally you can rest in peace.

The speech was powerful. It not only memorialized Tarō's life as worthy for the efforts the man made to improve it, but also presented an opportunity for the participants to review their morals and values. This memorial address was a final conversation with Tarō, which crystallized his life, magnetized the audience, and sparked personal memories of the deceased.

Thus, the funeral industry considers a memorial address to be an effective means of honoring and celebrating a person's life; from a business standpoint, however, it can create delays in a rigidly structured ceremony.

Cremation (Dabi)

The deceased's family and close relatives and the conductor are the predominant actors in the cremation; guests do not participate. Not all relatives are obliged to participate. I observed that on many occasions relatives stayed behind in the funeral auditorium or returned to the deceased's house.

After the Yamaha funeral ceremony ended, Doi took a shortcut to the crematorium in order to arrive before the hearse. He parked his car near the main office and quickly handed in the city government cremation certificate at the office. No one can be cremated without this certificate. He then hurried to the other end of the crematorium, greeted the crematory staff, and found out which incinerator of the fifteen had been allocated for the deceased.

By this time the hearse had arrived at the gate. Doi opened the door for Yamaha and carried the memorial tablet, which was later placed on top of the coffin. The cremators unloaded the deceased's coffin and laid it onto a stretcher-like dolly with which they smoothly rolled it into the building. The chief mourner followed the conductor and the cremators to the front of the incinerator. Immediately after entering the crematorium, the chief mourner handed a monetary gift (*sunshi*) to the oldest cremator without a word.[5] The cremator bowed and said "Thank you." Ten minutes later, the family and relatives had arrived by van and were also led to the front of the incinerator where they gathered around the coffin. The cremators prepared a table with lighted candles and incense. Doi asked the family and relatives to offer the final incense to the deceased. The family lined up in front of the table and one by one burned incense.

When they had finished offering incense, Doi guided them into a circle in front of the coffin.[6] Then a cremator switched the lever that opened the door of the chamber leading to the incinerator and rolled the coffin slowly and quietly through it. The door to the inner chamber closed, and the coffin was out of sight. A cremator stood at the chamber door and opened the switchboard with a key. He turned to the family and said, "It is time to ignite" (*soredewa tenka shite itadakimasu*) and asked the two chief mourners to step forward. Yamaha and Sanae went to the switchboard. Inside the switchboard was a red button they were to press to start the ignition. They hesitated for a moment, and both of them began to sob. This would be their last farewell to the deceased. The father and daughter looked into each other's eyes, finally decided, and pushed the button. The cremator asked all participants to press their hands together, and they remained in that posture for several minutes. Then the switchboard was locked and the key handed back to the chief mourner. The cremator informed them that when the process was completed there would be an announcement. Doi started to lead them to the waiting room of the crematorium. The relatives followed him, but the father and daughter remained in front of the closed door of the chamber. The father turned around first and began to move slowly away. The relatives returned to embrace Sanae and help her walk away, which she managed with difficulty.

The large waiting room on the opposite side of the building has chairs on the first floor and three tatami rooms on the second floor. (Tatami rooms can be rented by reservation.) The first floor looks like the waiting room of a train station: it contains a restaurant, an ice-cream machine, a candy machine, and soda machines all lined up against the wall. When the Yamaha family entered the hall it was noisy with families who were chatting, eating, and drinking alcohol. The family gathered at the end of the waiting room and ordered refreshments. Doi explained to them that it would take approximately an hour and a half for the cremation. The conductor paid his last respects and said farewell to the family. The chief mourner stood up, thanked him for his assistance, and bowed.

The red button that the chief mourners press looks as though it is the ignition button that begins incineration. The button, however, only signals the entry of a coffin into the inner chamber; this fact is not provided to the family, relatives, or any outsiders. I was told by the head cremator, Mazuda, that the idea for the ignition button came from the tradition of igniting the death flower with a candle flame during community funeral rituals. According to Mazuda, "The button was designed purposely and with much consideration on the part of contemporary crematoriums to mimic the candle ignition of traditional cremation. They wanted to reassure people that the ritual performance of ignition would be performed by the chief mourner." Pressing the ignition button used to have much the same meaning as igniting the death flower; performing that act made the chief mourner the inheritor and caretaker of the deceased, who was on the way to becoming an ancestor. "In the past, if the button was not pressed by the chief mourners, it could be a source of conflict within the family," said Mazuda. "One time the chief mourner disappeared when the coffin was laid in front of the chamber. Since he was out of sight, one of the other family members pressed the button. When the chief mourner came back, he and that man began to fight over the incident." Such quarrels, however, are very rare today because many mourners are reluctant to press the button. Because of this change in the psychology of contemporary mourners, the crematorium changed its policy by asking two chief mourners to perform this ritual action together.

The cremation process is monitored by two cremators in the computer station, while other cremators take turns checking on the body through two small circular windows, five inches in diameter, in the side of the oven. When the chief mourners press the red button, it signals the operators that the coffin has entered the inner chamber. They then turn on the switch that opens the channel and the electric roller slides the coffin into the oven. When the computer signals that the coffin is safely placed in the incinerator, the cremator presses the ignition button. Cremation starts only at that point.

Like most crematores, this one uses gas burners, and a large computer monitors the temperature of each incinerator. The temperature of an oven rises from 300 degrees centigrade to 800 degrees centigrade according to the amount of body fat of the corpse. The flow of gas and the amount of air are mechanically controlled, but cremators can adjust the strength of the heat according to the size and weight of each cadaver. At the lower portion of the oven, there is a lever, a steel rod, that can be inserted into the incinerator. Cremators occasionally use this rod to shift or slide the corpse to the center of the oven.

I watched through the small round window as the deceased was cremated. The gas heat was so strong that within seconds the outer coffin had disintegrated. Because the burner exhaust comes from the direction of the head, the deceased's hair and facial features are incinerated in less than a minute. Inside the oven, flames swirl swiftly in a circular motion. It is a world of red and black. The skull, the heart, lungs, and other organs glow red as if they are themselves made of flame. As the heart is immolated, it shakes and peels; red petals of ashes float in the eddies of air. For Buddhists the drama is at the climax; the deceased is at the boundary between the worlds of life and death. At this final moment of the physical body, the soul enters the world of the afterlife.

It was a powerful sight, with its own kind of beauty. Although the cremation is obviously both the climax and the transition of the deceased, families never observe it. Cremators told me that families rarely ask to view the cremation, and even if they do, cremators refuse to allow them to. When I asked why, I was told, "It is such a brutal and gruesome sight that we fear we might get complaints from the bereaved." Family and relatives thus begin their healing process at the waiting room, while the deceased is transformed into flames.

The office staff in the waiting room announced the name of the Yamaha family, telling them that the cremation was completed and the bones were ready to be picked up (*kotsu-age*). Family and relatives walked back to the hallway where the ovens were located. On receiving the key from the chief mourner, a cremator opened the switchboard and the inner chamber. The cremated remains, literally a skeleton on its back, appeared on the concrete platform. The cremator rolled the dolly into the ash-collecting room (*shū-kotsu-shitsu*) and the family followed. They gathered around the skeleton of the deceased. The cremated bones were white and dry. A cremator named some of the bones, pointing them out with a pair of metal chopsticks. Then he began to pick up bones from the deceased's toes and legs, moving toward the skull and setting them on a silver tray. It is believed that putting the bones into the ashpot working from the toes to the skull will properly place the deceased in a standing posture. The skull, whose shape is preserved even after incineration, cannot be put into the small ashpot as it is, so it is violently pierced with the metal chopsticks. The cremator explained to the chief mourner that the cremator must crack the skull to fit it into the pot. The chief mourners have no choice but to give their consent to this.

The family members were handed a pair of chopsticks, one bamboo and one wooden.[7] The chief mourner picked up the bones first and placed them into the ashpot. The chopsticks were then passed on to other relatives in the order of their relationship to the deceased. The last piece of bone, which connects the neck and the skull, was picked up by the chief mourner.[8] When this last piece was laid on top of the bones in the ashpot, the cremator closed the lid, placed the ashpot in a wooden box, and wrapped the box with a purple cloth. With the chief mourner tightly embracing the ashpot of the deceased, the family left the crematory in silence.

The incinerator of the crematorium in the Kyūshū area is designed so that the deceased's bones remain in the shape of the skeleton after cremation. It is also the custom of the Kita-Kyūshū area for the family to take only some of the bones of the deceased.[9] The entire skeleton cannot fit into the commercial ashpots. The cremators put the leftover bones back into the incinerator, where they are vacuumed through a pipe in the ceiling. The pipe runs to the far end of the building where the bones are pulverized twice into a fine dust. They are poured into sacks and kept at the back of crematorium where they cannot be seen by the public; when these sacks have accumulated, ash collectors take them away. (The destination of the leftover ashes is discussed in Chapter 6.)

SEVENTH-DAY MEMORIAL SERVICES

More than two-thirds of Moon Rise customers have the deceased's seventh-day memorial services (*shonanoka*) immediately after they have returned from the crematorium. The funeral staff call this seventh-day memorial service an advanced or elevated ritual (*age*), meaning that the mourning period has passed. Originally the mourning period lasted at least 49 days, during which the deceased was worshipped every seventh day by family members, other relatives, and priests. Funeral staff told me that seventh-day memorial services are carried out more and more often on the same day as the funeral because it is difficult to gather relatives on the 49th day. Most families have the event at home, but sometimes large families decide to have it in the tatami rooms of the funeral auditorium. Whether it takes place at home or at the auditorium, the seventh-day memorial is the final family gathering for the deceased until the first-year memorial service (*is-shūki*), held one year from the day of the deceased's death.

The funeral staff prepares purification salt and water for the family's return from the crematorium. Before entering the house or auditorium, the mourners sprinkle salt on their bodies and wash their hands as a ritual cleansing. Salt is considered effective to repel any spirits that might have followed the living from the crematorium.

Since the Yamaha family had used the auditorium, they reused the altar from the wake as the postfuneral altar. (A smaller version of the altar was also prepared by funeral staff at the Yamahas' house.) There was no conductor at this occasion; the female funeral assistant from the funeral ceremony helped the family prepare the feast. Yamaha first placed the ashpot at the center of the altar along with Yoshiko's photograph. The priest came and read the sutra for about twenty minutes. During this time the assistant set out the food. When the sutra recitation was finished, all the mourners offered incense to the deceased, who has been safely incorporated into the world of the dead. Finally they sat down to their meal of meat-based dishes, a sign of completing the mourning period. The meal began with beer and sake, also signs of the end of mourning, and lasted nearly three hours. Fifty hours after Yoshiko's death, the entire funeral process was complete.

Summary

"One can accept a person's death as a fact only if one can acknowledge what an abundant life that person has had during his or her life" (Himonya, 143). If family members could overcome the death of their loved ones sooner by finding value in the deceased's life, how might the funeral industry improve its services? What changes could the industry make in order to make up for its limited allocation of time? Kamatani, a funeral professional, suggested that "Modern funerals would have to increase the personal elements." A recent letter from him told about such a funeral. The deceased was a former photojournalist for Asahi Newspapers. During World War II, the deceased traveled from Nomohan, New Guinea, to Rabaul to cover battles, and he was one of the surviving journalists who had reported Hiroshima and Nagasaki immediately after the bombings. Kamatani wrote: "I selected twenty historical pictures, including a photo that showed the deceased in his early twenties. I made them into panels and exhibited them in front of the funeral hall. It had a great impact." He added, "Photos motivated attendees to start talking to each other about the deceased, and they had animated conversations about the good (and bad) old days. I later heard that some of the attendees had rented a hotel room for the second night because they didn't seem to know how to end their conversation. I had never heard of such a thing as a second funeral gathering, have you?" (*Osōshiki no nijikai nante kiita kotoga nai*). As Kamatani pointed out, in future ceremonies there will likely be more emphasis on the use of personal elements in order to partly compensate for the highly structured and compressed funeral form.

(Above) Buddhist coffin cover (*kan-ooi*)

(Below) Christian/Catholic and Shinto coffin cover (*kan-ooi*)

Ash pot (*honetsubo*)

(*Above*) Hearse (*reikyūsha*)

(*Below*) Entrance to a company funeral (*gōdōsō* or *shasō*). Photo courtesy of Junji Kamatani

A company funeral in an auditorium

Shinto funeral altar

Catholic funeral altar

Buddhist funeral altar in a hall

Closed oven at a crematorium

FUNERAL PROFESSIONALS AT MOON RISE

Who is responsible for the transition of the deceased from his or her wonderful life to beautiful death? Is this the task of a priest? The task of a doctor? I believe it is the responsibility of the funeral professionals to beautify the deceased. They are craftsmen of happy endings who transform death into poetic art.

—Ichijō Shinya, *Romantic Death*

As soon as Kuma, a funeral staff person in his late fifties, entered the office, we all knew something had gone wrong. His dark face had turned pink, his eyebrows were tightly drawn, and his eyes were burning with rage. After a moment someone dared to ask him, "What happened?" Kuma first burst out with swear words, then began to explain while taking off his shoes and socks. "I have just come back from the worst customer I have ever met in my life. This guy, Numata, wanted his deceased father to be taken to his apartment, so we took the deceased there. Arriving at his apartment we heard the yapping of Numata's dog. Upon entering the apartment and taking off my shoes properly, we smelled the dog's feces, and at the same time that I realized what it was, I stepped in it." [Apparently the son forgot to keep the window open for his dog to go out while he was away, and his dog went crazy.] "When we glanced around for a space to place the coffin, we realized that the apartment was full of dog's feces. We had to hold the coffin for a while because Numata had to clean a space for it. Then Numata dared to say he wanted to have a consultation there, but we couldn't find any location that had not been affected by the dog." [There was a tatami floor on which they had to sit directly, and Kuma is a tall, heavily built person.] "We just had to sit curled up in a little spot that was less smeared than others. On top of that Numata was arrogant!" By this time Kuma was washing his hands and feet at the sink. He turned around at us and uttered, "But you haven't heard the worst yet. That dog tried to piss on the coffin a couple of times when we were there."

Kuma's narrative received a burst of laughter from other funeral staff, who looked relieved that they had escaped this one. According to other funeral staff who went to Numata's apartment to set up a funeral altar later, he also had two cats hidden in a closet.

This was a worst-case scenario of the problems funeral staff experience in order to market a funeral. In this chapter I examine the professionals who worked for Moon Rise, the variations in their work, the pattern of personal relationships, and the differences in their power. Analyzing their task divisions will explain what motivates them to become funeral professionals and why they continue to do a job that can be very unpleasant at times.

The goal of the next two chapters is to illustrate how the division of work among funeral professionals reflects the perception of death pollution in contemporary Japan. The hierarchy of funeral professionals is determined by two factors: who engages in the inclusive handling of the corpse, and who provides comprehensive services to the bereaved. These two tasks allowed the funeral industry to replace community ties, and they are also the basis on which professionals are stratified. In short, the different degrees to which one is involved in the treatment of the deceased and the extent to which one has access to the bereaved are the key measurements that rank funeral staff in a hierarchy, because they are the very reasons that make them professionals. The specialization of work, in turn, produces the structure of habitus (Bourdieu 1977, 72–72) and contributes to the reproduction of current cultural practices.

The Funeral Staff of Moon Rise, Inc.

At Moon Rise, employees are divided into funeral staff (*eigyō*), female part-timers, funeral assistants, and conductors (*shikai-sha*). The status of each professional is determined by the rank of his or her department in the hierarchy, and by his or her personal characteristics. Gender differences, years of work experience, and age make distinctions within the same work group; in addition, the rank, status, and power of funeral professionals correspond to the nature of their tasks.

Funeral staff are hired at Moon Rise's funeral division, the Kokura Funeral Auditorium (Shiunkaku Eigyō-sho) and are full-time employees. There are seventeen funeral staff members working at Kokura Funeral Hall (Kokura Shiunkaku); fifteen are men. Their job includes transporting the deceased from the hospital, preparing materials for wakes and funeral ceremonies, and carrying the deceased in the coffin. The two young women who are on the funeral staff are limited to tasks like preparing and handling objects for funeral ceremonies. Naturally, their position is lower because their work responsibilities are fewer. This issue is discussed later along with the problem of professionalism and hierarchy. Here, I focus first on the male funeral staff members.

Contemporary funeral staff are unique in the sense that their role can shift from businessman to blue-collar worker during the course of a funeral. At certain points in the process, they are treated with more respect than businessmen, but at other times with much less than that of blue-collar workers. When funeral staff state, "This is a great job because no other job is appreciated by customers as much," they are at the same time expressing the contradictions they feel about themselves. They are proud of their work, and yet there is an underlying fear of being perceived as "nothing but a funeral worker" (*takaga sōgiya*). Their feelings of pride and shame alternate with their tasks.

If one imagines a funeral staff person looking like a laborer in a blue or khaki jacket, wide pants, and worn-out shoes, the reality might be a shock. Funeral staff are well combed, shaved, and outfitted. They wear suits, a white shirt, a necktie, and polished black shoes. A funeral staff person looks no different than millions of other male white-collar workers in Japan. During most of their working hours (including the time when they go to pick up the deceased), funeral staff wear their business suits as a uniform and cannot be distinguished from typical businessmen.

Impressed by how smart they look, one day I complimented Tomi. Tomi, who is in his early fifties, married, and has three daughters, has a reputation as a playboy. I jokingly told him that he looked so nice he could go to a bar straight after work. "Of course not." he said, with unexpected seriousness. I asked him why not. "Because we all smell like incense, or we smell like the perfume we spray on corpses. As soon as I sat near a stranger, that person would know immediately that I am either a priest or funeral staff. So it is important to change one's clothes before going out in public. This is a must for dating."

I did notice the smell of incense as soon as I began working at Moon Rise. However, I found the incense smell far more tolerable than the cigarette smoke that filled the funeral staff's office. Incense simply did not bother me, and it had never occurred to me that funeral staff were ashamed of the smell. I realized, however, that it is not the smell that is the problem, but the implications of the smell. In Japan, incense is a symbol of death. Walking around Harvard Square in Cambridge, I often noted various kinds of incense—pine, apple-cider, strawberry, and others—being sold on the streets and at the Body Shop. In America, incense is bought for its fragrance and is connected with relaxation. In a Japanese context, however, incense is used predominantly for Buddhist altars and funerals. No matter how nice the incense may smell, it is connected in people's minds with death and funerals; as such, it is outside of ordinary life. Funeral staff members' concern over smelling like incense derives from the fact that the smell distinguishes them from businessmen working in an office. At the same time, incense is the common denominator of all funeral professionals since its aroma lingers on everyone equally.

The distinction between the funeral staff and ordinary businessmen becomes even more pronounced when the staff have to pick up a corpse who has died an unnatural death (*henshitai*). This is the only occasion on which they put on their work jackets, gloves, and occasionally their black boots. Unnatural death often means that corpses are decomposed to a certain extent. Some corpses wash up on the shore after several months in the ocean and have been partially eaten by sea worms. Some corpses are not decomposed, but are disfigured by serious car or train accidents. Picking up these remains does not occur frequently, but it is something each employee must do at least once or twice a year.

When a phone call comes from a police station instead of a hospital or a private home, the funeral staff seems to freeze and quiet down for a moment. "Uh-oh . . . here it comes," someone will say. Before even hearing the news, a call from the police department is enough to bring immediate comments. After the phone call, there will be another couple of minutes during which the funeral staff whose turn it is to go try to persuade someone else to go instead. I heard one man say, "Not me, I just had my lunch thank you." Throughout the day, three people take turns picking up the deceased. If only a few deaths have occurred that day, two of these three members will go to pick up the corpse. If all three men have already been out on earlier calls that day, then the question of who should go is contested. Sometimes an experienced employee will volunteer to go, but otherwise Kamino, the director of the funeral staff, makes the final decision.

Picking up the corpse of a person who died an unnatural death is far worse than any blue-collar job. Kaku, in his late twenties, put it simply: "It is gruesome and miserable." Unfortunately, this happened to him on his first day on the job. "I can never forget that day when I had to go and pick up a body that was hit by a train. It wasn't even a corpse that we were removing. They were bits and pieces of body parts and organs, all spread along the rails. It took us hours to gather them." All funeral staff have had this kind of traumatic experience, which they later recount to the other staff. One night when there were no phone calls, the stories of these experiences turned into a contest of tolerance for the grotesque. A younger employee began talking about how horrible it was to handle the deceased who had committed suicide by slashing his neck. "It was bloody and moreover his neck was not properly attached! Imagine trying to put that thing in a pouch!" After more of these freakish stories, one of the experienced workers said, "You guys haven't experienced the worst yet." Then he told us his story of how he had to pick up a corpse that had been boiled in a gas-heated bathtub.[1] "This old person," he said, "presumably had a heart attack while he was in the bathtub and died. But the gas burner of the bathtub continued to heat. As a result, his upper body was intact while his lower body was completely cooked. It was like a chicken cooked in stock." His story was met with much laughter, exclamation, and admiration. What had begun as an occasion to tell stories and relieve frustrations soon turned into an opportunity to brag and demonstrate one's fortitude. In fact, the exchange of these grotesque stories was an expression of machismo, of personal strength. The more experienced one is with an abnormal corpse, the more one is respected.

During my fieldwork I once helped collect a corpse from the police station. The family called from the police station to tell the funeral staff that the person had drowned in a river. We had no information about the deceased's age or gender. I decided to go with Tomi and Otoba in spite of the funeral staff's concerns and objections. Otoba, a young man of 24, who was obviously not eager to go himself, said to me, "I strongly recommend that you don't go. You will have bad dreams for at least a week, and you will never be able to forget it."

At the police station, we proceeded directly to the left-hand side of the police building, which was completely hidden from the road. The coroner (*kenshikan*), a man in his late thirties or early forties, was wearing black rubber boots and an apron that hung down to his feet and was wiping his hands.[2] Tomi gave the coroner his name card and said, "Thank you for your work [*gokurō-samadeshita*]. We will do the rest from here," and made a polite bow. The coroner just nodded and pointed to a black trash bag lying behind him; the bag contained all the deceased's clothes and needed to be removed by the funeral staff.

The deceased was lying on a gray plastic sheet and covered with another similar sheet. There were no family members present. (They were upstairs at the police department for questioning and paperwork.) This was good news for the funeral staff because it meant they could wear rubber gloves, which would not have been possible if any of the deceased's family had been there. Wearing gloves would have suggested that the funeral staff were treating the deceased as a "corpse" (*shitai*) and not showing the respect due to the deceased's remains (*itai*).[3] After donning their gloves, Tomi, who was the more experienced, looked at Otoba and said, "Are we ready?" They removed the plastic cover, revealing a naked body that was somewhat bloated but not dramatically decomposed. The deceased was an elderly man in his seventies; his face looked peaceful. (We heard later that he had grown senile and often walked in his sleep.) "Not bad at all," said Tomi gratefully. But in spite of the chill air of early spring, the smell was strong. The funeral staff quickly unzipped the pouch and on the count of three shoved the deceased inside and pulled the zipper shut. Then the deceased was laid in the coffin with dry ice. There was a faucet nearby, and we all washed our hands with relief.

Frankly speaking, the whole event was not pleasant. To me it seemed that the experience contained the most repulsive sensations that a human can detect in the realms of smell, sight, and touch. It is the physical uncleanliness (*kegare, yogore, kitanasa*) more than heavy labor that drops the funeral staff below blue-collar workers at this phase of preparations for a funeral. As one of the funeral staff said, "It is a dirty job" (*kitanai shigoto*).

The night shift is an additional hardship on the funeral staff.

Not only is the night shift physically tiring, but it is also mentally exhausting. A night shift involves more than 36 hours of continuous work, which includes picking up the deceased, encoffining them, and consulting with the families. A staff person on the night shift begins work at 8:25 A.M. and is released finally at 9:00 the next evening, after the wake. Those not on the night shift may leave the office by 6:00 P.M. There are at least six funeral staff members on the job until 9:00 P.M.; three from the earlier night shift and three who began the cycle that day. After 9:00 the latter three and one part-time worker to answer the phone are responsible for everything until 8:25 the next morning.

"Luck determines one's load on the night shift," the staff used to tell me. If not many people died that night, the staff could go to sleep around midnight and might even get a whole eight hours of sleep. But more than half of the calls are received at night; it is more common for funeral staff to be awakened a couple of times in the middle of the night. There is a night-shift room next to the staff's office (*tōchoku-shitsu*) equipped with a bunk bed, two sets of futons, and a TV.

The funeral staff were astonished and somewhat annoyed by my decision to stay overnight with them. I was the first woman at the Kokura Auditorium to be permitted to join the night shift.[4] Their objections had to do with the gender difference and the boundaries of tasks, which I explain later in the section on female professionals.

That night, a call came in at 3:53 A.M. Without speaking much, Tomi prepared the coffin and Ibuse loaded other necessary objects to take to a hospital. The road was empty, and the city was asleep. The hospital stood between office buildings downtown. It presented an outmoded, worn-down, and decayed appearance. Our van drove up to the back door, the usual exit for transporting the dead in Japan; however, the door was locked. Ibuse went into the front to ask the guards where we should enter. We were directed to the other back door, where heaps of garbage were piled. Two hospital staff in white uniforms brought a stretcher and informed us that the deceased's room was on the third floor. We transported the coffin on the gurney and entered the quiet hospital.

I was struck by a strong antiseptic smell on my entry into the building. The inside of the hospital was as run down as its outside. When we arrived at the third floor we inhaled another kind of smell, coming from the bathroom beside the elevator. The door to the deceased's room was slightly open, and nurses were standing by. They led us in. A couple in their forties were standing in the room, and the woman was weeping. An old man was curled up on a filthy steel bed, like a bed in a jail. I wondered why the room was so dim and saw that one of the light bulbs on the ceiling was broken; there was no other light in the room. It was also icy cold, and I could see my breath turn white in the room. Since it was late December, I was wearing a winter coat, but I still felt the chill. I was stunned when Tomi pulled back the deceased's bedding. The cotton blanket-futon and futon mattress were only two inches thick, and the old man was wearing nothing but a thin nightgown (*yukata*). I suspected that he had died from the cold rather than old age. He was in a fetal position. Both of his arms and legs were folded up so tightly that the funeral staff could not stretch him out. They gave up trying to straighten him out, and the deceased was encoffined (on his side) with his legs and arms still bent. As we were leaving, I looked around the empty room, which contained nothing but a bed and two tables. There were no flowers, no TV, no food, no personal belongings, not even a radio or a book. There were bars on the only window, making the room look even more like a jail cell.

On the way back to the auditorium with the deceased, my thoughts swirled with questions about the old man's fate and the hospital. I asked Tomi if the old man might have frozen to death, why his room was empty, and why there were bars on the hospital windows. Tomi gave me a full explanation. He said that this hospital was famous for keeping elders who had been abandoned by their children; such hospitals are rare, but a couple exist in Kita-Kyūshū. Only seldom do children visit these parents, and when they do they do not seem to care how poorly their old parents are treated. This is because these children are not well off and their parents' health care costs are paid by the government; children are not willing to pay extra from their pockets or generous enough to bring anything to the hospital room. Because of such misery, old patients often become depressed and wish to commit suicide by jumping out the window. In order to avoid this, the hospital puts bars on their windows. "Who knows exactly why the old man died," Tomi added. "He might have died of cold or even starvation. To tell you the truth, that hospital is like a trash depot for elders" (*ubasuteyama*).[5]

The old man had indeed been treated as if his life had little value. Observing such a bad death filled me with pain and sorrow. The image of the way he had died in the darkness was enough to make me feel chilled to the bone. I asked Tomi, "How do you get over these terrible experiences?" He replied, "You never get over it. Once you face such bad deaths, they will always remain inside of you. But what you learn through these experiences is to try to live better so that you will not be like them."

I began to be able to tell who had worked the night shift the day before. Their faces showed exhaustion from lack of sleep, but there was also a mental and psychological exhaustion in their expressions. Night shifts entail accumulative experiences of physical filth as well as encounters with social and cultural defects. These combined elements force funeral staff into experiences beyond the normal. It is this that separates them from other businessmen and ranks them below blue-collar workers.

Why does anyone do this job? Is it simply for the paycheck? Is it because the funeral staff are uneducated people and have little chance to find better work? In fact, the funeral staff are paid 20 to 40 percent more than employees in other departments at Moon Rise.[6] In addition, the funeral staff is not as illiterate as one might assume. Out of fifteen men on the funeral staff, only three did not have a bachelor's degree; only four had worked at other companies. These four men joined Moon Rise in their forties, after leaving former jobs for various reasons, and were in their fifties at the time of my fieldwork. The other eleven men were all initially hired as full-time Moon Rise staff. They had completed Moon Rise's training program and indicated the department they wished to work in—finance, marketing, marriage hall, or funeral hall. The company executives consider each person's preferences, as well as their personalities and abilities. In general, about 80 to 90 percent of employee preferences are accepted, which implies that most of the funeral staff had chosen the job. Why? What makes the funeral department so special? By the end of my fieldwork I was convinced that the answer lies in the type of appreciation that the funeral staff receive from the bereaved.

During my stay I heard all of the funeral staff use the same phrase repeatedly to explain why their jobs were satisfying. When someone said, "My customers appreciated me, my day was great," the rest would always nod to each other. One man stated the value of the job in two sentences: "Receiving appreciation is like opium in this job. There is nothing that makes me happier than being accepted by my customers."

I have realized that receiving appreciation (*kansha*) is the key to understanding the job. What the funeral staff means by appreciation is the personal gratitude demonstrated by customers' deep bows and monetary tips; this attitude is explicitly distinct from a customer's gesture toward salesmen, delivery men, or clerks. A common interaction between a salesman and a customer is not a personal one; what they are exchanging is a commodity (tangible or intangible) for cash. In contrast, the funeral staff not only market ceremonies, but their services often provide emotional support to the bereaved. Their services include personal interactions that go beyond those of any other businessman.

One day Hosoi and I delivered boxes of gifts to a deceased's family. Tomi was there, too, dressed like the other attendants in a black mourning suit. I was surprised to see him there because it was his day off. Looking at his black suit, I immediately assumed that the deceased was one of his friends or relatives. "Was this funeral for someone close to you?" I asked him later. "No" he replied. He explained that the Watabe family had lost their grandfather two years earlier. At that time, Tomi had picked up the deceased at the hospital and arranged the funeral. The son, the present head of the family, had appreciated Tomi's work very much. When his mother died, Watabe called Moon Rise and asked for Tomi specifically. When told that Tomi was not there, Watabe called Tomi at home to ask for his help. "The son of the deceased was very nice to me. We got along together well, and I was glad to help," Tomi explained.

On another occasion, Tomi went to the home of the Sakai family who had lost their son, Jirō, a boy in his late teens who had committed suicide. When Tomi arrived, the son's body was still hanging from the ceiling and the Sakai family was in shock, especially the mother, Ritsuko, who was hysterical. (They had called the funeral hall, before calling the doctor, for guidance.) Upon arrival, Tomi took charge, first helping the family get the dead boy down and place his body on the floor. From the initial stage to the end, except for the doctor's examination and death certificate, Tomi handled all the details: making appointments with a Buddhist priest for the wake, cleaning up the gory mess in the house in order to construct a funeral altar, deciding what to say on the invitation card and speech, and keeping the fact of the suicide from outsiders. The parents wanted to have a proper funeral for their son while keeping the manner of his death secret.

Tomi performed and arranged the ceremony with such calmness that neither the relatives, guests, nor priests were suspicious. "The most important task was to calm down the mother," Tomi told me. A couple of days after the funeral, Ritsuko called Tomi. She invited him for lunch at the Sakai home. When he went, Ritsuko told him how guilty she felt about Jirō's suicide. According to her, the family's eldest son went to a prestigious university in Tokyo, and Jirō had just failed an entrance exam. Ritsuko had had high expectations for her second son, as high as for her first. "I have killed him," she cried to Tomi. "I felt very sorry for her," Tomi told me. "She and her husband had no one else to talk to about the accident because they were too ashamed to publicize it. She could talk to me because I was the only one who knew what had happened. After this she called me a couple of times later."

Tomi explained that the longer a funeral staff person stays in the job, the more one receives calls from former customers who want to talk about their deceased. In many families' eyes, Tomi and other funeral staff are not just businessmen who sell a product; they are people who know the circumstances of, and sometimes the secret behind, the deceased's death. Staff members also function as consultants who support the bereaved when they are too concerned about losing face to ask for help from relatives and friends. It is this kind of personal and intimate assistance that the funeral staff provide to the deceased's families. In turn, the bereaved express their gratitude with a monetary gift and/or a deep bow. The deep bow is different from a bow made to a businessman for his services. For a family that has experienced a tragic death whose circumstances it would like to keep private, the deep bow expresses indebtedness to the funeral staff who share the family's secret. I believe it is this sense of appreciation and touching people's lives that gives the funeral staff satisfaction, confidence, and dignity, and that justifies a job that can be miserable or degrading at times. Although their handling of the corpse is what degrades them, it is also what lifts them above an ordinary businessman and elevates them within their profession.

FEMALE WORKERS AT MOON RISE:
GENDER DIFFERENCES AND STRATIFICATION

Three different positions are open to women at Moon Rise: funeral staff, funeral assistant, and part-time worker. The full-time female funeral staff and part-timers are both hired by the funeral auditorium, and their work is limited to the auditorium funerals. The funeral assistants, who also work part time, belong to the Party Professionals branch of Moon Rise, and they work on funerals both within and outside the auditorium. Although their job descriptions overlap at several points, the women know the boundaries of their particular jobs and are careful not to cross them without reason. The problems that came up in this respect reveal not only the female workers' awareness of their distinct roles and tasks but also Moon Rise's managerial strategy for maintaining hierarchy in the profession.

At the Kokura Funeral Auditorium, there were two female funeral staff, Seki Risa and Mori Hiroko. Risa was twenty years old and a high school graduate, and had worked for two years. Hiroko was twenty-three, had graduated from a local college, and had worked for a year. They were both single. Both decided to work in the funeral department after finishing Moon Rise's training program. I was curious to know what attracted these young women to the funeral department instead of the wedding department. "Funerals are much more challenging than weddings. There is no one but the two of us who work on the funeral staff in Moon Rise's Kyūshū branches. It seemed like a new door opening for women's careers," Hiroko explained. For Risa, who lost her father when she was young and lives with her mother and a younger sister, the decision to work in the funeral department caused no trouble at home. "They were happy that I got a full-time job," Risa said. However, Hiroko's decision to work on the funeral staff was met with strong opposition from her parents; her father is the president of a local elementary school and cares about family face. "Even to this day, my parents will not tell anyone, relatives or neighbors, about my job. If someone asks what I am doing, they will say that I work at Moon Rise, hoping that the listener will think that I am working as a secretary or at the wedding branch. No further explanations are given." On one occasion, Hiroko brought bouquets of leftover flowers home from a funeral. There were too many flowers for one house, so her mother gave some to one of her neighbors. The neighbor, who was happy to receive such gorgeous flowers (lilies, roses, and carnations rather than just chrysanthemums), expressed admiration for Hiroko and said,

'How nice to have a daughter who works at a wedding hall!' "My mother did not contradict her and just smiled." Hiroko's job is an embarrassment to her parents.

According to Hiroko, her parents' opposition is a result of their status consciousness and not a reaction to the actual work. Although Hiroko and Risa were full-time funeral staff, their work responsibilities and tasks were not as great or as arduous as those of the men. They worked only within the funeral hall, were never expected to pick up a corpse from a hospital, and were never assigned to night shifts. Like women part-timers, their main tasks were setting up altars for wakes and funeral ceremonies, serving food and drink to the deceased's family and guests at funeral ceremonies, and taking care of materials after ceremonies. In short, unlike the male funeral staff, they did not touch the bodies at all. Since the handling of the physical remains within this profession is the source of power and corresponds directly to higher status, being deprived of any direct involvement with the corpse puts these women below male funeral staff in the hierarchy.

Hiroko and Risa, however, had unequal status within the funeral hall. Their unequal positions illuminate the unspoken strategy of Moon Rise. Hiroko, who had graduated from college, was given special attention by the funeral staff as well as managers. For example, the vice director of the funeral staff invited Hiroko to attend part-timers' monthly meetings to record documents. The executives also invited Hiroko when they offered me an introductory course on the funeral process. Risa acknowledged that Hiroko had certain abilities that she did not. For example, because Hiroko could use a computer she could help input customer information. However, the general acceptance of Hiroko by men in higher positions derived more from her family background and general behavior than from her abilities. For instance, Hiroko did not smoke, and Risa did. Not smoking was further interpreted as a sign that Hiroko, as a college graduate from a good family, is a model woman; smoking was a sign that Risa, who comes from a single-parent family and graduated only from high school, is a low-class woman. In fact, however, Risa was eager to do the work of the men and had the abilities to do so; she was strong and athletic, and she could drive, which Hiroko could not. Risa was always envious when I went along to pick up a deceased or when I went to funerals outside of the hall. Hiroko was satisfied with her job within the funeral hall; she liked paperwork and entering information into the computer. Whereas Risa was an outgoing person and not afraid of dirtying her hands, Hiroko's behavior tended to reaffirm her position as a white-collar worker.

The company's different treatment of these two women is not accidental. First, it is part of their conscious effort to increase the status of funeral staff in the eyes of the general public. At the time of my research, the training program that now provides the Funeral Director's Certificate did not yet exist, and the only way the funeral industry could gain higher status was by hiring people with a higher education.[7] Naturally, the company values workers with a college degree and proper family backgrounds because such employees will help project a white-collar image to customers. Hiroko fit the company's advertisement model. Second, the company wants to maintain men's superiority and regards any encroachment on the male funeral staff's territory as threatening. Men did not consider Risa's eagerness to be a positive characteristic, but rather a negative force that could threaten their position in the hierarchy and undermine their power.

Partly because of the company's strategy, Hiroko's and Risa's feelings about their work differed greatly. Risa, who had become frustrated and discouraged by the way the men on the funeral staff treated her, told me before I left that she had begun to think about marriage. "If I meet someone nice, I will quit the job and marry. The company does not want me anyway." In contrast, Hiroko told me that although she had a boyfriend she did not want to get married anytime soon. "Even if I do get married," Hiroko said, "I want to continue working because this job gives me a career path."

Both female part-timers and funeral assistants work part time.

During my tenure there, these women were between the ages of 35 and 55 (the majority are over 45), had all been married, and had children. One reason they chose the job was for the high hourly pay.[8] The other reason, which they often mentioned, was their own experience; attending parents' or relatives' funerals made them interested in the job. For example, one funeral assistant had lost her husband a few years earlier. At her husband's funeral she was comforted by people working in the funeral hall. When she decided to go to work, she immediately thought of funeral halls, where her age and tragic experience would be positive instead of negative credentials.

At first I was surprised to hear that these women were part-time workers; they were as energetic, serious, and professional as Risa and Hiroko. One part-timer told me, "The more I work in this job, the more I learn about death and funerals. The work not only pays me, but also provides me with a knowledge that enlightens my life." I was impressed when I saw them circulating books on death and funerals. Tanda Akiko, one of the part-timers, was interested in discussing Ichijō's *Romantic Death*. She was also curious what and how I would write about them. These women part-timers were extremely understanding and supportive of my research because many of them were taking care of elders, either their own parents or parents-in-law, and were going through their own search for the meaning of aging, dying, and death.

There were five women part-timers at the Kokura Funeral Auditorium. As stated earlier, part-timers only participate in funerals that take place at the hall. Within the department, they are supervised by the funeral staff. Hiroko arranged part-timers' schedules according to the number of funerals on the following day, assigning each of them to a separate funeral in rotation. Part-timers are expected to come an hour before and leave an hour after the funeral. Some of their tasks include putting up family name signs in the halls, helping full-time staff set up altars, arranging a bowl of rice and a plate of sticky-rice balls for the deceased, guiding guests to the halls, rearranging chairs and tables, and cleaning incense pots after a funeral. The women funeral staff and part-timers work side by side at the funerals, but the funeral staff are in charge, even though Hiroko and Risa were younger than any of the part-timers. The marked boundary between the part-timers and funeral staff is that part-timers are assigned to do tasks, such as cleaning, that are often behind the scenes, and they have less direct contact with customers than funeral staff or funeral assistants.

Unlike women part-timers, funeral assistants are hired through the Party Professionals (they use the term "Party-Pro"). Party professionals include conductors and assistants for funerals and weddings. There are ten funeral assistants for the Kita-Kyūshū region. On average, one funeral assistant and one conductor are allotted for a wake and a funeral, but if the funeral is large, more than one funeral assistant will be assigned. Funeral assistants and conductors attend wakes and funerals that take place both within and outside the funeral hall (e.g., in Buddhist temples, churches, and homes). The funeral assistant's job centers on serving and helping the deceased's family directly and has little to do with the material preparations for wakes and funerals. Their primary tasks are serving the vegetarian dinner before a funeral ceremony, serving tea and coffee to religious officiants, helping the women in the family put on their mourning kimonos, guiding and helping guests at wakes and funerals, and serving the meat-based meal after cremation of the deceased.

Assistants rank below conductors but maintain friendly relations in spite of the status gap. Conductors are careful to treat assistants politely; they are fully aware that assistants are their hands and feet and that miscommunications could affect the bereaved's evaluation of them.

There is some rivalry, however, between the part-timers and funeral assistants. At a funeral in the auditorium, a part-timer and a funeral assistant work simultaneously. They share few tasks because funeral assistants' jobs center directly on the deceased's family, whereas part-timers' work focuses on material preparations and the guests. Funeral assistants often demonstrate their superior position by distinguishing their tasks from those of part-timers. For example, assistants are the ones to serve tea or coffee to religious officiants. During my fieldwork I decided to add this chore to my schedule because it would provide a good opportunity to interview the priests. When I first asked funeral assistants for their permission, they gave me perplexing answers. They said, "I have to ask the conductor," or "I will think about it" (*kangaeteoku*). By avoiding a direct answer, they were saying no. (Later I was permitted to do this job by asking the head of the funeral auditorium and head conductor.) I had thought that the funeral assistants might welcome the opportunity to eliminate one task. In fact, I had heard them say that serving drinks to officiants is troublesome because it must be done immediately before the funeral finale and right before the coffin departure to the crematorium. So why did they reject my offer, and why did this offer become such a major issue that all the funeral assistants discussed it among themselves?

A funeral assistant later told me that they were not against me personally, but were protecting their territory from part-timers. Because I had been working with part-timers in the funeral hall and my uniform was different from those of funeral assistants, they categorized me with the part-timers and feared that if they allowed me to take over one of their tasks, then other part-timers might follow my lead.[9] Funeral assistants wanted to keep the task within their private domain; they counted their access to priests as one of their privileges.

The conflict between part-timers and funeral assistants became more apparent on another issue. Again the problem seemed simple on the surface: who should help the female family members get dressed in their mourning kimonos? Very few Japanese women today know how to wear a traditional kimono. When a kimono is necessary, as in funerals and weddings, many women make appointments with a hairdresser for a fitting. Thus Moon

Rise had decided, when it established its Party Professionals branch, that one of the funeral assistants' tasks would be to help the bereaved with their kimonos. During my fieldwork, however, the head of the funeral auditorium, Kamino, asked the Party Professionals branch to train part-timers in this skill as well. Kamino told me that this was in response to customer needs, to prepare as many women staff as possible to help the bereaved. Part-timers were more than eager to learn this new skill, which would give them an opportunity to interact with the deceased's family directly. Despite the fact that the training was carried out during off-work hours, at a distant location, and without pay, every part-timer attended every class. Tanda Akiko used to call the others the day before, saying, "Don't forget, tomorrow is the kimono lesson." Akiko was so excited that after each lesson she would report to me what they had learned.[10]

The funeral assistants were not thrilled with the news that they would have extra help. On the day part-timers began to help customers with their kimono fitting, the funeral assistants confronted part-timers afterward, saying that this was their job and that they did not require the part-timers' help. Part-timers complained vigorously about the difficulty of dealing with the funeral assistants. "They make me tired; don't they understand that we have the right to help as well?" They said the funeral assistants were being immature and narrow-minded: "It is about good service and not about a work boundary." The more part-timers learned about fitting kimonos, the more the conflict accelerated.

From the standpoint of part-timers, funeral assistants do have a privileged position. By directly serving the deceased's family, funeral assistants earn personal acknowledgment in the form of monetary or material gifts. Tasks such as serving tea and kimono fitting are important contacts, where funeral assistants fill the role (and incur the obligations) once held by other family members, relatives, and community members. The family often expresses their appreciation by giving funeral assistants tips (*sun-shi*) after the ceremony. This in turn gives funeral assistants a sense of pride and confidence; they consider these tips an affirmation of the quality of their work. Observing such situations, I sensed part-timers' envy. "No matter how much we work, we never receive as much appreciation from the bereaved as the assistants do," one of the part-timers explained. Learning funeral assistants' tasks and acquiring the same skills are the means by which part-timers attempt to improve their positions.

One may wonder why the supervisors at the funeral auditorium did not try to alleviate this rivalry when they became aware of the situation. It was only after the part-timers expressed their wish to use their kimono-fitting skills to the vice director of Kokura Funeral Auditorium that he publicly announced the message to funeral assistants. The announcement demonstrated the vice director's consent and confirmed that part-timers could do kimono fitting. But the conflict remained unresolved. Although I never saw part-timers and funeral assistants argue in public, they continued to talk behind each other's backs. Why is such conflict purposely unresolved, and who benefits from it?

A simple answer may be that hierarchical differences among employees are nurtured with a single purpose—to satisfy the customers. As long as they are unable to resolve the contested boundary of their tasks, part-timers and funeral assistants are compelled to compete and to expand and master their tasks. This tension seems to push employees to perfect their services. What is negative from the perspective of the employee is positive in the eyes of the employer. Task boundaries between workers seem to reflect the power structure within the company hierarchy.

FUNERAL CONDUCTORS

The conductors (*shikaisha*) are hired through the Party Professionals branch of Moon Rise. There were nine conductors in the Kita-Kyūshū area, six men and three women. They ranged in age from 38 to 72. The oldest, Fuku (who was called Grandpa Fuku) was hired when Party Professionals was established in 1972. In general, Moon Rise hires conductors who are older and married and have children, because the company prefers people with many experiences in life, who can understand pain and sympathize with the families of the deceased. For example, one male conductor was lame from a car accident. A female conductor who underwent a cancer operation years earlier told me that her experience of being near death was valued when she entered the profession.

Conductors are neither full-time nor temporary workers. They are paid by the number of funerals they perform each month. (I was told that they were paid more only for funerals in the largest hall at the Kokura Funeral Auditorium; otherwise, the pay rate was the same whether a funeral took place in a hall, a home, or a Buddhist temple.) Five of the nine conductors did not hold any other job. Among these five staff, three female conductors were housewives, and two men were retired from other jobs. The other four male conductors held second jobs, selling insurance, cosmetics, or cars. Moon Rise permits conductors to hold other jobs because the company cannot predict or guarantee the number of funeral assignments for each conductor.

All conductors gave the same reason for choosing their job. They said, "It allows independence." They are responsible only for their own assigned ceremonies, which are evaluated individually. In short, the work demands ability more than cooperation with other colleagues. All three female conductors began as funeral assistants and were trained later to be conductors. They told me that it was at first difficult to enter men's territory, but once they were experienced they were not treated differently from the men. Competition did not occur between men and women, but among all colleagues. The only inequality that exists is for company funerals. For the biggest funerals, which occur about ten times a year in the largest hall of the Kokura Auditorium, the assignment goes to a male conductor. A conductor and the director of the Kokura Auditorium explained that the customers for these large funeral ceremonies, which are often for company executives, prefer a male because he reflects the pattern of male dominance in their companies. But aside from these grand ceremonies, female conductors are appreciated as much as and sometimes more than male conductors, for their organizational skills as well as their sensitivity when caring for the bereaved.

The number of funerals assigned to each conductor varies with their abilities. Someone who is evaluated as "good" is called more frequently. One of the complaints I heard from conductors is that the job is stressful because of the constant competition. "I am always judged by customers and by Moon Rise," said Doi, the conductor who received the most assignments. "If I make mistakes, that will definitely affect my number of assignments. The job is like being an actor. One must work hard to get the fame, and one must maintain that quality to keep up the popularity. Once you start to lose fame, you will have fewer and fewer opportunities."

Conductors are judged by both the customers and the funeral staff. Naturally, the customers' evaluation carries more weight overall, but the funeral staff's opinions cannot be ignored. The funeral staff's evaluation is troublesome, not only because they control the assignments but also because their judgment may not concur with the customers'. This is especially true with the problem of timing. For the funeral staff and for the company, time is money. It is important to them that each wake and each ceremony begin and end promptly; the wake should be finished within two hours and the funeral within one hour. Two or three wakes and funerals take place every day. Most wakes begin at 6:00 and 7:00 P.M. and end at 8:00 or 9:00 P.M. A funeral ceremony can start anywhere between 9:00 A.M. and 3:00 P.M. according to the customers' needs, but the highest concentration is between 11:00 A.M. and 2:00 P.M. The funeral staff are pressed for time when several wakes and funerals overlap and they are simultaneously responding to calls about new deaths. A conductor is responsible for one funeral, whereas the funeral staff are responsible for many simultaneously. The funeral staff have to work longer hours and carry out their tasks in a more limited time frame. Delay at one funeral can delay the hearse drivers, who work closely with funeral staff. It takes an hour round trip to transport the deceased to a crematory. Delay at one funeral can delay all subsequent funerals. Thus, timing is crucial.

However, finishing funeral ceremonies on time is not such a simple matter from the conductor's perspective. Even the commoditization of funeral ceremonies cannot change the basic fact that a funeral is a human drama. A funeral is unpredictable. Once a farewell speech by a deceased's friend took longer than the conductor had expected. The speaker broke into tears while he was reading it and could hardly leave the stage. On another occasion, a conductor could not separate the family from the deceased during the last phase of the ceremony, when the coffin was opened for the bereaved to say farewell. Conductors observe the needs of the family more than funeral staff, who do not always stay for the whole ceremony. "I feel terrible," remarked Doi immediately after one funeral. It was a ceremony for a father who passed away leaving a young daughter and a mother behind. At the end of the ceremony, the daughter wept silently, resting one of her arms across the coffin. Doi had to gently remove her arm and ask her to step back. The coffin was then closed by the funeral staff and hustled into the hearse. "I wish I could have just left her the way she was, even for few more minutes, instead of shoving her away while she was in tears," said Doi. "It's not your fault," I said to him. "I know, but I feel bad anyway," he replied.

A conductor's prestige, however, rests on the customers' evaluations. No matter how good a relationship a conductor has with funeral staff, if a customer makes complaints the conductor will be instantly demoted. With time I came to realize that one male and one female conductor were more successful than the others (and were looked upon with envy). Both Doi Osamu and Shiroki Takako received high evaluations from customers and therefore more assignments from the funeral staff. What made them special seems to be the degree of effort they put into empathizing with the bereaved. Each one took a personal approach to the most delicate matters.

Shiroki and Doi both effectively assume fictive kinship roles in responding to the bereaved. According to the situation, they can play the role of parent, sibling, child, or friend. At the wake of Imai Tadashi, who had died in an auto accident, Shiroki was a mother figure to the deceased's fiancée, Inoue Lisa. The deceased, a Ph.D. candidate, was driving to school to hand in his dissertation when he crashed into a truck and broke his neck. He died instantly. The fiancée was speechless with shock, and the victim's family was heartbroken. Shiroki spoke to the fiancée as if she were her mother, saying, "Lisa-chan, what was his favorite food?" Lisa, looking as white as the deceased, answered that he liked cakes. Shiroki went to the store with her and purchased the sweets he had liked best. Then Shiroki asked Lisa to display these sweets in front of the altar. Giving her a task seemed to help Lisa shift her focus from her anguish. Lisa stayed close to Shiroki throughout the funeral ceremony.

Doi too had a way of identifying with the deceased's family. When a small boy died from an illness, his father was crushed with guilt for not being able to help his child. Doi put his hand gently onto the father's back. "I have a son myself," he said. "I try to do everything for him, but how can I save his life from the unknown? Nobody can blame you for that, and surely your son is not blaming you. Your son would be saddened by seeing the way you are reacting." Before the wake, Doi spent hours talking to the deceased's family. Shiroki and Doi conduct their work by plunging themselves into the midst of family tragedy. Shiroki put it this way: "One must have devotion to do this job. To use one's heart or sincerity [*magokoro* or *kokoro*] is the key to serving well." Later Shiroki told me that she always sent a sympathy note to the families whose funerals she has conducted. She and Doi built personal relationships with the families that went beyond their professional role. This psychological support is valued highly by the bereaved because it is no longer offered by community members.

The relationship between conductors and funeral staff was ambivalent. Although they seemed friendly with each other, comments they made behind each other's backs showed resentment. One member of the funeral staff despised the conductors, portraying their job as "trivial compared to ours." Conductors also claimed in private that "the role of a conductor is central in the funeral ceremony although the funeral staff do not accept it. Making a perfect ceremony depends on us, not them." Each group considers its role to be the more significant. On a practical level, however, they depend on each other; the funeral staff rely on conductors to conduct funerals, and conductors rely on the funeral staff for their assignments. Their relationships, which otherwise could be broken by resentment, are maintained by the necessities of the division of labor.

The work boundary between conductors and funeral staff is clear cut. Conductors interact with a deceased's family only after the deceased has been encoffined and the size, place, and time of the funeral has been arranged by the funeral staff. Conductors meet the deceased and the family for the first time several hours before the wake; their responsibility is to explain and to guide the bereaved from the wake through cremation. Conductors are not required to touch the body or to carry the casket. The core of their job is to provide service directly to the bereaved. Because conductors do not deal with the corpse, the funeral staff consider them amateurs; this is the reason conductors are ranked below funeral staff within the Moon Rise hierarchy.

Although customers appreciate the fact that the funeral staff handle the corpse, the bereaved often show more gratitude toward conductors, who advise and support the family. The fact that conductors do not handle the financial side of the business smoothes the way to a more personal relationship between conductors and the bereaved, which in some measure accounts for the kind of gratitude conductors receive.

The friction between funeral staff and conductor is further exacerbated by their differing social status in the eyes of the public. If marital status is considered one of the measurements of status, funeral staff rank lower than conductor. Because they handle corpses, many funeral staff have trouble finding a mate. A 23-year-old member of the funeral staff sighed and murmured, "As soon as I mention the fact that I am a funeral worker, that just ends the story." Another man who had just gotten married decided with his fiancée not to tell her parents or relatives about his job, fearing they would object to the match. The Moon Rise funeral staff often find marriage partners within the profession, either some-one working at Moon Rise or the siblings of one of their colleagues or bosses. By contrast, I heard no problems of this nature among conductors. Not only were they successful in finding marriage partners, some were also conducting extramarital affairs. If their ability to marry is any measure, conductors appear to be more highly regarded in the outside world than the funeral staff. However, within Moon Rise, the funeral staff are regarded as superior. The company alleviates their sense of inferiority by giving them the power to assign the conductors' work opportunities.

The ongoing friction between conductors and funeral staff is also partly a management strategy. Their tasks are intentionally kept separate so that conductors and funeral staff will compete to perfect their services and to establish personal connections with customers. Here again, from the company's perspective, distinct boundaries and the competition for power between the two positions are beneficial for the maximization of services and the expansion of commercialization.

Professionalism Among Funeral Workers

Unlike other businessmen who are accepted as professionals and can take pride in the legitimacy of their companies, the funeral workers at Moon Rise need to nurture their sense of pride as professionals throughout their career. This is especially apparent for the funeral staff, who work full time and are most responsible for the success of ceremonies. The process of boosting their own sense of professionalism coincides with the process of accepting the most distasteful, or "lowest," task in the funeral job and acting tough.

In the process of becoming a funeral professional, workers learn to control the expression of emotion. The ability to suppress emotions is the demarcation between funeral professionals and customers. Moreover, emotional restraint differentiates positions among the funeral workers themselves.

Contemporary Japanese often try not to show their emotions in public. This behavior contrasts with that of Chinese family members, who are required to lament, wail, and grieve openly as proper filial behavior (E. Johnson, 135).[11] Although public grieving existed in certain coastal areas and islands in the past, it was never a prevailing Japanese custom (Inoguchi 1954, 208–11). Japanese mourners rarely cry out loud during funeral ceremonies. Sometimes when I arrived at hospitals, the women of the family were in tears, but the men were silent. Instead of crying, Japanese men drink heavily at wakes. The emotional climax of the funeral occurs when the casket is opened so that family and close relatives can put flowers into it. At this point many participants break down and sob. Women weep while covering their mouth with their hands. As they add flowers, they sometimes talk to the deceased. Men lower their heads and quietly wipe their tears with a handkerchief. Another emotional climax occurs at the crematory, when the chief mourners push the button that sends the coffin into the oven. Often it is women who cannot restrain their tears and stand stiffly in front of the oven. Men, although in tears, immediately follow the conductor to the waiting room.

To be a professional in the funeral industry is to remain unmoved by death. The mourners may display their emotions, but the staff should not. Displaying one's emotion goes against the spirit of professionalism, which requires constant attention and rational decision-making. When I began my research, I wept at funerals. At that time, I asked the director of the Kokura Funeral Auditorium if he had cried when he began this job. "No. It is my job. If I take death emotionally, I can't do my job," was his reply. "Then how do you control your emotions?" I asked. "The key is not to connect the death of others to death in one's own family.

Concentrate one's spirit on the serving aspect and not on the suffering of the bereaved." Other male funeral staff also answered that they are not affected because the deceased is a stranger. They did, however, say that children's funerals make them emotional (they did not admit that they wept at these funerals). However, in reality, I observed that many male funeral staff did their best to avoid being present when the coffin was opened. I once noticed that a funeral staff member in his fifties (who had told me earlier that he never cried), had tears in his eyes while flowers were put into a coffin. When he saw me watching him, he quickly turned his back. It must have been an embarrassing incident for him because he did not talk to me for a while. I related my observation to another member of the funeral staff, who finally admitted, "It happens to me sometimes. But it is our job, and we must keep ourselves aloof."

A display of emotion and tears is taboo for professionals. To weep is to disgrace oneself, and the higher one's rank in the hierarchy the greater the disgrace. I never saw conductors in tears, and only once did I see a male funeral worker weep. In contrast, female funeral staff, part-timers, and funeral assistants are allowed to release their feelings without the same embarrassment. Hiroko and Risa, the women on the funeral staff, were in tears several times. They both agreed with me that the job is very emotional. At the same time I could see that they tried hard not to cry and avoided being seen in tears. I observed many part-timers and funeral assistants in tears during funerals. They explained that the funeral made them think of how they would feel if someone from their own family had died.

Thus, the expectation to suppress emotions is strongest for male funeral staff. The leniency toward women workers in the case of showing emotions corresponds to their hierarchical positions, the gap in responsibilities, and the boundaries of work among these professionals. Although controlling one's emotions is not a major determinant of status among funeral professionals, it has a significant function in determining their status among other colleagues. Likewise, the lower one is on the totem pole, the less shameful it is for one to cry.

Within the hierarchy perceived by funeral professionals, male funeral staff are ranked the highest, then conductors, female funeral staff, funeral assistants, and part-timers (see Figure 7). This ranking is expressed in several ways. For instance, President Sakuma makes inquiries about the business to the funeral staff and often asks them about conductors. In contrast, I rarely saw the president chat with other workers. Moon Rise's executives hire the funeral staff and conductors, while funeral assistants and part-timers are often hired by their supervisory branch. The pattern of commensality also reveals the hierarchical structure. Funeral staff eat lunch in their office adjacent to the funeral halls, and neither part-timers nor funeral assistants are invited to use the room. Conductors eat lunch somewhere outside the hall after funerals, and sometimes eat lunch with the funeral staff in their office. Corpse handling elevates the funeral staff to the highest rank; conductors rank second because of their direct and close interactions with the bereaved. The gap between female funeral staff and funeral assistants is small because they have about the same amount of access to the bereaved. The part-timers are ranked lowest because they neither handle the corpse nor interact closely with the bereaved.

What is at the core of the funeral staff's professionalism and sense of pride? Contrary to public opinion, handling the corpse is the underlying foundation of their professional confidence. The funeral industry was very successful in reconceptualizing funeral ceremonies as unpolluted and clean events. The only act that continued to be seen as filthy was touching the cadaver. All the young funeral staff told me that the hardest thing to get accustomed to in the job was handling the corpse. "I am used to it now, but in the beginning I hated the hard, cold, solid sensation of the corpse," explained one member of the funeral staff. However, this is exactly what all funeral staff must adjust to if they want to be respected by other funeral professionals.

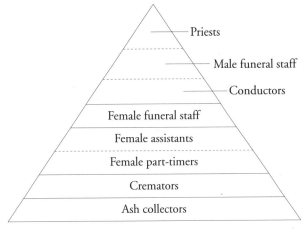

Note: Dotted lines indicate that the rank boundaries are contested.

FIGURE 7.   Self-perceived ranking of funeral professionals

I observed that the funeral staff used gloves only for deceased who had died in accidents, had suffered an otherwise unnatural death, or had been dead for several days. Otherwise all funeral staff grasped or touched cadavers with their bare hands, whether in a hospital or a private home, despite the fact that touching a corpse can be dangerous if the person had a contagious disease. "The trouble is," said Himonya, the president and the editor of the funeral magazine *Sōgi*, "funeral staff are not told of this risk and are not aware of it. Moreover, few doctors would mention the cause of death to a funeral staff member." But is it simply the lack of information that keeps the funeral staff from wearing gloves? In my opinion, ignorance is not the main reason. I observed that the funeral staff never forgot to wash their hands with antiseptic soap immediately after their return. They seemed to be fully aware of the health hazards. Ironically, their main reason for not wearing gloves may be the very same reason that they should wear them. If risking the existing danger fulfills their pride, then facing risk is a demonstration of courage, bravery, and machismo.

Therefore, it is handling the corpse that distinguishes funeral staff professionals and demarcates the boundary between them and others. At first I was not welcome when I accompanied them to hospitals, although they never seemed to mind my help with other tasks. But handling the corpse was their territory and the core task by which they dominated in the funeral profession.

There is no doubt that Kuma, introduced at the beginning of the chapter, disliked his experience at an apartment full of dog feces. But by completing the task he earned the respect of his colleagues, especially the younger ones. After he had left the office, other funeral staff praised him, "He has guts" (*konjō ga aru*).

FUNERAL PROFESSIONALS
OUTSIDE OF MOON RISE

Holiness and unholiness after all need not always be absolute opposites. They can be relative categories. What is clean in relation to one thing may be unclean in relation to another, and vice versa. The idiom of pollution lends itself to a complex algebra which takes into account the variables in each context.

—Mary Douglas, *Purity and Danger:*
An Analysis of the Concepts of Pollution and Taboo

Funeral professionals perform highly specialized tasks. For example, cremators are skilled at cremating and helping bereaved families collect the bones of their loved ones. Behind the scenes, cremators carefully monitor the progress of the deceased's cremation. Glancing through the small window of each incinerator, one cremator passes a message to another cremator, who mechanically controls the flow of gas and temperature: "This *hotoke* [Buddha or the deceased] is rising, we better switch to low." When I peeped, the body was bending upward. I asked how this happened. "It's like grilling a fish," he replied. "If the fire is too strong, the corpse curls up." Walking to the next incinerator, he stares into the window again. "This Buddha is not incinerating well" (*yakeguai ga warui*). Looking at his watch he says, "We need to raise the temperature. We don't have much time left for this one." While checking other incinerators he explained to me: "Cremating a human is much harder than grilling a fish. We have to prepare them perfectly. If well done [*yakesugi*], the bones crumble into ashes. If rare [*namayake*] the bones are too large to fit into pots." Being asked how he feels when the deceased has been cremated perfectly, he said, "I am really proud when the Buddha is prepared just right [*chodoyoi*], but it is also a pity because not all bones are collected by families and most go to waste." After getting to know some cremators, I learned that they all loved to fish and prepared their own sashimi (raw fish dish) and grilled fish (*yakizakana*). When asked if there was any connection between their job and their hobby, one replied, "It's a great feeling to catch a lively fish instead."

This chapter examines the funeral professionals outside of Moon Rise—the bathing service staff, cremators, ash collectors, and Buddhist priests. As in the preceding chapter, the differences in these professionals' roles is presented here with special attention given to two tasks, namely, handling the corpse and guiding the bereaved. On the basis of these two criteria, I draw a hierarchical scheme perceived by the professionals themselves. The hierarchy of funeral professionals reveals not only the new cultural values that commercial funerals are based on but also the preservation of current cultural practices through task specialization.

The Bathing Service

The bathing service staff are not Moon Rise employees. They work through the Kokura Funeral Auditorium but are hired by the Ceremony Special Car Service (CSC) company. CSC was the first company to market the bathing ceremony in Japan. I visited its headquarters in Osaka and interviewed the founding president.

The president, Kii Ryo, a 52-year-old man, used to work at one of the funeral companies as a funeral staff member in Osaka. He left that job in 1984 and, with the vice president, Hamada (age 51), established *Nyūyoku* Service, a bathing service for the elderly. Bathing services were performed by going to a customer's house with a van equipped with a bathtub, water heater, suction pump, container, and other necessary items. When one of his familiar customers passed away, Kii was asked by the family to give the deceased one last bath. For President Kii, who had worked on a funeral staff, "giving a bath to someone before or after death did not make much difference." He said, "I gladly agreed. I knew the old man well, and I felt that it was my last time to pay my respects. But to my surprise, the last bath I gave him was appreciated much more than I would ever have expected." The incident gave him the idea for starting a bathing service for the deceased. The president explained, "The bathing services for the elderly were contracted through the social welfare system and were not very profitable. We needed to find a different channel in order to survive." Starting with the simple idea of reinventing the bathing ritual, CSC had completely shifted its marketing within three years. The company kept its former name, Ceremony Special Car Service, because it continued to use similar vans.

By 1995 the company had expanded to 90 employees; they served funeral companies all over Japan (Kōbe, Kyōto, Nagoya, Hiroshima, Kyūshū, and Yamaguchi) that had contracted with CSC. Moon Rise and CSC signed a contract in the early fall of 1994 and the service began in November, when it was first introduced in the Kyūshū area.

Two bathing service staff from CSC attend morning meetings with Moon Rise's funeral staff, but they are independent from the rest of the Moon Rise personnel. They provide only bathing services, they are paid by CSC, and they have their own office at a different location. The bathing service staff maintain contact with the funeral staff by phone and fax to arrange for bathing ceremonies.

The two workers from CSC were Hirata Shigeru, a 28-year-old man who came from the main office in Osaka, and Oka, a 22-year-old woman who was hired from the local area after Hirata arrived in Kita-Kyūshū. Oka, a high school graduate, became interested in the job because of the high pay. She had worked previously at a trading company. Oka told me that she found the job through a newspaper advertisement that clearly stated that the job entailed giving a bath to the deceased. "I understood that it involved dead people," said Oka, "but I did not mind at all." Under Hirata's supervision, she quickly learned the job and came to enjoy it. She told me that her family did not object to her job. However, she said that she would quit if she met a future husband who disliked her job.

Hirata had been a typical laborer. His wife, Hirata Keiko, who had previously worked on the bathing staff, suggested that he try it himself. Many of the bathing staff were originally nurses who had been hired for the bathing service for the elderly. Keiko did not have a nurse's certificate but had worked as a nurse's assistant before working for CSC. Hirata stated frankly that the excellent pay was what attracted him to the job. Initially, he was not eager to touch the deceased, but he quickly overcame his reluctance. In fact, he not only got accustomed to the task but also began to find the job rewarding and satisfying. "I discovered that I receive a kind of appreciation from customers that no other job provides. The appreciation gives me the pride and enthusiasm that I need in continuing the work," said Hirata, who had been working for three years. "In this job, three years is considered very long. Many people quit after a year or two." This is because many staff conceal the job from their parents, fiancé(e)s, relatives, and friends, and once the secret is uncovered they receive so much opposition that they quit.

Similar to the members of a funeral staff, the bathing service staff must bolster their confidence by finding their own sense of professionalism. For them, demonstrating their superior knowledge of bathing the deceased is the key to their authority. The vice president, Hamada, told me that when she touches a corpse with her bare hands, showing respect, and handles it in a highly ritualized way, demonstrating professionalism, she receives admiration from customers that cannot be found in any other occupation. Despite her inferior status among the general public, she said, "The appreciation shown by families is of absolute importance. If one can positively accept it one can stand against any opposition, including that of social stigma."

Hirata is a good example of a person whose job changed him professionally and personally. According to the vice president,

Hamada, Hirata used to be a man who did not pay the slightest attention to elders. However, after beginning the job he began to be more aware of people who needed help. The job nurtured his sense of compassion and also gave him confidence to rise above the social stigma. Again, it was handling the corpse that generated Hirata's self-confidence: "Bathing the deceased rewards me with the bereaved's gratitude and fulfills my pride." As in the case of the funeral staff, handling the corpse is what makes the bathing ceremony workers professionals.

Cremators and Ash Collectors

The cremators (*onbō-san*) I interviewed were not employed by Moon Rise or any other private company.[1] All crematoriums in Kita-Kyūshū are owned by the city government, and the cremators are hired and paid by the city.[2] However, cremators have a certain autonomy and authority; they control affairs within the crematorium.

The job of the ash collectors (*haibutsu-kaishū-sha*) is to remove the leftover bones and ashes from the crematorium. I have concluded that the average Japanese rarely considers the existence of ash collectors. When the bereaved family is handed an ashpot with the partial remains of the deceased, some do wonder what happens to the bones and ashes left behind, but they seldom ask the cremators. The cremators, whom I came to know well, also told me that they had never asked the ash collectors. Perhaps they had not asked because of the natural reticence between the bereaved and the cremators as well as between the cremators and the ash collectors. Japanese may assume that the leftover ashes are buried somewhere but be reluctant to face the possibility that knowing where might be disquieting.

Mazuda, a 58-year-old, is a second-generation cremator. The South Crematorium, where he works now, is his third such workplace. He first worked with his father at the Tobata Crematory (Tobata Kasōba), which was built in 1921. At that time, the deceased were brought in during the evening and the bodies were cremated at night, confining the cremators' work to these hours. Until the 1960s, most funerals were over in the late afternoon, and crematories used coal, which could not generate the heat necessary for cremating a body within a short period of time. Thus cremators had to spend time firing the coal to the necessary temperature first. When the coal was ready, the coffin was put into the incinerator by laying it on top of two parallel bamboo sticks; the bamboo helped the coffin roll into the incinerator. Coffins were pushed into and taken out of incinerators manually. The body was turned with a stick during the cremation process. The body burned throughout the night and the cremated bones and ashes were picked up by the bereaved the next morning. "It was a heavy and grueling job," Mazuda recalled in front of other young cremators, pride tingeing his voice.

It was not until 1959 that Mazuda's work hours shifted to daytime. The second crematorium where he worked, Kiyomizu Crematorium (Kiyomizu Saijō), used oil for fuel, which shortened the cremation process. A deceased's family could pick up the ashes on the same day. "This one was a crematorium [*kasō-saijō*] and not a crematory [*kasōba*]," Mazuda emphasized. "The difference is that a crematory does not have a waiting room, and a crematorium does." The development of crematoriums with modern buildings, waiting space, and better equipment allowed cremators to become daytime workers. This was a great change for Mazuda. Nonetheless, the work still required manual labor. When the coffin was brought in, it was laid on a marble setting. The incinerator had iron rails on both sides, but the coffin had to be pushed by hand. The surface of the stone bed, where the coffin was laid, was brushed with wet brooms. This work seems to have generated strong memories for both Mazuda and his son, probably because they had to perform the task in front of the bereaved. Mazuda explained that to sweep the stone bed the broom had to be wetted first because the bed was steaming hot. "I always had to say to the mourners, excuse me sir, excuse me ma'am, please stand back while I sweep the ashes" (*suimasen, hakimasunode sagatteku-dasai*). Brushing the stone bed sent up white dust that covered everything. "The white lamps in front of each incinerator were always covered with a couple of centimeters of dust." After the family had taken the bones, the leftover bones and ashes were gathered into a bucket and carried outside, where they were thrown into a well with a shrine-like roof. When the well was full, ash collectors arrived to empty it. This old crematory space has been turned into a park today; cherry trees blossom where the old ash wells used to be.

Cremators who work at the South Crematorium today do less physical labor than cremators in previous decades. Since the establishment of South Crematorium in 1981, all cremators wear white coats (similar to the ones worn by doctors and pharmacists) that cover their upper body. Wearing a white coat was Mazuda's idea. The white coats, however, do not hide their shirts, black neckties, and handsome dark trousers. "I could not have worn such clothes in the old days because I was sweaty all the time," Mazuda said.

The crematorium is furnished with modern equipment that has eliminated or simplified most of the manual tasks. The coffin is easily transported with gurneys from the gate to the front of the incinerator; the coffin is rolled into the incinerator with a mechanical device; the incinerators use gas burners for cremation, and the temperature is monitored, controlled, and altered mechanically. "It has become so easy these days that I gained weight. I have to consciously reduce by doing exercises," Mazuda's son commented with a laugh.

The cremators still have to clear the leftover ashes from the incinerators, which they do with a vacuuming device that deposits the ashes and bones into a sack made of rough hemp. When the sack is full, after two or three days, it is put in storage at the back of the crematorium.

Although modern technology has eliminated the labor-intensive work from cremation, it is far from being a pleasant job. One of the cremator's most abhorrent tasks is cremating organs and other human body parts. Hospital trucks transport human parts, left over from surgery, to the crematorium once a month. These human parts are all frozen and wrapped in a plastic bag. Cremators wear gloves and masks to unwrap each part and lay it on the stone bed. "I got used to human parts, but I am still uncomfortable with aborted fetuses," Mazuda Jr. said. Other cremators nodded their agreement.

Cremators at South Crematorium, Mazuda in particular, control the crematorium. They supervise other workers, such as two male bookkeepers hired by the city government and the women who work in the café. Mazuda's wife, Kei, works part time in the crematorium office, but she also has influence over others in the crematorium. During a conversation, one of the Mazudas' daughters, Ruriko, mentioned that her mother has a very independent personality. "If my mother doesn't like someone [crematory workers or other funeral professionals who come in contact with her at the crematorium], the poor fellow will be rejected instantly by the whole staff working at the crematorium." Mazuda wields power over both the insiders and the outsiders. For example, he allows only well-behaved taxi drivers to enter the crematorium. Any driver who had been rude to mourners, looked down on the cremators, or was unmannerly was kept out. Mazuda would tell them, "I don't want to see your face here again," and that would be the end of it. Hearse drivers from Moon Rise are also very careful to be polite to cremators and are intimidated by Mazuda. It was obvious to me that hearse drivers did their best not to jeopardize their relationship with him because any complaints could lead to their dismissal. Mazuda even has control over ash collectors. As soon as the ash collectors arrived at the crematorium, they went directly to Mazuda, who acted like the president of a company and received their respectful bows. Although ash collectors are paid by the city government, it is the cremators who evaluate and assign the job to particular ash collectors. In this case, Mazuda is the commanding authority.

Where does Mazuda get his power? Does it derive from his wealth? Cremators are paid well, much more than the usual bureaucrats hired by the city government. They also receive money gifts from the chief mourners. To be accurate, however, their wealth is the result of their power, and not the other way around. In my observation, the source of their strength derives from the handling of the corpse and the Japanese fear of evil spirits and death pollution.

There is a conceptual distinction between funeral halls and crematories. Many guests do not mind staying for a cup of coffee after a funeral ceremony at an auditorium, whereas only close family members and relatives are willing to travel to the crematorium. The reason is not that crematoriums are unclean in the literal sense of the word. On the contrary, crematoriums today are not only extremely clean but also artistically beautiful: the building is modern with a high ceiling and large windows and skylights, and is set among gardens filled with flowers. It is fully air-conditioned in summer, and the incinerator is completely sealed off; the gas burner makes a constant, low, monotonous sound instead of the irregular sounds that tended to bother visitors; the smoke is filtered through a system that renders it mere vapor, with none of the black smoke released from the building; there is no chimney on the building and the vapor emitted is unrecognizable from the outside. After observing bereaved families at the crematorium, however, I was convinced that they still connected the crematorium with the notion of impurity and danger. Likewise, cremators are stigmatized. In fact, rarely do family members talk to cremators. When cremators make suggestions or provide information to the mourners, they are answered with a nod. The money gift is handed to a cremator silently when the bereaved arrive at the crematorium.

The body language expressed toward cremators is an important indicator of how they are perceived. The cremators' new clothes and improved background have not altered the way Japanese think about them. All the cremators except Mazuda himself have finished high school and look professional in their uniforms. All of these changes may have reduced the stigma attached to their profession since Mazuda was a child, but it has not disappeared completely. For instance, cremators have trouble finding marriage partners. Mazuda pointed to one of his subordinates and commented, "I have introduced more than 30 women to this guy, but he's still a bachelor." He also told me that his former subordinate quit because when he wanted to get married the fiancée's father had demanded that he choose between the job and his fiancée.

The stigma attached to cremators originates from their task. What led me to this conclusion is the persistent custom of the money gift, which the deceased's family gives to the cremators. Occasionally, the bereaved also present money gifts to conductors, funeral assistants, funeral staff, and part-timers. However, the implications of a money gift to the cremators and one that is given to the staff of a funeral company are fundamentally different. The money given to funeral staff signifies appreciation; the bereaved usually say a few words of gratitude at the time. It could also be considered a "return" or thank-you gift for their help.[3] It is important to note that the money gift to the staff is not obligatory, and furthermore, it is given after all the services have been carried out. From this perspective it can be considered a tip. In contrast, the money gift is handed silently to cremators as soon as the family arrives at the crematorium, before the actual cremation. In addition, such gifts to cremators are considered mandatory, an obligatory action. I asked the Moon Rise staff why it is still considered necessary to provide money gifts to cremators before the cremation. "Of course you need to give them money first," they all replied without hesitation. In the staff's opinion, the money was to make sure that the deceased would be incinerated properly and that the family would be able to collect the ashes. This explanation, however, generates questions rather than answers. Since the bereaved pay a standard fee for cremation that is set by the city government, one would assume that the deceased would be cremated properly. Why do people feel the need to pay extra money?

The deeper meaning of this money gift lies in the consolation and pacification (*kuyō*) of the deceased. The underlying sentiment is that if the corpse is not handled with care the deceased will turn into a vengeful evil spirit.

The idea of the deceased becoming a haunting spirit through mistreatment of the dead body has existed since the ninth century (Haga, 67), and its elimination was the central objective of community funerals. In contrast, commercial funeral ceremonies negate such a perception and treat the deceased as though they are alive. The act of cremation, though, implies a dramatic change; it draws a line between life and death. My observation is that the perception of death pollution or the fear of spirits is limited to those who engage in cremation and its aftermath. This impurity, however, is not contagious; it is contained within the crematorium and affects only its workers. In the commercial ceremony, the living are always impurity-free. Hence the belief in a fearsome ghost gives the cremators a fearsome authority; it is they who take the danger onto themselves in order to ensure the safe passage of the soul into the other world. It is this risk-taking that cremators are responsible for and are paid for. They control the fate of the deceased by putting themselves in jeopardy, and thus they control the living. However, cremators' power remains within the liminal state. As soon as the bereaved embrace the deceased's ashpot, their attitude toward the deceased quickly returns to peace and affection, just as suddenly as the subliminal fear arose.

Mazuda Jr. picked me up at 7:00 A.M., and we arrived at the South Crematorium at 7:25 on March 29, 1995.[4] Two assistants, who were in their forties, were already waiting at the gate of the crematory in their large shiny truck. Dressed in jeans and T-shirts, they looked like ordinary construction workers. Mazuda Jr. opened the gate and drove his car around to the back. The truck followed.

The Takeda Company (Takeda *Shōten*) is a private, family-owned business that collects ashes from various crematories. The two men I met were the second and third sons. The elder had inherited the position of president of the business that their father had begun 30 years earlier.

The history of their business parallels the development of modern crematories. In early crematories, ashes were buried at the back of the compound. When dramatic measures were taken to improve the condition and appearance of contemporary crematoriums, the modern buildings with their beautiful gardens became unsuitable places for dumping leftover ashes. With the modernization of crematories brought by the increase of cremation in Japan,[5] cremators also began to disassociate themselves from the manual labor (*jūrōdō*) involved in ash disposal, and the ash-collecting business was born.

The brothers of the Takeda Company told me that they collect ashes from the areas around Kyūshū, Chūgoku, and Shikoku. They have a contract with each crematory and are paid according to the number of visits they make. Since most crematories are government owned, it is the government (prefecture or city) that pays their salary. Listening to the conversations between the Takeda brothers and Mazuda, however, it was clear to me that their relationship with cremators is extremely important. The Takeda brothers went to greet Mazuda immediately upon arrival. They told me that city officials seldom come to talk to them. The cremators determine the ash collectors' job assignments by telling the city government which company they have hired.

Over the course of a year, the crematorium incinerates about 4,000 corpses. Ash collecting takes place four times a year, averaging 1,000 corpses' remains each time. The ash bags that were picked up on the day I visited were those that had been stored from mid-February through the end of March. During that month and a half, there was an accumulation of 39 ash bags. One ash bag weighs about 50 kilograms (110–120 pounds), heavy enough to require two men to lift it. At this crematorium the cremated bones are ground by machine into powder. According to the Takeda brothers, half of the crematories they work for do not have a grinding mechanism. In that case, bones are still in pieces; thus each bag weighs less than a bag filled only with ashes, but there are more bags to remove.

The Takeda brothers worked systematically. First they backed their truck into the garage behind the crematorium. They donned elaborate outfits that resembled biohazard suits. They wore masks, gloves, heavy boots, and blue nylon suits that covered them from top to bottom. In addition, they wore heavy black nylon aprons. After they had dressed, they used a two-wheeled cart to carry the ash bags to the truck. They manually loaded these bags onto the truck, making many trips. Each time a bag was lifted onto the truck, black smoke and dust filled the air; fortunately it did not smell. It was mainly the dust and the weight of the bags that seemed to make the job burdensome. It took them about twenty minutes to load all the bags neatly onto their truck. When the truck was fully loaded, they drove it out of the building and covered it with a thick green plastic sheet. With this covering in place, one could not differentiate the truck from any other truck carrying sand or construction materials. Then they carefully took off their masks and suits, put some water into a watering can, washed the dust from their boots, and went inside to wash their hands and faces. This entire process took an hour. The actual time necessary for the job is short, but since ash collectors and cremators agree that mourners should not be privy to this part of the process, ash collectors only pick up in the early morning.

I asked what was done with these ashes. Having asked this question of others, including priests, I knew they assumed that the ashes were buried in a large temple yard or at the back of a crematorium. Thanks to Takeda's frankness, I learned that they are taken to certain mountains and hills that the company owns and dumped into a hole, 8 meters long x 10 meters wide x 7 meters deep. After the holes are filled, cherry trees and conifers are planted. These grow rapidly and become huge. "In particular, the cherry blossoms in our place bloom more gorgeously than anywhere else," Takeda remarked proudly. These cherry trees attract many visitors, but few of them recognize the secret of the trees' beauty. During our interview the Takedas mentioned that they have a memorial tower (*kuyōtō*) on their land, and every March and September they chant sutras to placate the souls of the deceased. The nature of their job, and perhaps the stigma attached to it, seemed to have made them very religious. They have been believers of Sōkagakkai (one of the largest New Religions) for more than 39 years.[6]

The Takeda brothers are socially isolated people. During our meeting, they repeatedly expressed surprise that I was interested in their work. I noted that they were rarely spoken to and learned that they had little opportunity to interact with others outside their Sōkagakkai congregations. Even the cremators rarely talked to them unless necessary. The Takeda brothers possessed no business cards. Apologetically, they told me that they did not have cards because they avoid revealing their work to the public. Their occupation is inherited; even their marriage partners come from a family in the same occupational group.

It was noticeable that ash collectors rank below cremators in the social hierarchy. The cremators treated them as if they were lowly workers. They look down on ash collectors for being mere manual laborers who have no responsibility for the spirit of the deceased (and who risk no danger from those spirits), since ash collectors do not deal with the body in a liminal state. Cremators also pride themselves on their knowledge of cremation procedures and their skills in interacting with the bereaved. They differentiate themselves from ash collectors, who neither handle the corpse nor deal with the bereaved. The cremators call them *haibutsu-kaishū-sha*, literally, persons who collect trash. They are identified with garbage collectors and not with the remains of the deceased. Thus it is the combination of impurity, danger, responsibility, and knowledge that divides these two professions. In the eyes of the general public, both cremators and ash collectors are highly stigmatized. However, the ash collectors, stigmatized even by the cremators, are the contemporary untouchables—the lowest of the low. Interestingly, it is those who handle the corpse who rank higher in this occupational hierarchy.

Buddhist Priests

Religious officiants are an indispensable element of funerals. However, in recent years their position has been lowered by commercialized ceremonies, and this is particularly true for Buddhist priests.

As the main religious officiants, Buddhist priests participate in the majority of contemporary funeral ceremonies. Recently their lives have been influenced greatly by the shift from community funeral rituals to commercial funeral ceremonies. Unlike other religious officiants, Buddhist priests' financial security depends on death ceremonies (funerals and ancestral ceremonies) rather than on spreading their religious beliefs. Shintō priests, for instance, rarely engage in the rituals surrounding death, and they often support themselves by working at other jobs.[7] Neither are death ceremonies the main method by which Christianity and New Religions (*shinkyō-shukyō*) finance themselves and recruit new followers.

In contemporary funeral ceremonies the only power Buddhist priests have derives from the value placed on their religious services. The transition away from funeral rituals has lessened their authority and simultaneously impaired the once-close relationship between Buddhist priests and community members. Historical changes have threatened priests' economic standing, so that they have been forced to engage openly in the businesslike management of their temples. This, in turn, has also lowered their standing in the eyes of the community. Funeral professionals and family members of the deceased demonstrate a superficial respect—which is mere formality—toward priests at ceremonies. How Buddhist priests evaluate themselves and the ambiguous relationship they have with families of the deceased and with funeral professionals reveals their adjustment to their new roles in society.

The number of funeral ceremonies a Buddhist priest attends depends mostly on the number of families or parishioners affiliated with his temple (*danka*).[8] According to the priests I interviewed, the annual number of temple (or "temple-member") funerals they attend is about 10 percent of the total number of their parishioners, and accounts for 50 to 70 percent of the total funerals per year. The remaining 30 to 50 percent is made up of families who are not part of a temple but wish to have a priest at their loved one's funeral; these families are introduced to a priest by the funeral company. In general, Buddhist priests attend as many of these funerals as they have time for. When a priest accepts such a commission, the implication is that the bereaved family will become his temple's new parishioners or client and can be called upon to support temple finances.[9] Priests from newly established temples with few parishioners are the most eager to attend funerals because it is the easiest way to acquire new clients. For this reason priests must stay on good terms with funeral companies.

Buddhist priests have two major responsibilities in a funeral: to recite the sutra and to give the deceased a posthumous name. The purpose of these activities is to transport the deceased safely from the world of the living to the world of the dead in accordance with Buddhist beliefs. A priest first visits the deceased's house or a funeral hall to perform the sutra recitation (*makuragyō*) after the deceased has been encoffined. The priest returns again in the evening to recite the sutra at the wake. Sometimes a priest gives a short speech (*howā*) afterward about the deceased or the Buddhist interpretation of the afterlife. The priests' primary task is to recite the sutra at the funeral ceremony; usually only one priest attends the wake, but more than two attend the funeral. The priests arrive at the funeral hall about 30 minutes before a ceremony begins. Upon arrival they change from their ordinary robes into colorful and elaborate funeral robes. Frequently women funeral assistants are asked to help them change. When all the guests are seated, the priests enter the funeral hall while the funeral professionals greet them with deep bows to show respect (the guests remain seated without bowing). The priests sit and begin the sutra chanting, which takes approximately 30 to 40 minutes, about half the time of the total ceremony. When the priests' religious service and the ceremony of bidding farewell have been completed the priests leave the hall.[10] Buddhist priests rarely accompany the deceased's family to the crematorium, but they give another sutra recitation at the seventh-day memorial service (*shonanoka*), which in recent years is often held at the hall (or at home) immediately after the family returns from the crematorium.

The priests' other major responsibility is giving the deceased a posthumous name (*hōmyō* in the Jōdoshinshū sect, *hōgō* in the Nichirenshū sect, and *kaimyō* in other sects). The posthumous name is written in black calligraphy on the two wooden memorial tablets (*shiraki-ihai*). One wooden tablet is cremated with the deceased while the other is kept at the domestic Buddhist altar until the 49th-day memorial service. Later the posthumous name is rewritten by the priest in gold ink on a black-lacquered memorial tablet (*hon-ihai*), which is kept on the domestic Buddhist altar (*butsudan*).

The giving of posthumous names developed from a Buddhist ritual, *jukai*: when a new disciple entered the priesthood, he received a Buddhist name (Gorai 1992, 630–34). It then became customary to give the deceased posthumous names to ensure their Buddhahood (*jōbutsu*) in the afterlife. What is behind the posthumous name is the notion of beneficial regeneration; the deceased will be purified by becoming a Buddhist disciple, which in turn, allows the deceased to be regenerated into the world of Buddha (Gorai 1992). Besides turning the deceased into a Buddhist disciple, the posthumous name gives information about the age, sex, and status of the deceased. The status of a posthumous name (*ikai*) today, however, often parallels the amount of money the family offers the priests. For example, the rank of *koji* for males and *daishi* for females is more expensive than *shinji* for males and *shinnyo* for females. (The hierarchical scale of posthumous names is shown in Table 3.) The rank of the posthumous name can be purchased and altered by negotiations between priests and the bereaved. (If the bereaved's contribution is large, more priests will attend the funeral ceremony as well.) Thus it is not the deceased's deeds in life that determine a high-ranking posthumous name, but the amount of money donated by the family.

Buddhist priests are isolated from the whole funeral process[11]; their activities are limited to their religious responsibilities. They seldom influence the deceased's family in the decision-making at funeral ceremonies because they are not invited until funeral professionals have finished the preparation of the body, consultation with the family members, and preliminary decoration of the room. Although priests make decisions concerning the time of wakes and funerals, they are not wholeheartedly invited to join the deceased's family gatherings after the wake or the funeral.

During our interview, I noticed that priests were dissatisfied with the current situation. They repeatedly grumbled about contemporary families and the funeral industry. One priest said, "The problem is that families today are too ignorant about funerals, and they listen only to funeral professionals. Because they depend so much on funeral companies, they themselves behave like guests." The focus of their criticism, however, was the funeral companies and professionals. Many priests complained that the funeral staff do not prepare Buddhist objects in the correct manner. For example, a Buddhist priest from the Sōtō-shū sect told me of his irritation when the incense at the funeral altar was off-center. Although such an issue is not important to the bereaved or to the participants, the priest insisted that the idea of the "center" is very important in his religious sect, and he ridiculed the ignorance of funeral staff. Priests are also annoyed about the time limitations set by funeral companies. One older priest who had served for more than 40 years lamented, "If I recite the sutra in the proper way, it will take more than an hour and a half. But ceremonies are limited to an hour by the companies, and I am forced

TABLE 3
The Hierarchy of Posthumous Names

Rank		Male	Female
Lowest	Children	Dōji	Dōnyo
	Adults	Shinji	Shinnyo
		Koji	Daishi
		In-koji	In-daishi
Highest		Inden-daikoji	Inden-daishi

to cut many portions that I am supposed to recite. I am asked to shorten my recitations because they need time to read telegrams! Since when are telegrams more important for the deceased than sutra recitations?"

The priests' resentment of funeral professionals and the deceased's family is the direct result of commercialized ceremonies. The change has decreased priests' influence and control in funerals, which in turn has lowered their social status. Since Buddhist priests engage in spiritual matters and do not touch the corpse, their status remains much higher than that of those who handle the corpse. All the same, priests have lost respect and authority since the time of community rituals. The most important factor in this change has been the attenuation of the tie between temples and parishioners.

From the Tokugawa period (1600–1867) until the rise of the Shintō-state in World War II, Buddhist temples were certain to have parishioners. When the Tokugawa government issued an anti-Christian edict in the early seventeenth century, all households had to register with a Buddhist temple. Robert J. Smith, in *Ancestor Worship in Contemporary Japan*, writes that, "The effect of these anti-Christian edicts was generally to standardize and universalize practices for all classes and in all parts of the country so that the household everywhere became tied to the temple just as ancestor worship had become tied to Buddhism. For the parishioners the temple became primarily the place where the ancestors were worshipped, and the priest the chief officiant at ancestral rites" (Smith, R. 1974, 22).

The ties between households (*ie*) and Buddhist temples guaranteed that Buddhist priests were the officiants at the time of death. The importance of ancestor worship for the continuation of the household also supported the bond between each household and its temple. Each new generation followed the practices of the preceding one, and rarely did its members change their temple affiliation or their religious sect.[12] Thus, before the war, priests had stable positions in communities. An elder told me that the local temple priests were respected for their reading and writing skills. Priests also knew a great deal about local residents because they had many interactions with them. If a father was looking for prospective marriage partners for his sons and daughters, he would go to the priests for advice. The old man put it simply: "Priests had authority because they knew all about us."

Today, families do not hesitate to sever their ties to a local temple when they move to cities, even though they have no idea which temple to join once they have moved. As a result, Buddhist temples that have lost their old members are forced to find new families to sustain them. The families' only concern after setting up a new residence is to belong to the same Buddhist sect as their ancestors, and even this concern is waning in the face of a more practical concern—cost.

One crucial change that has affected the position of priests has been the increase of migration. Bereaved families now have the power to choose their temples and priests rather than depending on them. The consequence has been a competitive market for religious services and parishioner recruitment. The newly established small temples have to keep in close contact with funeral companies and build a personal network with funeral staff so that they will be introduced to the bereaved. At Moon Rise, I observed that priests who had close contacts with funeral staff officiated at more funeral services. For example, one member of the staff stated, "If a family asks me if I know any Jōdoshinshū sect priests, I always mention temple A because priest X of that temple is a nice guy." Having a good relationship with the funeral staff is the key to beating the competition.

The quest for parishioners continues even after the funeral ceremony is over. This is because families have the right to choose another temple to keep their deceased's ashes. I often heard stories about families who switched their temple affiliation because of the amount of money required for donations. One part-time female worker told me that she even changed her original family sect. "When my mother died I was introduced to an Ōbakushū sect temple. [This was her original household sect.] However, because of the high price of funeral services and the posthumous name at the funeral ceremony, I assumed that the temple's annual donations would also be costly, so I decided to preserve my mother's ashes in a large Jōdoshinshū sect temple." She said that because the latter temple has many members the donation of each family is lower.

Priests have become businessmen, and their services have become commercialized as a consequence of the unstable relations between families and temples. One may object to this perspective owing to the fact that even during the community funeral rituals Buddhist priests were paid either with money or rice and that from this perspective the contemporary temple management is no different from the past. It is, however, the nature of the donation that has been altered. The monetary or material donations in the community rituals were a kind of gift. They were not commercialized payments. A gift exchange reflects continuous personal relations, mutual dependency, and responsibilities. "The gifts themselves may be things that are normally used as commodities (food, feasts, luxury goods, services), but each transaction is not discrete and none, in principle, is terminal" (Kopytoff, 69). The monetary donations for today's funeral ceremonies are discrete; the family pays when the service is received. The exchange can be terminated at any time in the future if the family does not like the priests or the temple. The symmetrical relationship between the priests and families has been broken. This has transformed the priests' role; they have become providers of services, similar to funeral companies. The amount of money they receive as donations is objective and is a one-time payment. The services and posthumous names that the priests provide can be seen as commodities. The competition among temples, the freedom of choice that the bereaved possess, and the price negotiations between temples and families reveal the transformation of today's Buddhist priests into marketers of commercialized services.

Buddhist priests have also been transformed into businessmen through the marketing of gravesites and space in ossuaries. When a family or a person purchases a gravesite or ossuary space from a temple, that person becomes a parishioner. Formerly, cemeteries were owned by each community, by private households, or by temples. The Law Regarding Graves and Burial Sites, in effect since 1948, restricts their construction to certain areas that have received state permits. The law also limits ownership of cemeteries and ossuaries to the government or religious institutions. Many gravesites are advertised for sale by private real estate companies; they do not own the sites but have contracts with religious institutions to market them. Not only do priests have the right to own cemeteries and ossuaries, they can also expand their space. Thus the majority are owned and managed by priests, and this has become a stable source of income for Buddhist temples. Ossuaries in particular became a convenient commodity because they could be enlarged with less land and expense than graves.

City dwellers who have left their ancestral homes often do not own gravesites until someone in their family dies. Most people prefer to buy ossuary space, which is much cheaper than a gravesite. Most ossuaries are built within the Buddhist temple grounds and are taken care of by priests. In recent years both gravesites and ossuary space have been in high demand, and fewer family members are interred together. Most couples' ashes are kept together, but the next generation may not wish to use the same space as their parents. Purchasing space in an ossuary implies that one expends a large sum at the beginning and then makes payments (several times per year) until the deceased achieves ancestorhood (23 or 33 years after death). Buddhist priests send out a letter reminding families of their deceased's upcoming memorial date and letting them know it is time for ossuary donations. There is no doubt that the management of cemeteries and ossuaries is a profitable business at a time when there is a high demand for ash space. The cycle proceeds something like this: the more cemetery or ossuary space one owns, the more clients one can recruit; the more clients one has, the more graves and ossuaries one can construct. Cemeteries and ossuaries constitute a commodity that provides for temple expansion and priests' living expenses, and they are managed as other commodities are. Many priests I interviewed had members' addresses and payment information neatly organized on their laptop computers. "This way I can keep my management in order," one priest told me with a grin.

Buddhist priests' engagement in business is undeniable. However, it should not be assumed that all their profits go into their own pockets. "People think that we are profit makers [*bōzu maru-mōke*], but that is not true," one priest said to me. In 1985 the Japanese Religious Association (*Shūkyōhōjin*) stipulated that all temples must have an administrator (*sōdai*), selected from the temple's own parishioners, to be responsible for temple finances. This administrator is kept informed of the temple's budget accounts—that is to say, the temple's spending, the priests' salaries, and the revenues. Without the administrator's permission, a priest cannot use the money from any business activities. However, whatever the rules are, the head priest of the Buddhist temple seems to have great, if not complete, control over its finances.

Becoming accustomed to their changed role has not been simple or easy for Buddhist priests. On the one hand, they have had to maintain good relations with funeral companies, commoditize ossuaries, and set prices for monetary donations. On the other hand, they are embarrassed, almost ashamed, that their religious activities have turned into business enterprises. They despise their own business behavior as much as they despise funeral professionals, "who gain by someone's death." They are caught between the desire to lead a proper Buddhist life by following Buddhist precepts and the economic reality in which they must commercialize religious activities in order to survive. I encountered many Buddhist priests who criticized recent trends in their own profession. "Contemporary priests have lost their dignity and the values of earlier priests," they lamented. Buddhist priests were always dependent on funerals, but their activities were based on gifts, not payments. Some priests were unwilling to tell me how many parishioners their temple had. Others seemed embarrassed to tell me that their temples had few parishioners. If they considered themselves pure priests—whose main activity was to perform ceremonies for people—why should the number of parishioners or the size of the temple matter? Only if they were conscious of or judged by their business success would they have cause to feel proud or ashamed.

While possessing a small base in community settings, priests must commercialize their services, wearing their religious robes as business suits. The commercialization of religious services is certainly the basis for the general public's lowered regard, but the role of officiant-cum-businessman did not come about as a result of priests' choices; it was forced upon them by the historical transformations that caused migration to the cities, the disintegration of community ties, and the subsequent commercialization of funerals.

Summary: The Reproduction of Cultural Values and Practices

Status distinctions among funeral professionals correspond to differences in their tasks. Two major factors structure the hierarchy: the handling of the corpse, and direct interactions with the bereaved. The stratification among funeral professionals is perceived in fine gradations determined by task boundaries and power distinctions (see Figure 7 in Chapter 5).

Professionals stratify themselves rigorously, and even slight differences can create conflict. Priests, who possess the knowledge to guide the deceased and the bereaved according to religious teaching, are regarded more highly than funeral staff because they are better educated and have a license that validates their high status. However, because an increasing number of priests depend on funeral staff for recruiting parishioners, funeral staff have begun to act more boldly toward priests from smaller temples. One funeral staff member said, "They act as if they are important by wearing colorful gowns. In fact, we carry out the funeral, and they depend on us."

The relationship between funeral staff and conductors is also intensely competitive. Although funeral staff have some power over conductors (since it is the staff who assign their rotation), conductors regard their jobs as more important because they lead all participants during the ceremony. Women funeral staff, assistants, and part-timers are also conscious of their power differences. Part-timers may challenge funeral assistants by crossing work boundaries.

Cremators and ash collectors are belittled by other funeral professionals; according to one funeral staff worker, "They only handle the corpse at the last moment. Incinerating the body does not require much knowledge." The fact that cremators and ash collectors come from the lower classes (*buraku-min*) may also account for this attitude. Although the Moon Rise funeral staff did not distinguish between cremators and ash collectors, cremators unquestionably drew a boundary between themselves and ash collectors.

The stratification of funeral professionals is significant for understanding current cultural values and their continuation. The hierarchical structure implies that commercial funeral ceremonies are rational social and business events. In contrast to community rituals, the objective of commercial ceremonies is not to usher out a potentially malevolent spirit; instead, its purpose is to celebrate the deceased's life as well as strengthen occupational networks. According to this goal, the contribution of funeral professionals is to assist a family in creating a positive memory of the deceased, to remove and transform the corpse to ashes, and to provide the bereaved an opportunity to reinforce social ties.

The stratification of funeral professionals, moreover, enforces work boundaries, regulates the content of work, and develops the self-identity of each funeral professional. I believe it is the specialization of work that serves to produce, reproduce, and maintain cultural values and practices. In short, multiple circular movements between funeral professionals, consumers, and cultural values create cultural continuity.

THE COMMODITIZATION OF
THE BATHING CEREMONY

Mass goods represent culture, not because they are merely there as the environment within which we operate, but because they are an integral part of that process of objectification by which we create ourselves as an industrial society: our identities, our social affiliations, our lived everyday practices. The authenticity of artifacts as culture derives not from their relationship to some historical style or manufacturing process . . . but rather from their active participation in a process of social self-creation in which they are directly constitutive of our understanding of ourselves and others.

—Daniel Miller, *Material Culture and Mass Consumption*

The Transformation of Product to Commodity

On an autumn morning in late November, a grandmother in her seventies died in her sleep. Moon Rise's funeral staff picked her up at the hospital and took her home. When Tomi arrived at the house for a consultation, the family was gathered in the living room. The bereaved were very calm, probably because the deceased had passed away peacefully. It was under these circumstances that Tomi made his first attempt to sell a bathing ceremony.

During the consultation, Tomi spoke mainly to the chief mourner, but everyone in the family was involved in the financial decisions for the funeral. As the consultation neared its end, Tomi asked the chief mourner if he wanted to have a bathing ceremony for his mother. "Bathing ceremony? What is that all about?" was the reply. Tomi explained, "It is a ceremony to clean and to bathe the deceased. This ritual was an old Japanese tradition that ceased for decades, but our company has revived it and is the first to offer this service in Kyūshū." The chief mourner's wife said, "But she was cleaned by the nurses at the hospital." "Yes," Tomi answered.

"However, she was merely wiped with antiseptic, not bathed in warm water." The family looked at each other, considering the idea. One of the granddaughters broke the silence by asking, "How much do you charge for the service?" "¥50,000," Tomi replied. "¥50,000! That's expensive," she exclaimed. "Our grandmother was always frugal; I am sure she wouldn't want such a thing." As the rest of the family members nodded in agreement, Tomi did not seem to know what more to say to change their minds. The chief mourner said decisively, "The bathing ceremony is not necessary."

As I mentioned earlier, Moon Rise has a contract with the Ceremony Special Car Service (CSC), which specializes in bathing services. CSC had demonstrated the ceremony to funeral staff in the summer of 1994, and Moon Rise had started marketing the service in November of 1994, just after I began my fieldwork. I was able to observe the entire marketing process—from the product's entry into the market, to consumer acceptance, to sales growth— and trace the transition of the bathing ceremony from a product to a commodity.

The transition from a "product," meaning anything that is produced, to a "commodity," which is something a customer considers worth purchasing, does not happen overnight. The commoditization process includes designing, testing, producing, and marketing a product. The product is then exchanged, and at that point, consumed. When the product is exchanged for money, it is endowed with a value that may lead to further marketing, exchanges, consumption, wider distribution, and finally mass consumption.

A product achieves commodity status through actual exchange between producers and consumers. By tracing the marketing of bathing ceremonies, I observed that marketing does not automatically guarantee that a "thing," "service," or "product" will become a "commodity." In other words, exchange is meaningful because it provides opportunities for a product to embody values that will transform it into a commodity.

As seen in the unsuccessful story of Tomi's marketing of a

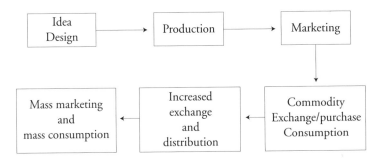

FIGURE 8.   The commoditization process

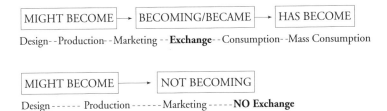

FIGURE 9.   The phases of commoditization and decommoditization

bathing ceremony, if a customer refuses a product or service, it remains just a product. The family saw no value in the bathing ceremony and therefore felt that they had lost nothing by refusing the service for their grandmother. If customers perceive no value or benefit from the bathing ceremony, it cannot become a commodity.

In this chapter I follow the life cycle of the bathing ceremony from product to commodity to show that the marketing and commoditization process are among the strongest forces that mediate and express cultural transitions. The commoditization of the bathing ceremony involves not only the reproduction of the traditional bathing ritual but also its reinvention: its form and meaning are drastically different from before. The transition of the bathing ceremony into a commodity shows how a product can become a commodity only if it incorporates the change of values taking place in a culture. Ultimately, successful commodity marketing is a happy marriage between a product and cultural values.

The objectification of values and the commoditization of services and goods are among the most significant processes that mediate cultural change. My analysis of this theme owes much to Grant McCracken's research on the culture of consumption. McCracken suggests that goods serve as an instrument of change and create an "object-code" that absorbs change (McCracken 1988, 131, 135). He further explains that, on the one hand, "goods are used as an opportunity for creativity and experimentation," and on the other hand, "they are used as a means of the internal and external reflection and disclosure which help shape and formalize the creative process" (135).

Although McCracken's analysis of the use of goods and consumption provides important insights about individuals and culture, his exclusive focus on these two aspects to explain cultural changes seems too narrow. The problem can be traced back to McCracken's model of the movement of meaning (Figure 10), in which he illustrated how cultural meaning descends from a "culturally constructed world," through "consumer goods," to "consumers" (72). What this model and McCracken's perspective on cultural change do not offer are an explanation of the complexities of meaning transfer and the various forces that bring cultural changes to the surface. I argue that shifts in meanings or values do not constitute a one-directional process and, as I suggested earlier, meaning is not transferred to all goods and services produced by industries. I agree with McCracken that the consumption of goods expresses cultural change, but he did not include in his model the dimension of changes over time.

I consider production, products, and consumption to be only part of a larger force that drives cultural change. Cultural changes are generated through interactions and negotiations between consumers, cultural values, and producers. By adding a time vector to

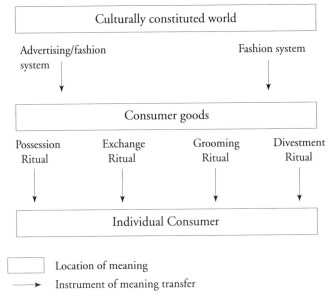

FIGURE 10.   Movement of meaning. *Source*: Grant McCracken,
"Culture and Consumption: A Theoretical Account of the
Structure and Movement of the Cultural Meaning of Consumer
Goods," *Journal of Consumer Research* (1988) 13:72.

McCracken's model of meaning transfer, I propose a tripartite interaction model in which changes in culture are generated by mutual interactions between values, producers, and consumers. The
changes in social relations, the objectification of values, the commoditization of a new product, and consumption all interconnect
to create cultural change. Instead of a uni-directional flow, cultural change is synthesized by the circular and repeated movements of A→B→C→A and A→C→B→A (see Figure 1). Here I
use the bathing ritual to examine the aforementioned theoretical
themes: I begin with the historical development of the bathing
ritual, move on to the invention and production of the bathing
ceremony, and finish by describing the commoditization of the
contemporary bathing ceremony.

The Development of the Bathing Ritual

The historical purpose of the bathing ritual was to purify death pollution and neutralize evil spirits. Water was seen as the medium in which all malevolent elements could be dissolved, and its symbolic power gave the bathing ritual its value.

Bathing in hot water became ritualized in the imperial court in the Heian period (794–866).[1] Outside of the imperial court, Buddhist temples also began to use bathing. According to temple records of Hōryūji, the temple bathing chamber (*yokudō*) existed as early as 747 (Takeda K., 14). There were bronze Buddhas in these bathing chambers for sutra recitation.

As Buddhism spread, temples began to open their bathing chambers to the sick. Water was considered a good way to get rid of the impurities that caused illness; in fact, bathing was regarded as a cure-all. As bathing became popular, many temples constructed new public bathing chambers, which became the prototype for bathhouses (*yusen*) (98). Moreover, taking baths at temples not only had a medical purpose. Alms-giving bathing (*seyoku*) had a spiritual purpose as well: for the salvation of their dead, people brought their memorial tablets (for ancestors or the recently deceased) to the bathhouses that had Buddhas. The money they paid for this bath took the form of alms for their deceased. Alms-giving bathing was also popular among the elite; the book *Gosaikan*, of the Kamakura (1185–1333) period, records that Minamoto Yoritomo (1147–99), the first shōgun of the period, performed alms bathing for 100 days (*hyakunichi-seyoku*) to console the spirit of the Emperor Goshirakawa, while providing free baths to ordinary people for the duration of the term (Takeda K., 101; Ochiai 1973, 40). By the Edo period (1600–1867), bathing had become common. "By around 1700, sentō [bathhouses] could be found in most neighborhoods of Tokyo. Baths were located on the first floor, and a place for relaxing, drinking tea, and gossiping with friends on the second" (Clark, 91).

However, the bathing ritual for the dead retained its earlier meaning. Through the medium of water, the bathing ritual purified the body and soul of the deceased, and those who bathed the dead were giving alms to the deceased's spirit. According to Gorai, moreover, the objective of the bathing ritual was to wash away the deceased's past sins so that he or she would be able to achieve Buddhahood; it was also for the bereaved, who would be able to receive the beneficial power of the deceased's spirit by virtue of conducting the ritual (Gorai 1992, 1002). Gorai also indicates that those who had been responsible for the ritual performance were household inheritors; if the deceased had no sons, then the closest family member performed the ritual (999–1047). Thus I infer that another function of the bathing ritual may have been to publicly confirm the inheritor as head of the household.

The Production of the Bathing Ceremony

Why did the bathing ritual disappear after World War II? How did Japanese people come to accept a funeral ceremony without it? After researching the traditional bathing ritual, the CSC president, Kii, concluded that the ritual's disappearance was due not to public preferences but to changing social conditions such as the loss of knowledge, the increase of hospitals, and the collapse of family and community solidarity. Perhaps losing many adult males and their neighbors in the war also made it difficult for the ritual to take hold again. A funeral industry developed from those conditions, but, purposely or accidentally, it omitted the bathing ritual from its services. Kii's conclusion was, "If funeral professionals do not provide it, who will?"

Facing an unknown market, Kii contemplated how he could market the bathing ceremony to funeral companies and consumers. The main problems were: How could he convince funeral companies of the importance of bathing ceremonies? How does a bathing ceremony contribute to the bereaved? What struck him as the essence of the bathing ritual was the chief mourner and the family's responsibility to perform it. "The bathing ritual was an absolute necessity and had to be performed by an inheritor and close family members," he said. "Today funeral companies are responsible for funeral services; therefore, it is they who are to be blamed for any failures or omissions in a ceremony." President Kii pointed out that although funeral companies have taken over handling the deceased, their focus has been on the material needs for the corpse, such as a coffin for transferring the body and presenting the deceased in front of an altar. According to Kii, this handling of the remains does not pay enough attention to the bereaved's psychological needs. "Although the current funeral industry treats the deceased's body with respect, it does not offer sufficient time for the bereaved to contemplate death because the deceased is immediately encoffined. I thought that the bathing ceremony would provide an opportunity for the funeral industry to start considering the customers' feelings," Kii commented. In his words, "The bathing ceremony should [help] fill the psychological void in contemporary funeral ceremonies." The idea of the bathing ceremony reflected the funeral industry's need to shift its emphasis from "hard" to "soft" services, those that focus on the feelings of the participants.

Reviving the bathing ritual necessitated reshaping it into a form the public would accept. With this in mind, Kii concentrated on three concepts he considered essential to his marketing strategy: authenticity (*dentō*), uniqueness (*kosei*), and effectiveness (*kōkateki*).

"Authenticity is the key," Kii explained. "Without this element customers will not perceive the bathing ceremony as traditional" (*dentōteki kanshū*). (The terms *dentō* and *denshō* are used in the advertisement of schools, shops, and products to imply that they follow traditional knowledge or practice.) The CSC designers intended to demonstrate the bathing ceremony's authenticity by presenting their knowledge of traditional bathing rituals. They chose specific elements of the bathing rituals to put the new ceremony into a traditional context. "I decided that the inclusion of these elements would verify our position as "the inheritor of tradition" (*dento wo tsugu*), Kii told me. For instance, CSC incorporated the ritual performance of mixing and pouring water. CSC professionals were instructed to follow the traditional method of adding hot water to cold, and to have the bereaved hold the wooden ladle (*shaku*) in the left hand while carrying the wooden bucket in the right hand.

To demonstrate their historical knowledge, CSC scheduled the water-pouring performance at the beginning of the ceremony. The CSC professionals (instead of the funeral staff) announced the beginning of the ceremony and explained the meaning of the performance (purification of the deceased). CSC's demonstration of its expertise was considered effective marketing for two reasons. First, a ritual that includes the family at the beginning creates a dramatic mood and gives the bereaved a sense of participation. Second, creating an opportunity for bathing staff to explain the process makes customers aware of their own lack of knowledge. Although the president did not say that this prelude was specifically designed to make customers feel ignorant or helpless, he stated, "In the prelude performance, we must act with dignity to demonstrate our superior knowledge of the past."

In addition to demonstrating their knowledge, CSC staff also emphasized the authenticity of the ritual by introducing themselves as experienced specialists in bathing patients, presenting themselves as caretakers of the elderly and the deceased. By stressing the caretaker or nursing role, they intended to imply that their profession was similar to that of medical staff and to project an image of sincerity, kindness, generosity, and benevolence. The president's categorization of their task as "an extension of public health services" hides the profitable aspect of the bathing ceremony and associates the business with the helping professions. Professionals wearing white jackets resembling doctors' lab coats were a key element of this strategy. Identifying themselves with health services was a way to provide credentials and avoid being criticized for the high cost of the ceremony.

Uniqueness or *kosei* is a second important element of CSC's marketing strategy. The term *kosei* has a positive connotation; in this context, it implies that something is attractive and fashionable and that it may become part of the present culture.

"What is attractive about a bathing ceremony?" Kii had wondered. "What had inspired the bereaved family [for whom he performed his first bathing ritual] to ask me to bathe their grandfather after he passed away?" He did not believe that the family's request derived from their knowledge of the traditional bathing ritual; rather, it came from a sincere affection for their grandfather: "They simply thought that he would be happy to have one last bath before departure. What underlay their request was, as simple as it sounds, the Japanese fondness of bathing. Just look at the retired people and yuppies today. A passion for bathing and visiting hot springs are the only things that both generations have in common." As Kii pointed out, trips to hot springs and saunas and the installation of larger bathtubs at home became major trends in the 1980s and 1990s. CSC decided to emphasize the concept of bathing more than purification in its bathing ceremony for the deceased.

This was not a simple matter, however, since purification was the reason for the traditional ritual, and part of CSC's claim to authenticity was its knowledge of tradition. Moreover, for sanitary reasons, the deceased's body could not literally be soaked in warm water. In order to emphasize bathing, however, CSC limited the use of the term "purification" to its introductory explanation. For the remainder of the ceremony, the bathing, washing, or refreshing of the deceased (*okarada wo arau*) was emphasized. The rest of the performance was designed to follow the pattern of bathing in everyday life as closely as possible. Although they do not actually immerse the body in the bathtub, the bathing staff scrubs, shampoos, and showers the deceased. The common meaning of bathing was interpreted here as relaxation after a long day of work, and also as a family activity, a time for nurturing the sense of belonging.[2] "The deceased need baths," the president of CSC claimed, "because they worked hard during their lives and it is time for them to relax, and because it is their last chance to do so while surrounded by their family." To create a sense of the uniqueness of its bathing ceremony, CSC made a qualitative analysis of popular culture that synchronized the bathing ceremony with the general implications of bathing. As will become apparent, what CSC claimed as unique became the hallmark of the bathing ceremony as a commodity.

Two factors that make a product effective (*kōkateki*) are acceptance (*nattoku suru*), which comes from suiting the modern way of life, and content (*manzoku suru*), which comes from customer satisfaction. President Kii's response on both counts was to treat the deceased as if they were alive and free of impurities. He predicted not only that the bereaved would appreciate the treatment of their deceased loved one as a person, but also that CSC's attitude would strengthen the bereaved's focus on bathing and cleaning. He said, "When I was working at a funeral company, I realized the importance of treating the deceased as a person and not as a corpse. In contemporary Japan the notion of the deceased being an impure corpse is almost a taboo." He thus decided to exclude most of the religious aspects of the ceremony, discarding all those performances from the traditional ritual that treated the deceased as physically and spiritually impure or dangerous. For example, CSC decided to perform the bathing ceremony only during the day; the bathing staff do not wear headbands to ward off evil spirits; water is not thrown away under the deceased's house or in a field; rice wine is not drunk before or after the ceremony as a purification technique; and CSC does not advise the bereaved to take a bath themselves after the ceremony.

CSC rationalized (*riseika*) or modernized (*kindaika*) its service through the acts of its employees and the use of modern technology. The cleanliness aspect of the ceremony is conveyed by the attitude of those who bathe the deceased and the way water is used and discarded. CSC employs professionals who project an image of youth and cleanliness. The bathing staff are fairly young; men are under 40 and women under 30. The women professionals I met were all young, charming, and attractive. The vice president herself told me that one of the reasons for hiring pretty young women is to create a pleasant and fresh (*sugasugashiku shinsenna*) atmosphere. Naturally, their uniforms are neat and attractive; men wear white medical coats with black trousers, and women wear a white or light blue flowered apron over skirts.

CSC also uses modern technology to create a positive environment for the bathing ceremony. Water is boiled in the van, vacuumed back into the van, and channeled into the sewage when the van returns to Moon Rise (or another funeral hall). CSC uses a shower head to sprinkle water onto the deceased, and the temperature can be adjusted as in a normal bath system. These practices shifted the meaning of the ceremony from the negative notion of purifying death pollution to the positive notion of providing relaxed bathing for the dead person.

Treating the deceased as a person meant that the bathing staff had to use the same care and gentleness with the deceased as a nurse with a patient. Making a face (e.g., turning one's head away in reaction to the smell of the corpse) or causing injury to the deceased's body (e.g., cutting the face while shaving or cutting nails too short) is regarded as disrespectful to the deceased and to the family.

Finally, the product's effectiveness was measured by the difference in the deceased's physical appearance before and after the ceremony. "If customers feel that the deceased has become extremely clean and looks good after our service," Kii explained, "customers are content and feel that the cost is justified." To produce satisfactory results, CSC concentrated on the visual and olfactory aspects of the ceremony. The deceased is bathed and washed entirely and dried with many bath towels; his or her hair is shampooed, rinsed, dried, and combed; the deceased is either given a fresh shave or made up with cosmetics and is dressed in a new robe. When the deceased is encoffined, cotton frames the face and neck, just beneath the coffin window. These are some of the visual touches that create a marked change in the deceased's appearance after the ceremony. Furthermore, the effectiveness of scent cannot be underestimated. The shampoo, conditioner, and liquid body soap used during the bathing ceremony are all products of Shiseidō, a brand well known for its strongly scented products. CSC's strategy is to fill the room with fresh fragrance (with the help of hot-water vapor). The liquid body soap not only looks modern but also emits much more aroma than common bar soap. The bathing ceremony was designed to maximize the power of invisible perfume to appeal to people's sense of cleanliness. To suit the tastes of contemporary Japanese, CSC designed its bathing ceremony as a relaxing bath for the dead.

Marketing, Exchange, and Consumption

At the beginning of this chapter I argued that no matter how sophisticated the product it cannot be considered a commodity unless it moves from the hands of a producer to the hands of consumers, because this exchange generates the value that turns a product into a commodity. Value is conferred by the positive interaction between producers and consumers; successful marketing triggers a favorable perception, evaluation, and judgment by customers. Depending on the value that appears through the exchanges, the social life of a commodity may be short or long. The important factor in the generation of value is that this value is not born in a vacuum or imposed by collective anonymous forces, but comes into being gradually, through verbal negotiations and interactions between consumers and producers. Whether an exchange leads to more distribution, more exchange, and finally to mass consumption, however, depends on the practical match between values, consumer judgments, and a product.

CSC's initial marketing of the bathing ceremony targeted funeral companies. After expanding its business successfully in the Osaka area, CSC began contracting with funeral companies elsewhere. Moon Rise was the first funeral company in the Kyūshū

TABLE 4

Bathing Service Sales by CSC, 1987–1994

Time period	Sales per month
1987	1–2 services
1988	20–40
1989	100
1990	average of 150
1991	average of 200
1992	average of 500
1993	average of 1,000–1,300
1994	average of 1,800

SOURCE: Interview with CSC president, 1995

area to have a contract with CSC, and therefore the first company to market the ceremony locally. According to the contract, the funeral staff would market the ceremony and CSC would perform it (see Table 4).

Once the contract was signed, CSC gave demonstration sessions to executives and funeral staff to show them what they would be marketing. When Tomi's initial marketing endeavors (discussed at the beginning of this chapter) were met with complete rejection by customers, Moon Rise managers immediately formed a team to create a sales guidebook. The team, composed of Moon Rise managers and funeral staff, developed scripts of sample conversations between funeral staff and customers in various hypothetical situations to show their staff how to convince customers to purchase the ceremony. The following are some examples:

Marketing Example 1

CUSTOMER: "The deceased has already been disinfected by antiseptic at the hospital. Therefore, extra cleaning is not necessary."

MOON RISE FUNERAL STAFF:

> "The reason for the bathing ceremony differs completely from that of sterilization measures in hospitals. The purpose of the bathing ceremony is not disinfection. It is to refresh the deceased, who could not bathe or shower while hospitalized."

Marketing Example 2

CUSTOMER: "I feel that the bathing ceremony is an excessive expenditure and that it is not central to the funeral ceremony."

MOON RISE STAFF:

> "In the past, the bathing ritual was pivotal; it was a major responsibility of family members to perform the rite. Unlike hospital disinfection, a bathing ceremony is bathing and washing [*onagashi*] with care for the deceased. It is an important part of the farewell performance for the bereaved and for the transition of the deceased's soul."

The guidebook gave the funeral staff the basic ideas for marketing. Naturally, the conversations leading to actual sales are more complicated than the guidebook examples. And customers may reject the ceremony no matter what arguments the funeral staff present. The key to success is finding, through interactions with customers, the feature that will interest a particular customer. Success depends on a combination of assumptions, intuition, and the persuasive skill of each professional.

At the initial stage of marketing, the funeral staff often repeated what they had read in the guidebook. They did not offer second and third explanations after an initial rejection. Moon Rise, however, did not give up; it was aware that CSC had successfully marketed its services in Osaka. In order to create a real market in the future, the director of the funeral staff allowed CSC to market bathing ceremonies at a reduced rate. (This was put into practice after an executive decision.) A member of the funeral staff would ask the bereaved if they wanted to purchase the bathing ceremony. For the first couple of months, most answered that they did not. As an alternative, the funeral staff offered to take ¥50,000 (the same price as the bathing ceremony) off the price of the funeral altar or funeral hall for customers who wanted the bathing ceremony. This strategy worked well; soon about 30 percent of all funerals included the bathing ceremony. (After this discount was stopped, a similar percentage of people bought the bathing ceremony; see Table 5.) While the service was being offered for a reduced fee, funeral staff began to develop an understanding of what was significant about the bathing ceremony.[3] During this period, they observed and analyzed the reasons the bathing ceremony was rejected, accepted, or appreciated. This testing period served as an on-site learning session for funeral staff, and their rejection-acceptance experiences were critical to the future marketing of the ceremony; through these exchanges, staff were able to eliminate factors that obviously were not attractive and actively incorporate factors that created customer satisfaction.

The Development of Marketing

The first real sale was finally made by Tomi after a couple of weeks of failure. A son had lost his mother in her nineties. The deceased was in a nursing home, and the chief mourner was the son, a retired man in his seventies. The consultation took place in one of Moon Rise's tatami rooms. The deceased's sisters were also present.

Tomi asked the family if they would like to give the deceased a bathing ceremony. They answered that she had been cleaned at the nursing home. Tomi this time emphasized that the bathing ceremony was like "giving her a bath for the last time." The sisters of the deceased and the son looked at each other and finally one

TABLE 5

Bathing Ceremony Sales by Moon Rise, 1994–1995

Month	Year	Funerals	Bathing ceremonies	Percentage of funerals with bathing ceremonies
November	1994	77	27	35%
December	1994	107	40	37
January	1995	156	38	24
February	1995	106	32	30
March	1995	105	24	22
April	1995	82	37	45
May	1995	94	31	32
June	1995	89	35	39
July	1995	95	25	26
August	1995	82	35	42
September	1995	78	42	53
October	1995	93	53	56

SOURCE: Moon Rise, Inc., 1995

of the sisters said, "Kōsuke-san, your mother would appreciate your giving her a last bath." "Did you have a chance to give her a bath?" Tomi asked. "I haven't given her a bath for a long time, not since she went to stay at the nursing home," the son replied. Tomi quickly added, "I am aware that ¥50,000 is a little expensive, but if you realize that this is the final bath you can provide for your mother, it is not expensive at all. And in fact, this is your last chance; it will be too late when she is nothing but bones" (*okotsu ni natte karadewa osoidesukara*). Under this pressure the bereaved agreed to purchase the bathing ceremony. This was the moment when the product became a commodity; and for Tomi it was his first marketing success.

The value of a product or service is generated by the customer's reaction to it. The bereaved mentioned in the story above were surprised by the Western-looking bathtub and shower equipment. They were sincerely impressed that the equipment could be brought to a tatami room and taken away without leaving a mess. They admired the professional preparations and performance of the ceremony, as well as the finished appearance of the deceased. They appreciated the respectful way the bathing staff treated the grandmother and the family. As I described in Chapter 5, the family often thanks the bathing ceremony staff for honoring the deceased by bowing deeply to them at the end of the ceremony. Although the bathing ceremony is actually a shower, the bathtub imprints the image of bathing in customer's minds. Moreover, when the ceremony was completed, the son said to the bathing staff, "I am so glad I decided to do this. I feel like I carried out my filial duty, and now I don't have to feel guilty." Thus, the bathing ceremony enabled the deceased's family to allay guilt and to feel virtuous and satisfied that they had expressed the appropriate appreciation and gratitude to the deceased. In this way the exchange of the bathing ceremony took on value.

THE FIT BETWEEN A PRODUCT AND CUSTOMER NEEDS

The commoditization of the bathing ceremony has been achieved. Statistical data obtained from Moon Rise demonstrate the steady proliferation of the product in funerals (Table 5). The decrease in sales during summer is natural since Japanese deceased are not embalmed — the corpse decomposes quickly in the summer heat, making it difficult to take the time for a bathing ceremony.

The marketing strategy for the bathing ceremony effectively incorporated the four Ps: product, price, place, and promotion (Kotler, Ang, Leong, and Tan, 114). The design and features of the service were well thought out, and the quality of service was high. The ceremony in Kita-Kyūshū was priced at ¥50,000; this was lower than in other metropolitan areas like Tokyo or Osaka, but higher than in less populous suburbs. As discussed earlier, Moon Rise provided a discount during the introductory stage of the product. The use of a van provided flexibility as to the location in which the service could be rendered; the van allowed the service to take place at a house or funeral hall, though it was limited to the first floor. The timing of the service, however, was the weakness of this product. Because the service took one to two hours, if there was much customer demand on a particular day, Moon Rise could not allocate the best times to all customers. In addition, since funerals were never advertised on TV or in other mass media, the promotion of the bathing ceremony was dependent upon funeral staff.

Perhaps the only exception to this was when a journalist interviewed me and I mentioned my interest in the bathing ceremony. A week later, together with the story of my fieldwork, Moon Rise's bathing ceremony was featured in a newspaper article. But generally, the bathing ceremony was promoted by funeral staff upon meeting a new customer. They also relied on the bereaved who had purchased the ceremony to spread the word to their friends and colleagues. In addition, the decision to leave the coffin windows open until the funeral ceremony allowed the proud family members to show off the cleanly bathed deceased to visitors.

Ultimately, however, the strength of the bathing ceremony derives from the perfect match between the customer's needs and the product. I believe that CSC's president accurately foresaw a window of opportunity in the funeral market. The success of the bathing ceremony is intimately tied to changes in the Japanese perception of death, which otherwise had little representation. Let me explain what I am suggesting by the fit between the product and the Japanese attitude on death.

One of the characteristics of Japanese elderly today is longevity. The average life expectancy in 1992 was 76 years for men and 82 years for women; in 1955 it was 63 for men and 67 for women (Keizai-Kikakuchō, 43). One consequence of longevity is a decrease in the size of estates transferred to the next generation because elders' life savings are drained over time. Erdman Palmore had already noted in the mid-1970s that people older than 70 and those in rural areas did not have adequate incomes (Palmore, 83–85). According to the Ministry of Public Welfare, the welfare pension provides 50 percent of the income for elders above 65 today. Furthermore, the pension constitutes the only source of income for half of those who receive it (NLI Research Institute, 252). Among survey respondents, only one out of three was receiving a salary of some sort, while 86 percent of the remaining elders were receiving a public annuity (*kōteki-nenkin*). The economic insecurity of elders is reflected in the number of parents who had received a monetary gift from their children. Although the amount of the gift was not sufficient to substitute for a pension, three out of four elders responded that they had received monetary gifts from their children (ibid.).

The changes in the life expectancy and smaller inheritances are at the core of the bathing ceremony's success. Traditionally, the inheritance was significant because it was the integral apparatus of household succession and ancestor worship. The transfer of property, including family graves and the Buddhist altar (*butsudan*), to a chief mourner structured the household perpetuation (see, e.g., Ariga 1972; Cornell and Smith; Ooms 1967; Smith, R. 1974; Yanagita 1975a). What was important was the balanced relationship between the living and the dead (Suzuki 1998, 184): "Just as the living would not exist without the ancestors, the ancestors exist only because the living remember and memorialize them" (Smith, R. 1992, 3).

In Chinese funerals reciprocal exchanges also took place between the deceased and a chief mourner. A chief mourner in a Chinese funeral received inheritance property and in turn was required to absorb the largest portion of death pollution (Ahern 1973; Freedman; Watson, J. 1982). Likewise, I believe that in Japan the performance of a chief mourner in providing a bathing ceremony for the former head of the household was important to ensure both the right of inheritance and his succession to household head. However, in contemporary Japan, the relationship between the living and the ancestors of the household, which had

been sustained by economic succession as well as spiritual exchanges, became asymmetrical as a result of social changes. This
asymmetric relationship between the living and the dead generated a condition in which the feelings of the living dictated the
funeral decisions.

It was during this transition in the cultural environment that
the values of the bathing ceremony found a fit. First, family members who had a deep relationship with the deceased wished to express their love in a visible form. As inheritances grew smaller, funerals came to be seen as less of an obligation and more of a
goodwill gesture by the bereaved. Second, some men wanted to
express guilt and apologies to the deceased because they took so
little care of their parents in their old age. Robert J. Smith noted
in the 1980s that there was a "developing trend for the prospective
heirs to assign inheritance rights to the married daughter who
took on the care of aged parents."[4] As a result, more daughters are
inheriting property because they are often responsible for taking
care of their parents in old age (NLI Research Institute, 271–72).[5]
In another scenario, the parents of a man whose wife is not willing to take care of them often end up in an institution for the elderly. There is a strong stigma attached to these institutions, and
even their residents refer to their fate as a contemporary example
of "disposing of the elderly" (*ubasuteyama*)—a phrase from an old
Japanese legend (Bethel, 131). The story goes that a village somewhere in Japan used to abandon its old and frail grandparents in
the woods. As in the story, elder-homes are considered places for
aging parents who were discarded by their unloving children.
Since taking care of parents is no longer an obligation but is considered an act of love and moral uprightness among children,
those who have neglected this task feel ashamed and wish to express their feelings or compensate for their neglect by visible
means.

With the changes in attitude toward death came values that
were not tied to an objective form. The success of the bathing ceremony can be attributed to its bridging of the gap between values

and form; it came to fulfill the needs of the mourners. Marketing success grew with the funeral professionals' promotion of the value of bathing, which represented the contemporary Japanese perception toward the deceased. Values such as traditional Japanese baths (Clark 1992), refreshment for the deceased, expressions of appreciation for and apologies to the deceased, sympathy for the deceased, resolution of past grudges and conflicts, and the generosity and benevolence of the living were emphasized instead. The strategy of the funeral staff to ask about the circumstances of the deceased's death and observe the behavior of the bereaved allowed them to market the features of the ceremony that most closely matched the deceased's family's values. For example, when a young daughter had been killed in an accident, the funeral staff emphasized the sympathy and guilt-absolving aspect of the bathing ceremony. "By giving her a final bath," Tomi said, "it might moderate the guilt you feel because the deceased will appreciate what you have done for her." The bereaved agreed, and they were content with their decision.

Sales stabilized as the values of the bathing ceremony became established and the funeral staff mastered the art of conveying them. Consequently, the bath—this vital comfort in Japanese living—acted as the fulcrum in transforming a traditional ritual for the dead into a commodity for the bereaved.

Summary

Successful marketing is the process by which a product gradually acquires new values. Initially, the bathing ceremony had no meaning in the contemporary setting. CSC produced and began to market the ceremony using concepts such as authenticity, uniqueness, and effectiveness. Customers did not absorb these concepts directly, however. The value of the bathing ceremony emerged through the repetition of services and interactions among salespeople, ceremony staff, and customers. The salesmen became aware of which factors were rejected, which were positive, and what the ceremony meant for different customers and in different situations. By objectifying customers' interpretations and reactions, salesmen ascertained the values that customers found meaningful in the product. These values were then verbalized and attached to the product. Georg Simmel has suggested that "every exchange leads back to a value which in turn leads back to an exchange" (Simmel 1971, 48). It is this acquisition of values, through dialectical exchanges between individuals and an object, that makes a product metamorphose into a market commodity.

The commoditization of the bathing ceremony was also possible because the perception toward death and dying had been transformed in postwar Japan, and standard funeral ceremonies lacked a means for the bereaved to express that change. The combination of this absence and the popularity of bathing in Japan seems to have contributed to the significance associated with the bathing ceremony. Thus, the commoditization of the bathing ceremony demonstrates that the new product contributes to the "vital, tangible record of cultural meaning that is otherwise intangible" (McCracken 1986, 73).

The successful marketing of a commodity leads to mass consumption, a process through which people assimilate and adopt values that a commodity embodies. Marketing is thus a powerful force that can change consumer customs. During my fieldwork, I observed that the cumulative exchanges of the bathing ceremony have changed the former funeral practices by incorporating the bathing ceremony into a funeral. This cultural transition, however, did not come about as the result of manipulative marketing. In order to assume that the consumption of goods has any significant implications for cultural change, other changes—for example, in social relationships, values (such as the perception of death), industries, and products—must also be present. What propels cultural change are the multiple interactions of consumers, industries/producers, and the value system. Simmel points out the complex interactions that are in motion when he states that "some particular circumstances are always involved when one attaches a feeling of value to an object. Every such feeling of value is lodged in a whole complex system of our feelings which is in constant flux, adaptation, and reconstruction" (Simmel 1971, 52). If, however, as Marshall Sahlins states, "the product that reaches its destined market constitutes an objectification of social category and so helps to constitute the latter in society" (Sahlins 1976, 183), one must also be aware of the dynamic processes of products that reach their destined market. The commoditization and consumption of the bathing ceremony were possible only because of the transformations in social relationships, the advancement of health care, and changes in the perception of death and dying. In consequence, I hope that adding the aspect of interactions among industry, products, social relationships, and values to McCracken's model of meaning movements will offer a better understanding of cultural changes (see Figure 1).

Tomi, who experienced repeated rejections at the initial stages of marketing the bathing ceremony, is now one of the top salespeople. "I know what to emphasize, and I know what a bathing ceremony means to the bereaved," he told me. Without a perceived value, the product could not be assimilated into culture or ultimately change cultural practices. The traditional bathing ritual, once an obligatory performance for purifying death pollution, has been transformed into a commodity that encourages the living to believe they are communicating with the dead. The commoditization is thus "performative" (Tambiah 1981); it serves as a psychological bridge between the living and the dead through the objectification of values.

CONCLUSION:
THE SHIFT TO COMMERCIALIZATION
AND MASS CONSUMPTION

Death reminds us not only of our own mortality but also of the fragility of our social institutions and groups.

—Rubie S. Watson, "Remembering the Dead"

Consumption is a major factor in the potential return of culture to human values.

—Daniel Miller, *Material Culture and Mass Consumption*

On February 2, 1995, President Sakuma of Moon Rise held a banquet for the Moon Rise staff at one of the most expensive Chinese restaurants in Kita-Kyūshū to celebrate their superb sales record for January.[1] The banquet took place in a large tatami room, where 80 funeral staff members from three Kita-Kyūshū branches were served a full-course meal, accompanied plentifully with beer and sake. The banquet opened with the president's speech praising funeral staff for their marketing efforts; after dinner, the banquet became a karaoke party. The president, who was well prepared, sang first. When he finished singing he waved his hand to me. I took a bottle of freshly warmed sake and went to sit beside him.

The inebriated president was in a good mood and called me by my first name. "Hikaru-chan," he began, "you might think that we are being immoral to celebrate funerals and the death of others. But you see, business is both a competition and a contribution. Becoming competitive means providing the most affectionate, intimate, effective, and well-organized services to customers." At first I thought that the president was making sure that my thesis would not turn into the usual indictment of Japanese funeral companies as immoral money-gougers. As the conversation continued, however, I realized that he was explaining the interdependency between companies and consumers. The president continued, "As you know, contemporary funeral companies have developed through marketing the Mutual-Aid System.[2] Of course, I cannot deny the fact that companies who joined the National Wedding and Funeral Mutual-Aid Association saw great business opportunities in marketing funerals. However, the main reason we were attracted initially was its honorable mission, a venture to replace the attenuating functions of communities. We considered this work to be not only profitable but also meaningful to people's lives." His point was that while production, marketing, and commercialization are not derived from altruism, neither do they cause social conflict. The marketing and consumption of funeral services are two sides of the same coin; one cannot exist without the other.

Thinkers such as Marx, Engels, Simmel, and Weber considered the capitalist mode of production antagonistic to the well-being of men (Marx and Engels; Simmel 1990; Weber). Marx especially portrayed a stark picture of bourgeoisie vs. proletariat, products vs. men, and use-value vs. exchange-value, assuming that the development of industrial production would alienate people from each other because "the relations connecting the labor of one individual with that of the rest appear not as direct social relations between individuals at work, but as what they really are, material relations between persons and social relations between things" (Marx and Engels, 321). His view of capitalism as replacing direct relations between people with indirect relations between things derives from his emphasis on production and not on consumption. As President Sukuma suggested, commercialization can also be seen as the mirror of consumption, and people can be directly connected through the act of consumption. De Certeau suggested, "Ways of reappropriating the product-system, ways created by consumers, have as their goal a therapeutics for deteriorating social relations" (de Certeau, 24).

Consumption, moreover, is a practice determined by consumers; production does not oblige or coerce people to consume. I do not consider mass consumption or mass culture the result of the culture industry—the view propagated particularly by Adorno, who suggests that culture is the means by which the elite and capitalists control the masses. Instead, I view consumers and producers as possessing equal suasion; consumers can influence producers by making consumption choices, and producers can influence consumers by marketing products.

This chapter presents social and cultural changes that emerged with the transition from the community funeral ritual to the commercial ceremony and the role played by the funeral industry in maintaining them. I have analyzed this transition in a fashion analogous to the study of the shift from gift exchange to commodity transaction,[3] contrasting the differences between the personal relations, values, and structure of social integration in the two cases,[4] as well as highlighting the similarities.[5] The transition from community rituals to commercial ceremonies does not appear as a polar opposition but as part of the process of modernizing. It can also be seen as the "process of individuation" brought about by modernization and industrialization (Dore 1958). Dore postulates that greater educational opportunity, the division of labor, professionalization, migration to the cities, and salaried income have loosened Japanese ties to their households. However, Dore stated that this "does not of itself necessarily imply anything which can be called a triumph of individualism." (154). He argued that when Japanese are individuated they are also deprived of the security of binding primary ties and hence become even more vulnerable to pressures to conform with the anonymous mass (392). In this context, commercialization and mass production emerged as a means for social cohesion. I argue that this function is what the funeral industry has been enacting in contemporary Japanese culture.

Personal Relations, Values, and Social Integration in Community and Commercial Funerals

Funerals provided one of the most important opportunities labor exchanges between *kumi* members.[6] The labor that the cooperative group provided for the deceased's family was a continuous obligation, to be returned in kind in the future. The exchange of labor was based on a long-term reciprocal dependency that operated on the calculated principle that "if I help the other person now, I will be helped next time." This exchange benefited all members equally because both the ritual knowledge and the materials used in the funeral were held in common. Moreover, the amount of incense money and the size of the condolence gift was fixed. Participation in funerals was a symmetrical exchange in a continuous cycle of reciprocation among *kumi* members. As one elder stated, "The relationship between *kumi* members was more important than [the relationship to] one's distant relatives."

The values expressed in funeral rituals were based on the belief in death impurity. These values, however, were connected directly to the economic and political ties between the bereaved family and community members. The exchanges in community funeral rituals emphasized the continuous relationship of the deceased's household to its *kumi* more than the bereaved's ties to his or her patrilineal line.[7] The key indication of this was shown by the person who took charge of the dangerous spirit and risked death pollution. In community funeral rituals, it was the immediate family and the community members who handled the corpse and took responsibility for the spirit in transition.

As in China, the major concern of the Japanese funeral ritual was to placate the malevolent spirit, which had to be managed in some way and could not be left to pollute the cosmos (Watson, J. 1982, 182). Whoever participated in the act of absorbing the heaviest pollution demonstrated his willingness to maintain strong ties with the deceased's family. The Japanese eldest son or the inheritor took on the most responsibility by bathing (as discussed earlier in bathing rituals) and encoffining the deceased's body. However, interviews with Kita-Kyūshū elders revealed that *kumi* members shared the danger as much as the bereaved family did by handling the physical remains of the deceased. It was the *kumi* members who walked in the procession, held the white cloth tied to the coffin, dug the grave, and buried the deceased. The community took upon itself the responsibility of sending the deceased's soul safely to the afterlife.

The depth of their involvement entitled all *kumi* members to eat a vegetarian meal at the end of the ritual. The rice brought by relatives and *kumi* members as the condolence gift (*kōden*) was consumed at this meal,[8] which emphasized the continuing relationship between the bereaved family and community members. Proof of this relationship was the fact that this dinner was referred to as "bone-biting" (*hone-kami*—see note 15 to Chapter 2), a phrase implying that the whole *kumi* shared the "bone" or "spirit" of the deceased.

Community funeral rituals in Japan were similar to Korean funerals, where "the proper ushering of the [spirit] into the afterlife help[ed] to hold village society together" (Dredge, 91). Thus the exchange of labor among the living and the exchange between the deceased and the living in funeral rituals demonstrated the integration of a household to its community as much as the perpetuity of the household line itself. The exchanges of labor and values among *kumi* members in funeral rituals solidified their integration; here, the shared handling of the corpse was the bond that held them together.

COMMERCIAL FUNERAL CEREMONIES

What Moon Rise emphasizes most in its marketing is building networks. Its aim is to form personal ties between its company and bereaved family members. Salesmanship is critical to the creation of these new ties. There are three major ways in which

Moon Rise attempts to attract customers: marketing Mutual-Aid Cooperative membership; establishing contracts with Elders' Clubs (*rōjinkai*) and other institutions; and holding festivals as a means of advertisement.

During my tenure at Moon Rise, the majority (about 70 percent) of funeral ceremonies it provided were for MAC members. Since its establishment in 1966, Moon Rise has used its MAC membership as the primary means of expanding its business. At the peak period of MAC membership sales (1973–85) there were about 200 sales staff members, and even in the late 1990s there were about 70 salespeople who specialized only in MAC membership sales in the Kita-Kyūshū area.[9] The ultimate goal of these sales professionals is naturally to sell MAC memberships; however, the marketing process is considered as important as the actual sale. During marketing, the salespeople acquire information about a family or an individual who will, they hope, recommend the product to others.

The experienced salespeople do not push the product to customers on the first visit. They are fully aware that creating a personal relationship and sense of trust with each customer is an important part of selling the product. During multiple visits these salespeople gather information about the individual, his or her family structure, the age and sex of family members, their occupations, and the individual's preferences for funeral ceremonies. The fact that sales staff visit their customers after they have purchased the MAC membership demonstrates that constructing personal ties is at the core of the sale. During my fieldwork I often met a bereaved family member who mentioned the name of the person who had originally sold him or her a MAC membership. Sometimes when a MAC member dies, the family calls a familiar salesperson instead of the main number of the Moon Rise Funeral Auditorium.

In recent decades, Moon Rise has also pursued a new form of tie with Elders' Clubs all over Kita-Kyūshū.[10] The clubs are local recreation groups with low membership fees. Moon Rise offers them special reduced fees for their funerals if the club is willing to make a "volunteer contract." It is a volunteer contract in the sense that although it is signed by the head of an Elders' Club, members do not have to use Moon Rise for their funerals. The contract applies only when an elder's family decides to ask Moon Rise for the funeral services, based on the deceased's earlier request.

One feature of the contract is that 10 percent of the price of the funeral altar is given to the Elders' Club, providing cash support for its activities. (The deceased's family, who pays for the altar, also receives a 10-percent price reduction.) This offer does not apply to members who already have MAC memberships with Moon Rise, but to other elders who are not members of a MAC. This marketing strategy targets those elders who have closer ties with other elders than with their own children.

Moon Rise has similar contracts with other institutions and companies; it is usually the executives of a company who sign the volunteer contract with Moon Rise.[11] When an employee of such a company dies and the deceased's family decides to use Moon Rise, it pays a discounted price, and the company gets a refund from Moon Rise. What makes the volunteer contract so successful is that it appeals to the loyalty of Japanese workers and their families to their own companies, organizations, or clubs.

Special festivities held at the Moon Rise Funeral Hall are another method of making contact with future customers, and they convey the image of the funeral hall as a place for people to visit. Moon Rise often holds parties, seminars, and exhibitions for both wedding and funeral ceremonies at its auditorium. One of the largest events is the Funeral Festival (*Sōsaihaku*), which takes place every July. Admission is free, and it is open to the public. Moon Rise began this festival in the mid-1980s in order to minimize the distance between itself and local residents, and designed it to draw a large audience, from children to elders. The event begins with a summer dance party (*bon-odori*) the night before the festival. Food stands offer popcorn, beer, cotton candy, and Japanese fast foods.

The main festival takes place on the following day at the

Kokura Funeral Auditorium and consists of exhibitions of ceremony arrangements, explanation/planning sessions for funerals,
seminars about death, and a Buddhist memorial service for the
dead (*hōyō*). On the morning of the festival, Buddhist priests
from Nanzōin temple, one of the largest Buddhist temples in
Kyūshū, perform a memorial service for the deceased who have
had their funerals at Moon Rise. In the afternoon, a popular
movie star gives a talk about his or her view of life and death.
Throughout the day, visitors can peruse the Tibetan Buddhist
texts owned by the Nanzoin Temple, the collections of Buddhist
scrolls owned by President Sakuma, and photographs of different
funerals. They can also attend a seminar that explains the funeral
ceremony or receive a lesson on the practice of Chinese *chi-kong*
exercises. In the main hall, many tables and stands are set up, and
staff members are available to answer questions about funeral ceremonies and memorial services. At these tables, experienced funeral professionals provide free advice and ideas for planning future funerals. The majority of the visitors are elders who are
concerned about their own funerals, but in recent years the number of younger people interested in preparing a good funeral for
themselves and their parents has increased. Ultimately, the festival
provides an excellent chance for the company to communicate
with and draw in potential customers.

INTERPERSONAL RELATIONS IN THE COMMUNITY RITUAL
AND THE COMMERCIAL CEREMONY

In community funerals, relationships were made among *kumi*
members or between households, whereas in a commercial ceremony ties are formed between funeral companies and individuals
or family members. In the creation of new relationships in the
commercial ceremony, it is the funeral professionals who bridge
the gap between the institution and individuals.

The power relations in the exchange also differ in the two
cases. The reciprocation among community members was more
or less symmetrical; they had no one but each other to rely upon.

The fact that reciprocity among themselves was their only choice ensured a balanced exchange relationship. In a commercial ceremony, however, the exchange relations between the funeral industry and customers are sometimes symmetric and sometimes asymmetric at different points in the transaction. For example, family members depend completely on the funeral professionals to handle the physical body and lead them through the ceremonial process. But before choosing a funeral company the bereaved family has the advantage: it can choose among competing companies. Moreover, once a funeral is over the family once again has the upper hand, since it can refuse to pay or pay a reduced fee if it was dissatisfied with the services.

The degree of interdependency is also different in the commercial ceremony than it was in the performance of the community ritual. The ties between community members were strong. Exchanges were continuous and returned. In order to keep up the interdependency, the time factor in the flow of exchange was critical. As Bourdieu points out, "Until [the bereaved] has given in return, the receiver is 'obliged,' expected to show his gratitude towards his benefactor . . . lest he be accused of ingratitude and stand condemned by 'what people say,' which is what gives his actions their social meaning" (Bourdieu 1977, 6). In contrast, commercial ceremonies do not create further obligations and commitments between the company and the bereaved. A customer pays for the services, and this payment clears the debt. But despite the loose interdependency between funeral companies and their customers, the commodity exchange of a funeral ceremony is not as impersonal and discrete as it appears to be.

What community rituals and commodity ceremonies have in common is a long-term strategy. In community settings, the members enforced mutual aid among *kumi* members, and this in turn maintained their relationship over a long period of time. Funeral companies also calculate their long-term interests. Their strategy is to keep up the ties with their customers even after the transaction has been completed. MAC membership sales staff continue to visit the deceased's family so that their customers will renew membership. Funeral professionals also keep up their relationships with the deceased's family. Many professional conductors send cards to the bereaved families after the ceremony. Other funeral professionals call or visit families at home to express their sympathy. It is true that these exchanges cannot be expected or guaranteed as they were for community rituals, because the degree of dependency is one-sided; it is the funeral industry that wants to maintain ties with consumers rather than the other way around. However, the ties established in funeral ceremonies are not completely broken; they are often kept up by the work of individual professionals. Thus, a commercial funeral is not an entirely discrete transaction between a company and an individual; each transaction possesses the potential for reproducing the exchange in an unlimited time frame.

Hence the commercialization of funerals reflects the shift of personal relationships from a community to an institutional base. Mutual Aid Cooperative membership, which began in 1948, was so named because the industry wanted to replace the interpersonal relationship between community members with one between companies and families. Although the power relations of the actors and the degree of interdependency differ from those in community rituals, the commercial funeral ceremonies represent a strategic exchange between the industry and individuals that allows them to continue their interpersonal relationship.

THE TRANSFORMATION OF VALUES

The idea of corpse pollution has faded along with the idea of death pollution during the funeral ceremony. (The idea of pollution remains during cremation, which I have elaborated on previously.) Funeral ceremonies today are becoming like other commodities that are neither pure/polluted nor yin/yang; they are becoming neutral.[12] Members of the younger generation in particular demonstrate no concern about death pollution. For example, young women attend funerals in the kind of fancy, sexy black dresses and high-heeled shoes typically worn to parties, and leave their hair loose. After a large funeral, the masses of flowers left over from the ceremony are given away to the participants. In the earlier days of community funeral rituals, nobody would have dared to take those flowers because, as the elders told me, "They are bad luck." But today participants of all ages, particularly women, choose their favorite flowers to take home after a funeral.[13] The funeral industry may be credited for its efforts in changing the image of funerals by improving the funeral space.

A coffee shop in the Kokura Auditorium was very popular among funeral-goers. Those who arrived a little early stopped there for beverages, and those who had missed lunch could buy a snack. After the ceremony, old friends and colleagues could talk about the deceased over a cup of coffee. One housewife with no funeral business even frequented this coffee shop in the funeral auditorium. I first noticed the woman because she was wearing normal street clothes. I thought she might have arrived from out of town for a funeral the following day, which would explain her clothing. But I saw her often after that. She always ordered the same thing, a cup of black tea with toast. If she was not attending a funeral then what was she doing there, I wondered. When asked, she answered simply, "I like the toast set here. You make wonderful tea. The place is peaceful and besides, this coffee shop is on my way home." As far as she was concerned she was enjoying afternoon teatime and nothing more. I told this story to president Sakuma, who obviously appreciated it; he commented that such visits would not be possible if people considered funeral auditoriums impure places.

What is emphasized in commercial funeral ceremonies today is a positive remembrance of the dead. Funerals have become an occasion for family, friends, and colleagues to share and crystallize their memories of the deceased. The most crucial part of constructing a positive memory is the memorial address (chōji).

Funerals for elders often lack a memorial address because their close friends and colleagues have already passed away. Sometimes chairmen simply cannot find participants who are willing to give memorial addresses for the deceased. Well-written and well-presented memorial addresses have tremendous power to move the audience and fix the deceased's best qualities in participants' memories.

What makes a good funeral is the beautification of the deceased's life: honoring their contributions; appreciating their kindness, their generosity, and their social achievements; and learning from their good deeds. One might say that the objective of the funeral industry is to generate an occasion for remembering only the virtues and merits of those who have died. The faults of the deceased in his or her lifetime may be amended, resolved, and forgiven by the participants at a good funeral. As one funeral professional said, "A good funeral is said to be the one that erases the deceased's bad deeds" (*yoi sōgi wa kojin no kakono ayamachiwo keshisaru*).

The values expressed in community rituals and commercial ceremonies differ not only in content but also in how they are exchanged between the living and the dead. In community rituals, belief in the dangerous spirit maintained a symmetrical balance between the living and the deceased until the 49th day after death, when the deceased was considered to have been transformed into a peaceful spirit. Their relationship was symmetric; the living owed the dead the property they had inherited and considered caring for the dead their obligation. When the fear of a malevolent spirit waned and the prospect of inheritance declined, the fate of the deceased came more under the control of the living.[14] In funeral ceremonies, the living now have more power; they decide how much honor should be given to the deceased. The personal memories created during a funeral ceremony are a direct result of the living's affection for the one who has died. The dead are now at the mercy of the living, because it is the living who evaluate the deceased's life.

THE CONTINUATION OF SOCIAL INTEGRATION

The process of commercialization paralleled the estrangement of death and dying from communities. "These days I don't even know if someone is sick or someone has passed away in my neighborhood unless I see a mourning paper attached to the doorway or ceremonial dried flowers [*zōka*] on the gate of the house," stated Uchiyama. He also said that he has not handled a corpse since World War II. "Usually it is the funeral professionals who are called first while neighbors are informed last. People do not depend on neighbors anymore," he said. After the war, his *kumi* was amalgamated into the village association (*chōnaikai*), which was determined by larger residential divisions. Today the head of the village association receives a call from the deceased's family only to be informed of the time and place of the wake and funeral.[15] Unlike in the past, when a community functioned as a cooperative mutual-aid organization, contemporary neighbors rarely assist the bereaved.[16]

The removal of death rituals, and death itself, from communities was brought about by various factors, one of which was the increased use of hospitals. In 1965, 36.5 percent of the deaths in Kita-Kyūshū occurred in hospitals and 50.1 percent at home. By 1975 the figure was reversed: 57.1 percent died at hospitals, and 31.7 percent died at home. By 1992, 83.4 percent of deaths occurred in hospitals and only 11.9 percent at home (Kita-Kyūshūshi Hokenkyoku, 11).

Also, even as funeral professionals were beginning to provide comprehensive services that handled the physical remains of the deceased, many youths were migrating to cities to become "salarymen" (businessmen). Such shifts and attenuated ties between community members allowed funeral companies to expand their businesses to villages. As discussed earlier, the responsibility to care for the physical remains was at the core of religious, economic, and political solidarity in the community. When this base crumbled, the symmetrical exchanges between community members fell apart. Moreover, with the gradual decrease of community elders who knew the traditions and customs, the knowledge of how to prepare the corpse for funerals was lost. The discontinuation of reciprocity among community members enabled funeral companies to extend their tasks from handling the physical remains and arranging materials to providing comprehensive services and dominating the entire funeral process.

The basis for the commercialization of funeral ceremonies—in which handling the physical remains plays a key part—was the acquisition and subsequent monopoly of funeral knowledge by funeral companies as communities became alienated from the rituals of death. The loss of knowledge in the communities helped funerals evolve into commodities because the discrepancies between those who possessed such knowledge and those who didn't became clearly demarcated.

Four areas are the sole province of the funeral industry: the handling of the deceased; the funeral ceremony (both services and material arrangements); the funeral-supply market; and funeral sales. First, families now are as dependent on professional knowledge of how to treat the deceased's body immediately after death as they were on doctors when the deceased was alive. The knowledge of encoffining and transporting the deceased, as well as access to coffins and hearses, belongs to the funeral companies. Second, despite the wide availability of books and video tapes about funerals, the general public knows little about how to conduct a ceremony or the role of the chief mourner. Moreover, the funeral altar and the arrangement of the altar have become so elaborate that ordinary people are discouraged from engaging in these preparations. Third, firms that manufacture items used in funeral ceremonies produce for and target sales to the industry— that is, directly to funeral companies rather than individuals.[17] Last, the prices of funeral ceremonies are presented to customers as fixed according to their size, similar to the way in which products in department stores are sold with price tags. Customers can observe the qualitative and quantitative differences between services, but it is difficult for them to judge the value of the services without knowing how much funeral companies actually spend to provide them. As it is for many commodities, the real price of the funeral ceremony and the funeral companies' profits are obscured. The product conceals the use-value of the ceremony as well as the profit it generates for the funeral companies.

The loss of funeral knowledge that was once passed from generation to generation, and the acquisition of this knowledge by the industry, has discouraged ordinary people from conducting funerals themselves. Consequently, funeral companies with specialized knowledge have come to dominate the field and have widened the knowledge gap between professionals and consumers.

In the performance of community funeral rituals, community members were important participants and actors and reaffirmed their ties to one another. Contemporary ceremonies, however, are more likely to emphasize the ties between individuals and their workplace, and even ties between companies. The deceased's coworkers (or those of the deceased's spouse or parents) and the partners of that company comprise the majority of attendants. For example, Yoshiko's colleagues and former schoolmates (described in Chapters 3 and 4) attended her funeral, but more than half of the participants were her father's colleagues from work. In company funerals (provided by the company for someone who had been in a high executive position), the emphasis on individual ties to the company and alliances between companies predominates. For such funerals, selecting funeral committees becomes a critical matter; the company's intention is to exploit the occasion to reaffirm its alliances. For the funeral of the president of the Kyūshū Tea Company (see Chapter 4), eight funeral committee members were carefully chosen from its own company and its parent company, Tokyo Tea, and its rival company, which also had branched out from Tokyo Tea, was ignored. The special incense burning (*tokubetsu-shōko*) by these guests was vital in confirming the relationship between the two companies. Even memorial addresses are used to confirm ties between individuals and their workplaces and between different companies. Commercial ceremonies emphasize the deceased's connection to an institution rather than a community and thus demonstrate the shift from community solidarity to occupational solidarity.

Commercial ceremonies have been standardized by fixed prices and are differentiated by the quality and the quantity of the product and the labor. Some of the items that vary in price are the funeral hall, rented funeral altars, coffins, ashpots, flowers, return gifts, invitation cards, and dinner. The variety of items available makes possible countless permutations; but in actuality, people's selections are often determined by the choice of a funeral altar. An expensive altar affects the selection of the funeral hall, coffin, flowers, ashpot, gifts, and food items. In short, the choice of a funeral altar reflects the social position, age, and gender of the deceased and the social status of the family.

The funeral altar has become increasingly stratified over the years. Moon Rise has 21 different prices for funeral altars, starting at ¥60,000 and ranging up to 10 million yen. The price varies according to the design and size of the altar, the number of chrysanthemums on the altar, and the decorative gardens beside the altar. For example, the cheapest altar has two pairs of small chrysanthemum pots on the altar, which is about 72 inches in length, and no decorative garden. Altar prices also vary according to the types of flowers used. Most of the flowerpots are filled with chrysanthemums (flowers native to Japan), but as the price rises above ¥60,000, plenty of nonnative flowers (lilies, roses, carnations, irises, daisies, and other flowers associated with weddings or celebrations) are displayed (see Table 2 in Chapter 4).

A smaller altar (less than ¥360,000) will likely be arranged in a tatami room or at home, whereas a hall is necessary for an altar that costs more than ¥420,000. For altars more expensive than 2 million yen, the ceremony will take place in the largest auditorium hall. The size of an altar also prescribes the number of funeral professionals at a ceremony and the quality and quantity of bouquets that decorate both sides of the coffin, making clear to funeral-goers how much money has been spent.[18]

The standardization of funeral ceremonies has stratified materials at different price levels, which in turn has enabled customers to purchase the product that matches the deceased's and their own social standing. There were distinctions between the rich and poor in community rituals, but the hierarchy was not as clearly marked as it is in commercial ceremonies. The variety of materials available for community rituals was small; while the hierarchical differences may have been obvious to the people in the community, they did not offer a common measurement that could be understood within a larger scope. In general, community funerals minimized the precise rank differences of individuals, and this strengthened community solidarity. In contrast, standardized ceremonies enable individuals to rank themselves among others.

The situating of oneself and others on a single hierarchical scale is part of a process of overall homogenization. Mass consumption of commercial funerals that provide a standardized measurement or reference point has created what Wilk calls "structures of common difference," which are "built through processes of commoditisation and objectification that do produce an appearance of artificiality and homogeneity" (Wilk, 118).[19] The point is that a homogeneous structure coexists with differences, and moreover, homogeneity expands its differences. The consumption of different variations within a common apparatus creates a homogeneous culture because the diversity in commodities and services is "not of content, but of form" (ibid.). Once the mass consumption of funeral ceremonies made commercial ceremonies a cultural norm, contemporary Japanese were impelled to purchase services in order to save face in front of their colleagues and friends. In this way the mass consumption of funeral ceremonies serves to express differences within a common structure. Thus commercialization and consumption function together to homogenize Japanese culture.

Summary

The commercialization of funeral ceremonies has become possible through changes in various social factors, such as large-scale migration to the cities. These social changes resulted in the removal of death rituals from community settings, the cessation of caring for the corpse by family and community, and the specialization of knowledge by funeral professionals. Marketing and repeated consumption have led to mass consumption, which has deterred ordinary people from providing funerals and has allowed funeral companies to dominate in their specialized task.

Commercial ceremonies differ from community rituals in the interpersonal relationships they foster, the values they promote, and patterns of integration. Commercial ceremonies have become secular and rational, emphasizing personal memories of the deceased. Commercial funerals create new ties between individuals and funeral companies and reconfirm the individual's relationship to the workplace. The commercialization of funerals is part of the larger process of mass consumption, which has stratified individuals by a common denominator and dissolved local heterogeneity into a homogeneity of cultural practice.

At the banquet mentioned at the beginning of this chapter, President Sakuma said that he was planning the construction of a Moon Rise shrine and would register it as a religious institution (*shūkyo-hōjin*). He actually took this action just before the completion of my fieldwork.[20] The idea behind the building of the shrine, I was told, is expressed in the term "well-being," which is also the name of Moon Rise's monthly magazine. "Well-being stands for our aim to culturalize and assimilate ourselves to consumers' culture, and not the other way around. In order to serve consumers well, one must balance competition and contribution. Companies cannot exist by ignoring the needs of consumers," the president explained.

The commercialization of funerals can be summed up as both

marketing and mass consumption that composed and have re-composed the Japanese funerary culture. On the one hand, fu-neral companies have made a continuing effort to perfect their services by replacing the tasks of the bereaved and cooperative community groups. On the other hand, commercial services have become the norm, not because the funeral industry imposed its will on consumers, but because people found value and meaning in commercial funeral services. Although many distinctions can be made between the community funeral's gift exchange and the commercial funeral's commodity-exchange patterns, the commer-cialization of funerals did not alienate individuals or eliminate a funerary culture, but rather substituted one culture for another, reflecting changes in Japanese society. Commercialization brought new forms of dependence, which replaced the old one based on communities, and new pressures to conform to them. As Daniel Miller states, "Consumption can be examined as an intra-class phenomenon used in establishing social cohesion" (Miller, 197). The development of the funeral industry and the shift from com-munity to commercial funerals led to the mass consumption of fu-neral services, which serves as a basis of social and cultural cohe-sion in contemporary Japan.

INTRODUCTION

1.   Living 100 years, or more than the average lifespan, is considered
      lucky and an event that should be celebrated.

2.   Other Japanese books on contemporary funerals, such as
      Himonya; Inoue H. 1990, 1994; Kosugi; Nakajō; Ichijō 1992a;
      and Inose are written for lay audiences. One section of Bestor's
      Neighborhood Tokyo captures a contemporary funeral in progress;
      he portrays both the community members' and a funeral
      company's involvement in a commercial district of Tokyo
      (Bestor, 199–205).

3.   Ichijō Shinya is the pseudonym of Sakuma Tsunekazu.

4.   "The process of individuation is proceeding as the individual's
      education, employment, recreation and political activity become
      increasingly divorced from the household, and the number of
      overlapping groups in which he is involved, each claiming a
      separate allegiance, increases" (Dore 1958, 155).

5.   *Nishinihon* Newspaper (Morning Edition) 21 January 1995 and
      Mainichi Newspaper (Evening Edition) 6 April 1995.

CHAPTER I. DEATH RITUALS IN ANTHROPOLOGY
AND JAPANESE FOLKLORE STUDIES

1.   Victor Turner explained transitional rites or the liminal period
      with the expression "betwixt and between," in which a being is
      in a state between classifications of the existing cultural criteria
      (Turner 1967, 93–111). He later came to view liminality as the
      state of unstructured "communitas" that functions to propel the

structured social life in a dialectical manner (Turner 1969, 94–130).

2.   In his examination of the transitional stages of the living and the dead, Van Gennep does not presume both time periods to coincide in all cases (Van Gennep, 147). Moreover, the duration of transitions varies according to the sex, age, and social position of the deceased (146).

3.   Watson's research was conducted in San Tin and Ha Tsuen village in the Hong Kong New Territories.

4.   Emily Martin Ahern describes the rules of worship for Ch'inan people in Taiwan as:

   (1)   If X inherits property from Y, he must worship Y
   (2)   If X is a direct descendant of Y, he may or may not worship Y
   (3)   If X is Y's only descendant, he must worship Y
   (4)   If X is the most obligated descendant, he must worship Y (1973, 148). She also points out that the importance of the obligation of worship is "created by the inheritance of rice land" (151).

5.   The LoWiili inherit all property patrilineally, while the LoDagaba inherit all immovable property patrilineally and movable property matrilineally (Goody 1962, 8–9).

6.   Thompson on the other hand considers the pig's head and tail to represent a renewal of the unity and the continuity between them (96).

7.   The various studies suggest two models. One model is the dualism of *hare* and *ke* (Yanagita 1962b; Wakamori 1981; Tsuboi 1982, 1983), or *hare* and *ke*, including *kegare* within the scope of *hare* (Sakurai 1981; Namihira 1974). The other model is the triangulation of *hare*, *ke*, and *kegare* (Sakurai 1981; Miyata).

8.   Although the consumption of rice is now common in Japan, it used to be eaten only on special occasions, such as funerals and during the performance of other rituals.

9.   There is a huge amount of literature on Japanese households and communities that discusses ancestor worship (e.g., Ariga 1972, 1979; Embree; Beardsley, Hall, and Ward; Cornell and Smith; Dore 1958, 1978; Nakane; Norbeck 1954, 1978; Smith R. 1978; Vogel 1963).

10. "The dōzoku is a set of households that recognize their relationship in terms of *honke* and *bunke* and which, on the basis of this relation, have developed a corporate function as a group" (Nakane, 90–91).

11. Under the Tokugawa regime, the edict of the parochial system (*danka-seido*) decreed that every Japanese household had to affiliate with a Buddhist temple (Kitagawa, 211).

12. Yanagita mentions *muenbotoke* or the *hokajoryo* as outsider spirits but does not state that they are ancestral spirits of the household (1975b, 217–18). He does point out, however, that any deceased, even one without a household, can become a *hotoke*, which refers to becoming the Buddha or a disciple of the Buddha (221).

    In contrast, Takeda suggests that *muenbotoke* are in a peripheral or lower position than ancestral spirits (Takeda C. 1979, 35).

13. In recent years, however, with the increase in cremation, the use of the double-grave system has declined (Shintani 1985, 37).

CHAPTER 2. THE HISTORY OF JAPANESE FUNERAL TRADITIONS

1. These rituals are supposed to be conducted in this sequence, but in practice sometimes rituals are transposed (Akata 1986, 88).

2. My description of funerals is based on interviews with elders living in the Kita-Kyūshū area (where I conducted my fieldwork at Moon Rise) and documents about local funeral customs published by the Kita-Kyūshū Education Committee.

3. Inoguchi documents another method of giving last water— spraying water directly onto the dying person's face (Inoguchi 1954, 34). Gorai argues that last water should be considered death water (*shini-mizu*), given after death (Gorai 1992, 737). He draws examples from the north of Japan where last water or death water was given by placing a wet brush on the deceased's lips or placing a piece of wetted paper into the deceased's mouth (ibid.). Gorai considers last water and death water to be the same thing; however, the elders I interviewed indicated that they are two separate things, requiring two separate actions. In Kita-Kyūshū death water was a cup of water placed near the deceased's bedside as an offering.

4. Villagers called a doctor only after the family was certain of a

person's death. Because of the expense, people rarely received medical care during their lifetimes. Except for the very rich, people died at home; therefore, a doctor saw most people for the first time at death.

5. *Kumi* was organized around residential divisions in Kita-Kyūshū and was a reciprocal organization responsible for weddings, funerals, and other events that needed labor cooperation. Sometimes *kō*, an organization based on religious activities, overlapped with *kumi* and was called "*kō-gumi.*" For more examples of *kō* and *kumi* see Norbeck 1954; and Beardsley, Hall, and Ward.

6. *Shikabana* is written in characters three different ways: as death flower, paper flower, and four-flower. It is made out of four thin wooden sticks about seven inches long. The narrow white paper (I saw a different funeral company using silver paper) is cut and rolled onto these sticks to look like flowers. The four sticks are then erected on a square of wood. A narrow piece of black paper tied around the four corners makes a sort of container. The memorial tablet is then placed in the middle. The death flower was traditionally placed on the grave. Gorai explains that the death flower indicated the whereabouts of the deceased's burial site for the living. At the same time, it marked the boundary between the world of the afterlife and the world of the living for the soul of the deceased (Gorai 1992, 250–51).

7. Two *tatsuguchi*, one male and one female dragon, were made from bamboo sticks and paper. The head of the dragon was made by slicing the bamboo stick, and the body was wrapped with black and white paper. These were carried by the person who led the coffin and family members to the burial site.

8. Three types of box roofs, *akoya, tengai,* and *roppōkan,* were used in Kita-Kyūshū. *Akoya* (Buddha's house) is made out of paper shaped like a triangular house roof. It was placed on top of the coffin during the procession and left behind on the burial mound. Beautiful paintings of lotus flowers or a phoenix were drawn on it by community members. However, not all communities in Kita-Kyūshū used the same shape of roof. An elder told me that in Sarugai a wood-framed shrine-like roof called "*tengai*" was used instead. The *tengai* (heaven cover) was attached to a

bamboo stick and held over the coffin by a *kumi* member during the procession; it was not left on the grave but kept by the carrier. The shrine-like roof was covered with gold and white paper each time it was used. In Tanoura, instead of these wooden roofs, they used a *roppōkan* (six-sided container) that was composed of two pieces. The top piece was hexagonal with a hat-like roof, inside which a round coffin was placed. The bottom piece was a large tray on which the top piece was laid; it was carried by two kumi members. After the procession it was stored in a community warehouse and used only at funerals.

9. *Hi* were substitutes for candles; usually six units were placed on both sides of the road that led to the burial site. They were also called *kōshō* because they were made out of short bamboo sticks on top of which a red pepper (*tōgarashi*, or *kōshō* in this region) was tied. The red pepper was supposed to ward off evil spirits (*mayoke*) (Saito, 114). The six *hi* represented the six levels of incarnation in Buddhism: heaven, the human world, the world of carnage, the animal world, the world of devils, and hell. However, other communities, such as Tenraiji, Ideura, Tanoura, and Honjo, used six candleholders made out of thin bamboo sticks (*rokudō-shōmei-shokudai*), which were placed on the road just before the procession.

10. The family ate only vegetarian food for 49 days after the death. It was believed that for that period of time the soul of the deceased lingered on top of the house and that vegetarian food prevented the household from succumbing to its impurity.

11. The trays and plates were usually kept in the communal warehouse and were used for other rituals, such as weddings.

12. The function of dress is similar in the Chinese case; see Wolf 1970. Japanese mourning dress, however, was not as colorful as the Chinese, reflecting less stratification among kin.

13. On incense money and kōden exchanges, see Bestor 1989.

14. Sometimes the deceased's house was too small to allow all the priests and the bereaved to sit behind the coffin. In those cases, a stage was made at the outside space directly behind where the deceased's coffin lay. The priests sat on chairs (*kyoku-roku*) and a community member held an umbrella over them.

15. "*Hone-kami*" was also referred to as "*hone-kaburi*" and "*hone-

koburi." The term was used in the Kita-Kyūshū area to mean the dinner served after cooperating in the labor for the funeral.

16. The timing of the final rites (*tomurai-age*) varies throughout the country, but most favored are the 33d and 50th anniversaries of death (Smith 1974, 96).

17. *Yakko* were servants of the warriors. Apart from carrying out errands for their masters, their main task was to perform in a parade at processions.

18. Based on an interview with the current vice president of the Nakamura-gumi-Sōgisha, Kakuda Chiaki, on March 7, 1995.

19. In 1897 the Meiji government announced the Prevention of Infectious Disease (*Densen-byō-yobō-hō*), which informed citizens of the danger of corpses. This edict was a supplement to the Regulations Concerning Graves and Burials (*Bochi-oyobi-maisō-torishimari-kisoku*) issued in 1894; it restricted the location of burial sites, the time of cremation, and the treatment of cremated bones and ashes (Asaka and Yagisawa, 68).

20. Before the decree concerning infectious disease, the Meiji government issued the edict of Prohibition of Cremation (*Kasō-kinshirei*) in 1873 as part of agitating Shintoism. Only two years later, however, the government lifted the ban (Asaka and Yagisawa, 58).

21. Taishō Democracy refers to the movement of liberalism and democracy that arose during the 1920s. Socialism, the Protection of the Constitution movement, and the universal suffrage movement arose during this period.

22. Sakai Toshihiko (1870–1933) was a socialist, one of the founders of Heimin-Shimbun (Newspaper for the Ordinary People), and a pacifist who participated in the establishment of the Japanese Communist Party and the Japanese Socialist Party.

23. Inoue Shōichi believes that the shape of the shrine-like roof, which is adopted from the litter model of the lower class, indicates the assimilation of lower-class practices by the upper class. This phenomenon, he states, parallels the rise of a middle class (*taishū*) in Shōwa (Inoue S., 153–55).

24. The funeral industry comprises contemporary funeral companies and funeral homes that perform funeral ceremonies; it performs

a different role than that of funeral parlors during traditional funeral rituals.

25. The contract of the National Wedding and Funeral Mutual-Aid Association stipulates that candidates must satisfy three conditions for enrollment: the candidate who conducts weddings and funerals must have full capacity to carry out modern funerals; the candidate must have the appropriate facilities, management skills, and disposition to perform within the Mutual-Aid System; the candidate must submit recommendation letters from local association members or officials (ZGR 1974, 159).

26. The charges for these services are extra and are excluded from the cost of membership.

CHAPTER 3. THE PHASE OF NEGATED DEATH

1. This is a direct result of the differences between health care in the United States and Japan. Japanese health care is socialistic; the government provides health care to all Japanese. Thus, city, prefectual, and public university hospitals have little money to spend on decor or patient conveniences.

2. The room for the soul in Japan and a morgue in America are different. The former is a single room (it varies in size) for one corpse, whereas in America the dead share one room.

3. Funeral staff do not use cord to tie the hands as the nurses do, although it would greatly facilitate arranging the beads between the deceased's pressed hands. Any action that makes it appear as if it causes pain for the deceased is strictly prohibited among funeral staff. The reason the funeral staff is prohibited from performing the same action that the medical staff is allowed to perform is a complex structure of perspective that illustrates the linguistic difference between "corpse" (*shitai*) and "a deceased's remains" (*itai*). The latter term implies the body of one's family, relative, or a close friend. It is a term that demonstrates respect to the deceased and the family. In contrast, the use of the word *shitai* implies a cadaver that has no relationship to anyone; it is a thing or an object. Thus, the "deceased's remains" need to be treated as if the person were still alive. The funeral industry must

treat the deceased with extreme care so that the family does not believe the funeral staff have treated the deceased as a "corpse" and thus without respect.

4. The head cloth is not placed on the deceased's head until the encoffining.

5. Usually nurses send off the deceased from the hospital, but doctors are sometimes present. I was told by the funeral staff that the number of medical staff sending off the deceased depends on the number of gifts the deceased's family has given them during the period of hospitalization. The more gifts that were given, the more medical staff are willing to send him or her off.

6. A seal is a character-based stamp that is used as a signature. The person who is the chief mourner and is responsible for payment, in this case Yamaha, is required to provide his or her seal.

7. The coffin is never placed directly on the floor. The window on the coffin is made so that the two small doors on the coffin open outward. The window has a transparent plastic cover instead of glass so that it can be incinerated during cremation. Often the plastic cover became smeared with tears; part-time workers wipe off the plastic cover with cloths after the wake or on the morning of the funeral ceremony.

8. All these displayed foods are placed into the coffin after the funeral ceremony and incinerated with the deceased; they are to sustain the deceased on the journey to the other world.

9. I later found out from their conversation with the conductor that the deceased's mother had passed away earlier.

10. For more detailed information on altars see the Conclusion.

11. Relatives and guests often give these flowers as gifts. They may also purchase the item by calling Moon Rise. The name of the giver or the company name will be inscribed on the plate.

12. Dried-flower wreaths (*zoka*) are nearly three meters tall. The circular top, which forms a third of the whole object, is arranged with large flowers, and the rest of the structure consists of two wooden poles connected at the top. Between the two poles, a cloth sheet is attached to indicate the giver's name. The dried-flower wreath is often purchased for funerals that take place at home because they can be the marker for visitors to find the house. I have noticed, however, that companies and institutions

purchase them as often as real flowers because they indicate the giver's name more visibly than the fresh-flower arrangements, which use a narrower name plate.

13. The cremation certificate is obtained at the Family Registration Department (*Koseki-gakari*) of a city, village, or town government. The Family Registration Department is open 24 hours a day so that cremation certificates can be picked up at any time.

14. The majority of the wake and funeral ceremony photos are in black and white. Men are usually pictured in suits and women in mourning kimonos; if a family provides a color photograph of the deceased, the funeral company uses computer technology to make the clothes black.

15. The traditional bathing ritual is discussed in Chapter 7.

16. According to statistics from the Kita-Kyūshū Department of Public Health, in 1992, 83.4 percent of all deaths occurred in hospitals, 1.9 percent in clinics, 0.1 percent in nursing homes, 11.9 percent at home, and the rest (2.7 percent) elsewhere.

17. The tasks of CSC and its development are discussed in Chapter 6.

18. The private parts of the body were given a more cursory cleansing to preserve the modesty of the deceased.

19. Uchiumi, who works at the coffee shop at the auditorium, told me a story that she remembers clearly. A couple of years earlier, the son of two famous doctors committed suicide. The son was carried directly to the Moon Rise Auditorium. His grandmother was the only attendant at the wake and the funeral. Nobody was invited or notified. On the blackboard of the funeral staff's office, where ordinarily the deceased's names are written, a sign said "Secret" and "Do not Disturb." Uchiumi said that the incident was concealed from the public because the son's parents were highly regarded doctors in the local area who feared their son's suicide would harm their reputations. Uchiumi explained to me, "Suicide destroys the family name. It is considered the most shameful way to die."

20. There is no set amount for the donation to the priest. See Chapter 6.

21. Many families who have moved away from the residence of their parents and ancestors do not belong to or have contact with a temple. Although each family needs a priest for the funeral and

a place for the deceased's ashes, the family does not necessarily join the officiating priest's temple. Like the funeral services purchased from a company, the priests' services can be a single transaction. The relationship between Buddhist priests and families is discussed in Chapter 6.

22. For wakes at home, family members take turns staying up, but when a wake takes place at the auditorium, only one or two relatives remain in most cases.

CHAPTER 4. THE FUNERAL CEREMONY

1. See Chapter 2, note 6.

2. The hearse, a renovated Cadillac, has room for the driver, one passenger, and the coffin. The back of this Cadillac was decorated like a grand room, with the walls painted gold and lanterns hanging from the ceiling.

3. At a *missō*, a wake (*kari-tsuya*), funeral, and cremation are carried out. Since a company funeral, called *honsō*, takes place after the missō, it inlcudes only a wake (*hon-tsuya*) and a funeral ceremony, but no cremation.

4. On the day of a company funeral, no staff members are permitted to take the day off, not even part-timers. This also applies to those who had previously arranged for a day off that day.

5. The meaning of this gift is discussed in Chapter 6.

6. If a priest had come with them they would have chanted the sutra as well. Priests rarely accompany a family to the crematorium except in the Nichirenshōshū sect. Most priests immediately return to their temple after the ceremony.

7. In 1959, after consulting with a priest, Mazuda, the head cremator, decided to use one wood and one bamboo chopstick. He said it "simplifies the process of picking up and allows the family members to pick up the bones more quickly." Traditionally, however, two pairs of chopsticks, one of wood and the other of bamboo, were used. (There are crematoriums in other parts of the country that still follow this practice. The two mourners, one with a wooden pair and the other with a bamboo pair, picked up the bones together.) The custom of two people using chopsticks to pick up bones is to differentiate the practice from every-

day life, where people will avoid picking up food at the same time as another person.

8. This piece of bone is called the Adam's apple (*nodo-botoke*, literally "throat-Buddha." It is so called because it looks like a Buddha sitting cross-legged. The cremators, however, told me that the bone called the Adam's apple is not really from the throat but from the spinal cord; it is the bone that connects the neck and the skull.

9. There are two patterns of collecting bones in Japan. One is the complete collection (*zenbu-shūkotsu*) and the other is partial collection (*bubun-shūkotsu*). The custom is divided around the latitude line of 35 degrees; above the line, complete collection is common, whereas below the line partial collection is predominant (Yagisawa, 46). I was told by the head cremator, Mazuda, that in complete-collection areas, funeral companies provide larger ashpots that will hold the entire skeleton. The incinerators of these crematoriums also differ. They are designed to leave the cremated bones in a heap at the bottom of the incinerator. The incinerators also use a higher temperature, which leaves the bones in smaller pieces.

CHAPTER 5. FUNERAL PROFESSIONALS AT MOON RISE

1. Many bathtubs in Japanese houses use manual gas burners that are attached to each bathtub. This is because many Japanese houses still maintain separate gas systems for the kitchen and the bath.

2. I noticed that the coroner stared at me as if he had never seen a woman before. Later Suke told me that it must have been the first time he had seen a woman arrive to pick up the corpse of someone who had died an unnatural death.

3. In Japanese the connotations of the terms for "corpse" (*shitai*) and the deceased's "remains" (*itai*) are different. *Shitai* implies cadaver or dead body. *Itai* means the body of one's family or acquaintance, and it implies respect for the deceased as well as for his or her family.

4. I stayed up reading in the funeral office, in one of the customer's rooms, or in the salon in the funeral hall while I waited for calls.

5. *Ubasuteyama*, literally "a mountain where grandmothers are abandoned," is based on a story that in certain parts of Japan when a woman became old and useless her family sent her to a mountain to die.

6. Their monthly salary was 20 percent higher than that of other Moon Rise white-collar workers, but with the additional payment for the night shift, it could be 30 to 40 percent higher. Staff were paid according to the number of deaths on the night shift.

7. The exam and certification system was established in 1996, after I had left.

8. Most part-time jobs paid ¥500 an hour, but the funeral hall employees were paid ¥1,000 an hour.

9. My uniform was like that of the female funeral staff and resembled the uniform of the part-timers.

10. Wearing a silk kimono is not as easy as one might think. It requires wearing layers of undergarments so that the final layer, the kimono, will be free of wrinkles. For example, in order to make the bodyline straight, one must wrap a bath towel around the waist. Tying a silk *obi* (the thick outer "belt") into the proper bow shape also requires much practice. Since contemporary women have few opportunities to wear a kimono, they also have few chances to learn such skills. Those who wish to learn often take courses on kimono fitting.

11. Also see Naquin, 39; and Watson, J. 1988, 12.

CHAPTER 6. FUNERAL PROFESSIONALS
OUTSIDE OF MOON RISE

1. According to Mazuda, the head of the crematorium, the term *onbō* (written in two characters, *on* meaning "hide" and *bō* meaning "priest") is derived from the term for a low-ranking priest who used to carry the deceased on his back to a cremation or burial site.

2. In 1988, there were about 3,000 active crematoriums in Japan, each with an oven, a chimney (exhaust pipe), and a building. Of these crematoriums, 85 percent were owned by the city, the town, or village organizations (Asaka, 40).

3. At community funerals before World War II, the bereaved provided small gifts to all villagers in return for their assistance with the rituals.

4. Mazuda Jr. told me that ash collectors usually arrived at 7:00 A.M. or earlier but had changed their schedule for me that day.

5. The cremation rate in Japan has changed as follows (Asaka, 43):

1896	26.8%	1914	71.8%
1909	24.8%	1915	79.2%
1910	55.7%	1916	86.5%
1911	54.0%	1917	91.1%
1912	58.6%	1918	94.5%
1913	63.1%	1990	97.1%

6. According to Helen Hardacre, most Shintō priests today have primary jobs outside the priesthood and engage in Shintō affairs as a sideline occupation.

7. New Religions include all religious groups that have developed since the nineteenth century, including Tenrikyō, Kurozumikyō, Sōka-gakkai, and Kōfuku no Kagaku. "They are very much products of the Japanese religious environment, taking elements from the various interpenetrating traditions, Shintō, Buddhist, and folk, that form the framework of the Japanese religious world" (Reader, 197). They have filled the varying spiritual needs in Japan and tend to be highly organized with strict disciplines.

8. Temple affiliation indicates that a family's ancestors are taken care of by the temple priests: either they visit the ancestral altar at home on the deceased's death date, or they keep ancestors' ashes in the temple grave or an ossuary. In return, the bereaved family periodically makes donations to the temple. Affiliation with a temple does not necessarily imply that the family members belong to a particular Buddhist sect. The bereaved are more like clients who have received death services for their deceased family.

9. Once a temple priest provides a funeral service, he stays in touch with the family, following up with ancestral ceremonies and preserving the ashes of the deceased. These acts imply that the family members have become parishioners of the temple and allow

priests to ask for donations from the family. If the donations requested seem too high to the family, they can cut their ties with the temple anytime. Often dissatisfaction with the size of the required donation is the reason families change temple affiliation.

10. The bereaved who invite and who do not invite priests to join them for drinks after the services (as a formality) are about equal in number. Even with an invitation, however, priests generally do not attend this family affair. This is because priests rarely have personal ties with the family, and most of the invitations are extended as a formality or polite gesture.

11. A funeral is composed of priests' services (sutra chanting and burning incense) and the ceremony of bidding farewell (reading eulogies and telegrams), as discussed in Chapters 3 and 4.

12. During the Tokugawa period membership in a Buddhist sect was determined by the social status of the household.

CHAPTER 7. THE COMMODITIZATION
OF THE BATHING CEREMONY

1. The rites of bathing (*oyudono no gi*) at court were performed on the occasion of a birth, the accession of an emperor, a marriage, a change in office, moving to a new residence, and the New Year, and after a period of illness as an extension of earlier purification rites (Takeda K., 74).

2. Most bathtubs in Japan are deep vessels that are filled with hot water only once per bathing occasion. Family members do not wash their bodies inside the tub but soak in the tub after they have finished washing and showering outside the tub. Since the tub is filled only once, family members take turns soaking, one right after another. This makes bathing a family affair. Instead of taking an individual shower at any time of day, Japanese families bathe "together" in the evening.

3. This took place from November to the beginning of January. The reduced-price strategy was an "open-secret" and was carried out quietly among the funeral staff.

4. Personal communication by e-mail, March 1997.

5. "In some cases all the children but one and the widow will renounce their claim after it has been agreed that one of the

children will accept both the assets and the responsibility for the care of the mother in her old age" (Smith, R. 1987, 13).

CONCLUSION

1. The company conducted 156 funeral ceremonies in January 1995. This was nearly double the usual number.
2. The Mutual-Aid System is based on recruiting members, who by paying the membership fee can receive a funeral or wedding when needed. See Chapter 2.
3. Since examples of "pure" gift exchange or commodity exchange are empirically difficult to find (Yan, 217), I examined a more gift- or commodity-oriented economy.
4. See Mauss; Gregory; Taussig.
5. See Appadurai; Sahlins 1972; Tambiah 1984; Yan.
6. In areas like Tōhoku where the *dōzoku* kinship organization prevailed, community members overlap with kinship networks. But here I want to emphasize that it was the residential association that mattered most in people's daily lives.
7. It goes without saying that the continuation of the household and ancestral line was important in Japanese death rituals. However, I believe that the emphasis on the household was prevalent in ancestral rites and much less emphasized in funeral rituals.
8. Gorai stressed the importance of this meal. He states that the bereaved were obliged to serve the community members no matter what the conditions were and that the community members had a right to demand this food (Gorai 1992, 851).
9. The decrease of MAC membership sales is due to the saturation of the market by funeral companies. Also, in recent years people have begun to spend much more than the price of MAC membership for funerals, demonstrating that more people can afford to pay in a lump sum.
10. Elders' Clubs exist in most villages and cities in Japan and usually consist of about twenty members age 70 older. In principle, one can join the local Elders' Club at age 60, but few people do.
11. The content of contracts—i.e., the size of the price reduction and refund—varies from company to company.

12. I use "becoming" because elders who are older than 70 continue to dislike funerals and consider them unlucky and polluted. It is younger people who are not concerned with danger in funeral ceremonies.

13. Men do not object to the concept of taking flowers, but they told me that they are "too embarrassed to be carrying flowers back to their office."

14. Inheritances became insignificant as a result of massive migration to cities, longevity, and the high cost of hospital care. Unless one is extremely rich, one's wealth is spent before death and little is left for children to inherit.

15. The role as head of the village association is passed from house to house in turn.

16. On rare occasions, villagers might bring food to the wake or the funeral. But it is more common for the bereaved to purchase ready-made packaged foods.

17. Legally, it is possible to purchase these funeral items, but since they are not advertised to the public it is difficult for ordinary people to find them.

18. An arrangement of ¥50,000 flower bouquets has three pots on a stand, a ¥40,000 one has two pots, and a ¥30,000 one has only one. The types of flowers also differ; the most expensive arrangement comes with extravagant Western flowers like Casablanca, lilies, and white roses; the middle range comes with the same kind of Western flowers but fewer; the cheapest one is dominated by chrysanthemums and has only a few Western flowers.

19. Richard Wilk uses the term in his study of globalization and localization in Belize, but I think his idea applies to the general context of changes in consumption practices in different cultures.

20. Because only registered religious institutions are allowed to construct gravesites and ossuaries, the establishment of the Moon Rise shrine may be an initial attempt to expand ossuaries, a much-needed service for consumers today.

Abegglen, James. 1958. *The Japanese Factory*. Glencoe, Ill.: Free Press.

Adorno, T. 1991. *The Culture Industry*. London: Routledge.

Ahern, Emily Martin. 1973. *The Cult of the Dead in a Chinese Village*. Stanford: Stanford University Press.

———. 1975. "The Power and Pollution of Chinese Women." In *Women in Chinese Society*, edited by Margery Wolf and Roxane Witke. Stanford: Stanford University Press.

———. 1988. "Gender and Ideological Differences in Representations of Life and Death." In *Death Ritual in Late Imperial and Modern China*, edited by James L. Watson and Evelyn S. Rawski, 164–76. Berkeley: University of California Press.

Akata Mitsuo. 1980. *Saigi shūzoku no kenkyū* (Research on the custom of rituals). Tokyo: Kobundo.

———. 1984. "Girei denshō" (The traditions of rituals). In *Nihon minzokugaku*, edited by Akata Mitsuo. Tokyo: Kobundo.

———. 1986. *Sorei shinkōto takai kannen* (Ancestor worship and the afterlife). Kyoto: Jinbun Shoin.

———. 1988. *Ie no denshō to senzokan* (Household traditions and the perception of ancestors). Kyoto: Jinbun Shoin.

Anderson, Perry. 1983. *In the Tracks of Historical Materialism*. New York: Verso.

Appadurai, Arjun. 1986. "Introduction." In *The Social Life of Things*, edited by Arjun Appadurai, 3–63. Cambridge, Eng.: Cambridge University Press.

Ariga Kizaemon. 1972. *Ie*. (Household). Tokyo: Shimbundō.

———. 1979. "Hotoketo iu kotobani tsuite." (Concerning the term *hotoke*). In *Sōsōbosei Kenkyūshūsei*. Vol. 3: *Senzokuyō* (Research on funeral and burial traditions: Ancestor worship), edited by Takeda Choshu, 93–113. Tokyo: Meicho Shuppan.

Asahi Shimbun Chōsabu, ed. 1994. *Asahi-nenkan 1994: Asahi Data Book*. (Asahi year bok). Tokyo: Asahi Shimbunsha.

Asaka Katsusuke. 1991. "Kasōba towa? Hensen wo tadori kangaeru." (What is a crematory? An inquiry into its history). *Sōgi*, 1, no. 6: 40–43.

———, and Yagisawa Sōichi, eds. 1983. *Kasōba* (A crematory). Tokyo: Daimeidō.

Barth, Fredrik. 1981. *Process and Form in Social Life: Selected Essays of Fredrik Barth*. Vol. 1. Boston: Routledge & Kegan Paul.

Baudrillard, Jean. 1979. *La Société de consommation: Ses mythes, ses structures*. Trans. Imamura Hitoshi and Tsukahara Fumi. Tokyo: Kinokuniya Shoten.

———. 1993. *Symbolic Exchange and Death*. Trans. Iain Hamilton Grant. London: Sage Publications.

Beardsley, Richard, John W. Hall, and Robert E. Ward, eds. 1959. *Village Japan*. Chicago: University of Chicago Press.

Bell, Catherine. 1992. *Ritual Theory, Ritual Practice*. New York: Oxford University Press.

Bernier, Barnard. 1975. *Breaking the Cosmic Circle: Religion in a Japanese Village*. Ithaca, N.Y.: Cornell University.

Bestor, Theodore C. 1989. *Neighborhood Tokyo*. Stanford: Stanford University Press.

Bethel, Diana. 1992. "Alienation and Reconnection in a Home for the Elderly." In *Remade in Japan: Everyday Life and Consumer Taste in a Changing Society*, edited by Joseph J. Tobin, 126–42. New Haven, Conn.: Yale University Press.

Bloch, Maurice. 1981. "Tombs and States." In *Mortality and Immortality: The Anthropology and Archaeology of Death*, edited by S. C. Humphreys and Helen King, 137–47. New York: Academic Press.

———. 1982. "Death, Women, and Power." In *Death and the Regeneration of Life*, edited by Maurice Bloch and Jonathan Parry, 211–30. New York: Cambridge University Press.

———, and Jonathan Parry. 1982. "Introduction." In *Death and the*

Regeneration of Life, edited by Maurice Bloch and Jonathan Parry. New York: Cambridge University Press.

Bourdieu, Pierre. 1977. *Outline of a Theory of Practice*. New York: Cambridge University Press.

———. 1984. *Distinction: A Social Critique of the Judgement of Taste*. Trans. Richard Nice. Cambridge, Mass.: Harvard University Press.

———. 1991. *Language and Symbolic Power*. Trans. Gino Raymond and Matthew Adamson. Cambridge, Mass.: Harvard University Press.

Brown, Keith. 1979. *Shinjo: The Chronicle of a Japanese Village*. Pittsburgh: University Center for International Studies.

Clark, Scott. 1992. "The Japanese Bath: Extraordinarily Ordinary." In *Remade in Japan: Everyday Life and Consumer Taste in a Changing Society*, edited by Joseph J. Tobin, 89–105. New Haven, Conn.: Yale University Press.

Cole, Robert E. 1971. *The Japanese Blue Collar: The Changing Tradition*. Berkeley: University of California Press.

Cornell, John B. 1964. "Dozoku: An Example of Evolution and Transition in Japanese Village Society." *Comparative Studies in Society and History* 6: 449–80.

———, and Robert Smith. 1956. *Two Japanese Villages*. Ann Arbor: University of Michigan, Center for Japanese Studies. Occasional Papers No. 5.

Damon, Frederick H., and Roy Wagner. 1989. *Death Rituals and Life in the Societies of the Kula Ring*. De Kalb: Northern Illinois University Press.

Danforth, Loring M. 1982. *The Death Rituals of Rural Greece*. Princeton, N.J.: Princeton University Press.

De Certeau, Michel. 1984. *The Practice of Everyday Life*. Trans. Steven Rendall. Berkeley: University of California Press.

Dempsey, D. 1975. *The Way We Die: An Investigation of Death and Dying in America Today*. New York: McGraw-Hill.

Dore, Ronald P. 1958. *City Life in Japan: A Study of a Tokyo Ward*. Berkeley: University of California Press.

———. 1973. *British Factory–Japanese Factory: The Origins of National Diversity in Industrial Relations*. Berkeley: University of California Press.

————. 1978. *Shinohara: A Portrait of a Japanese Village.* New York: Pantheon.

Douglas, William A. 1969. *Death in Murelaga: Funerary Rituals in a Spanish Basque Village.* Seattle: University of Washington Press.

Dredge, Paul C. 1987. "Korean Funerals: Ritual as Process." In *Religion and Ritual in Korean Society,* edited by Jaurel Kendall and Griffin Dix, vol. 12: 71–92. *Korea Research Monograph.* Berkeley: University of California.

Durkheim, Emile. 1965. [1915] *The Elementary Forms of Religious Life.* New York: Free Press.

————. 1984. [1893] *The Division of Labor in Society.* Trans. W. D. Halls. New York: Free Press.

Ebersole, Gary L. 1989. *Ritual Poetry and the Politics of Death in Early Japan.* Princeton, N.J.: Princeton University Press.

Edwards, Walter. 1989. *Modern Japan Through Its Weddings. Gender, Person, and Society in Ritual Portrayal.* Stanford: Stanford University Press.

Ei Rokusuke. 1994. *Daiōjō* (Happy ending). Tokyo: Iwanami Shoten.

Embree, John. 1939. *Suye Mura: A Japanese Village.* Chicago: University of Chicago Press.

Forman, Shepard. 1980. "Descent, Alliance, and Exchange Ideology Among the Makassae of East Timor." In *The Flow of Life: Essays on Eastern Indonesia,* edited by James J. Fox, 152–77. Cambridge, Mass.: Harvard University Press.

Frazer, Sir James George. 1933. *Fear of the Dead in Primitive Religion.* Vol. 1. London: Macmillan.

Freedman, Maurice. 1979. "Ancestor Worship: Two Facets of the Chinese Case." In *The Study of Chinese Society: Essays by Maurice Freedman,* edited by G. William Skinner. Stanford: Stanford University Press.

Goody, Jack. 1959. "Death and Social Control Among the Lodagaa." *Man* 204: 134–38.

————. 1962. *Death, Property, and the Ancestors.* Stanford: Stanford University Press.

Gorai Shigeru. 1992. *Sō to Kuyō.* (Death rituals and worship). Osaka: Tōhō Shuppan.

————. 1994. *Nihonjin no shiseikan.* (Japanese perception of life and death). Tokyo: Kadokawa Shoten.

Gregory, C. A. 1982. *Gifts and Commodities*. London: Academic Press.

Habenstein, Robert W. 1962. "Sociology of Occupations: The Case of the American Funeral Director." In *Human Behavior and Social Process: An Interactionist Approach*, edited by Arnold M. Rose, 225–46. Boston: Houghton Mifflin.

Haga Noboru. 1987. *Sōgi no rekishi* (The history of funerals). Tokyo: Yūzankaku.

Harada Toshiaki. 1970. *Shūkyō to Minzoku* (Religion and folklore). Tokyo: Tōkaidaigaku Shuppan.

Harada Toshihiko and Hirayama Harujirō. 1969. *Nihon shomin seikatsu shiryō shūsei* (A history of the lifestyles of ordinary Japanese people). Tokyo: Sanyosha.

Hardacre, Helen. 1989. *Shinto and the State, 1868–1988*. Princeton, N.J.: Princeton University Press.

Haris, Olivia. 1982. "The Dead and the Devils Among the Bolivian Laymi." In *Death and the Regeneration of Life*, edited by Maurice Bloch and Jonathan Parry, 45–73. New York: Cambridge University Press.

Harmer, R. M. 1963. *The High Cost of Dying*. New York: Crowell-Collier.

Harrison, Simon. 1992. "Ritual as Intellectual Property." *Man*, n.s., 27: 225–44.

Hart, Keith. 1982. "On Commoditization." In *From Craft to Industry*, edited by Esther N. Goody. New York: Cambridge University Press.

Hertz, Robert. 1960. [1907] "A Contribution to the Study of the Collective Representation of Death." In *Death and the Right Hand*. Trans. Rodney and Claudia Needham, 27–86. Glencoe, Ill.: Free Press.

Himonya Hajime. 1994. *Osōshiki no manabikata*. (Learning about the funeral ceremony). Tokyo: Kōdansha.

Hirade Kōjiro. 1968. *Tokyo Fūzokushi*. (Customs of Tokyo). Tokyo: Harashobō.

Hobsbawm, Eric, and Terence Ranger, eds. 1983. *The Invention of Tradition*. New York: Cambridge University Press.

Hori Ichirō. 1959. "Japanese Folk Beliefs." *American Anthropologist* 61: 405–24.

———. 1968. *Folk Religion in Japan: Continuity and Change*. Chicago: University of Chicago Press.

Hozumi Nobushige. 1943. *Ancestor Worship and the Japanese Law.* Tokyo: Hokuseidō.

Huntington, Richard. 1973. "Death and the Social Order: Bara Funeral Customs (Madagascar)." *African Studies* 32, no. 2: 65–84.

Ichijō Shinya. 1991. *Romantic Death.* Tokyo: Kokusho Kankōkai.

———. 1992a. *Tamashii wo dezain suru: Sōgitowa nanika?* (Designing the soul: What is a funeral?). Ed. Ichijo Shinya. Tokyo: Kokusho Kankōkai.

———. 1992b "Nijū-isseiki no sō wo kōsō suru." (Designing funerals for the twenty-first century). *Bukkyō* 20 (July): 168–70.

Idota, Hirofumi. 1993. "Saishi jōkō no kaisei to hōkōzō" (The amendment to the articles on worship and the legal structure). In *Kazoku no hō to rekishi* (History and family law), edited by Idota Hirofumi, 183–213. Kyoto: Sekai Shisōsha.

Ikeda Yōichirō. 1998. "Sōgi no kiyomejio yamemasu: 'shi wa kegare' wo hitei." (The halt of the salt-purification rite in funeral ceremonies: Denial of the concept of death impurity). In *Asahi Shimbun* (Asahi newspaper), 8 September.

Inoguchi Shōji. 1954. *Bukkyō izen* (Before Buddhism). Tokyo: Kokin Shoin.

———. 1959. "Sōshiki" (Funerals). *Nihon Minzokugaku Taikei* (Japanese folklore studies)(Tokyo), no. 4: 291–329.

———. 1965. *Nihon no sōshiki* (Japanese death ritual). Tokyo: Hayakawa Shobō.

———, ed. 1979. *Sōsōbosei Kenkyūshūsei.* Vol. 2: *Sōsōgirei* (A collection of funeral and grave studies: Funeral rituals). Tokyo: Meicho Shuppan.

Inose, Naoki. 1987. *Shiwo mitsumeru shigoto* (An occupation that faces death). Tokyo: Shinchōsha.

Inoue Haruyo. 1990. *Gendai ohaka jijō, yureru kazoku no nakade* (Contemporary placement of graves with shifting families). Osaka: Sōgensha.

Inoue Shōichi. 1990. *Reikyūsha no Tanjō* (The birth of the hearse). Tokyo: Asahi Shimbunsha.

———. 1994. *Ima sōgi ohakaga kawaru* (Funerals and graves are changing now). Tokyo: Sanseidō.

Itō Mikiharu. 1974. *Inasaku girei no kenkyū* (The study of agricultural rituals). Tokyo: Jiritsu Shobō.

Johnson, Coleen Leahy. 1974. "Gift Giving and Reciprocity Among the Japanese in Honolulu." *American Ethnologist* no. 2: 295–308.

Johnson, Elizabeth L. 1988. "Grieving for the Dead, Grieving for the Living: Funeral Laments of Hakka Women." In *Death Ritual in Late Imperial and Modern China*, edited by James L. Watson and Evelyn S. Rawski, 135–63. Berkeley: University of California Press.

Kaji Nobuyuki. 1990. *Jukyō towa nanika?* (What is Confucianism?). Tokyo: Chūōkōronsha.

Keizai Kikakuchō Chōsakyoku, ed. 1994. *Keizai-youlan* (Economic survey). Office of General Affairs, Census Bureau. Tokyo: Ōkurashō Insatsukyoku.

Kirby, R. J. 1911. "Ancestor Worship in Japan." *Transactions of the Asiatic Society of Japan* no. 38: 233–67.

Kita-Kyūshūshi Hokenkyoku (Kita-Kyūshūshi Health Department). 1992. *Eisei Tōkei Nenpō* (Statistics on health). Kita-Kyūshū Health Department. Kita-Kyūshū: Kita-Kyūshūshi Hokenkyoku.

Kita-Kyūshūshi Kyōikuiinkai (Kita-Kyūshū Education Committee), ed. 1988. *Kita-Kyūshūshi minzokuchōsa hōkokusho* (Report on the investigations of customs in Kita-Kyūshū). Vols. 1, 2. Kita-Kyūshū: Bunshindō.

Kitagawa, M. Joseph. 1987. *On Understanding Japanese Religion*. Princeton, N.J.: Princeton University Press.

Kopytoff, Igor. 1986. "The Cultural Biography of Things: Commoditization as Process." In *The Social Life of Things*, edited by Arjun Appadurai, 64–91. Cambridge, Eng.: Cambridge University Press.

Kosugi Teppei. 1992. *Sōshiki* (The funeral). Tokyo: Asahi-Shimbunsha.

Kotler, Philip, Swee Hoon Ang, Siew Meng Leong, and Chin Tiong Tan. 1996. *Marketing Management: An Asian Perspective*. New York: Prentice Hall.

Kübler-Ross, Elisabeth. 1969. *On Death and Dying*. New York: Macmillan.

Kurata Ichirō. 1979. "Kōden no konjaku" (The past and present of Kōden). In *Sōsō Kenkyūshūsei*. Vol. 2: Sōsōgirei (A collection of funeral and grave studies: Funeral rituals), edited by Inoguchi Shōji, 219–25. Tokyo: Meicho Shuppan.

Lay, Hyde Arthur. 1891. "Japanese Funeral Rites." *Transactions of the Asiatic Society of Japan* no. 19: 507–44.

Leach, Edmund. 1976. *Culture and Communication*. New York: Cambridge University Press.

Malinowski, Bronislaw. 1954. [1925] *Magic, Science and Religion and Other Essays*. New York: Anchor Books.

Marx, Karl, and Frederick Engels. 1978. *The Marx-Engels Reader*. New York: W. W. Norton.

Matsudaira Narimitsu. 1963. "The Concept of Tamashii in Japan." In *Studies in Japanese Folklore*, edited by Richard M. Dorson, 181–97. Bloomington: Indiana University Press.

Matsunami, Kodo. 1992. *Sekaino Sōshiki* (Funerals of the world). Tokyo: Shinchōsha.

Mauss, Marcel. 1990. [1950] *The Gift*. Trans. W. D. Halls. New York: W. W. Norton.

McCracken, Grant. 1986. "Culture and Consumption: A Theoretical Account of the Structure and Movement of the Cultural Meaning of Consumer Goods." *Journal of Consumer Research* no. 13: 71–84.

———. 1988. *Culture & Consumption*. Bloomington: Indiana University.

Metcalf, Peter. 1982. *A Borneo Journey into Death*. Philadelphia: University of Pennsylvania Press.

———, and Richard Huntington, eds. 1991. *Celebrations of Death: The Anthropology of Mortuary Ritual*. New York: Cambridge University Press.

Middleton, John. 1982. "Lugbara Death." In *Death and the Regeneration of Life*, edited by Maurice Bloch and Jonathan Parry, 134–54. New York: Cambridge University Press.

Miller, Daniel. 1987. *Material Culture and Mass Consumption*. New York: Basil Blackwell.

Ministry of Justice Japan. 1960. *The Constitution and Criminal Statutes of Japan*. Tokyo: Ministry of Justice.

———. 1962. *The Civil Code of Japan*. Tokyo: Ministry of Justice.

Mitford, Jessica. 1963. *The American Way of Death*. New York: Simon & Schuster.

Miyata Noboru. 1979. *Kami no minzokushi* (The folklore history of Kami). Tokyo: Iwanami Shoten.

Mogami Takayoshi. 1959. "Shigo no matsuri oyobi bosei" (Afterlife rituals and the grave system). *Nihon Minzokugaku Taikei* (Japanese folklore studies) (Tokyo), no. 4: 331–61.

———. 1963. "The Double-Grave System." In *Studies in Japanese Folklore*, edited by Richard M. Dorson, 167–80. Bloomington: Indiana University Press.

———. 1979. "Muenbotokeni tsuite" (Concerning wandering spirits). In *Sōsōboseishūsei*. Vol. 3: *Senzokuyō* (Research on funeral and burial traditions: Ancestor worship), edited by Takeda Choshu, 386–93. Tokyo: Meicho Shuppan.

———, ed. 1979. *Sōsōbosei Kenkyūshūsei*. Vol. 4: *Hakano shūzoku*. (Research on funeral and burial traditions: Grave customs). Tokyo: Meicho Shuppan.

Moji-kyodokai-kaihō. 1961. *Moji ga Seki* (Moji Peninsula). Moji: Moji-Kyodokai.

Moore, Sally Falk. 1981. "Chagga 'Customary' Law and the Property of the Dead." In *Mortality and Immortality: The Anthropology and Archaeology of Death*, edited by S. C. Humphreys and Helen King, 225–48. New York: Academic Press.

———. 1986. *Social Facts and Fabrications: "Customary" Law on Kilimanjaro, 1880–1980*. New York: Cambridge University Press.

Mori Kenji. 1994. "Ideology toshiteno sosensaishi to haka." (Ancestor worship and graves as an ideology). In *Hakakarano jiyū*, edited by Sōsōno jiyū wo Susumerukai, 49–73. Tokyo: Hakaihyōronsha.

Mori Senzō. 1969. *Meiji Tokyo Itsubunshi* (Unheard stories of Tokyo during Meiji). Vol. 1. Tokyo: Heibonsha.

Murakami, Kyōkō. 1991a. "Sōgi no kindaika to sōsaigyō no hensen" (The modernization of funeral ceremonies and the transformation of the funeral profession.) *Sōgi* 1, no. 1: 75–79.

———. 1991b. "Toshika, kindaika to sōsō girei no henyō" (Urbanization, modernization and the transformation of death rituals). *Sōgi* 1, no. 4: 105–9.

———. 1992a. "Sōgi hihanron no hihanteki kōsatsu" (A critical analysis of funeral criticisms). *Bukkyō* 20 (July): 171–80.

———. 1992b. "Sōgi to iu kōi wo dō yomi tokuka: Part I." (How to analyze the funeral ceremony). *Sōgi* 2, no. 4: 101–5.

———. 1992c. "Sōgi to iu kōi wo dō yomi tokuka: Part II." (How to analyze the funeral ceremony). *Sōgi* 2, no. 5: 101–5.

Naikaku Sōridaijin Kanbō Kōhōshitsu (Office of the Prime Minister, Bureau of Public Relations). 1992. *Yoron-chōsa-nenkan* (Annual public research). Tokyo: Ōkurashō Insatsukyoku.

Nakajō Takako. 1991. *Tezukuri-Sōshiki* (Home-made funeral). Osaka: Kansaishoin.

Nakamura Ikuo. 1988. *Kami to hito no seishinshi* (The cosmological history of deity and people). Kyoto: Jinbun Shoin.

Nakane Chie. 1967. *Kinship and Economic Organization in Rural Japan.* New York: Humanities Press.

Nakano Eizō. 1970. *Yusen no rekishi* (The history of bathing). Tokyo: Yūzankaku.

Namihira Emiko. 1974. "A Study on the Structure of Japanese Folk Belief." *Nihon Minzokugaku Kenkyū* 38, nos. 3 and 4: 230–56.

———. 1992. "Sōgi to gurīfu serapī" (Funeral and grief therapy). *Bukkyō* 20 (July): 50–58.

Naquin, Susan. 1988. "Funerals in North China: Uniformity and Variation." In *Death Ritual in Late Imperial and Modern China,* edited by James L. Watson and Evelyn S. Rawski, 37–70. Berkeley: University of California Press.

NLI Research Institute. 1994. *Nihon no kazoku wa dō kawattanoka* (How Japanese families have changed). Tokyo: NHK Shuppan.

Norbeck, Edward. 1954. *Takashima: A Japanese Fishing Village.* Salt Lake City: University of Utah Press.

———. 1978. *Country to City: The Urbanization of a Japanese Hamlet.* Salt Lake City: University of Utah Press.

Ōbayashi Taryō. 1977. *Sōsei no kigen* (The origins of the death ritual). Tokyo: Kadokawa Shoten.

Ochiai Shigeru. 1973. *Arau bunkashiwa* (Cultural stories of washing). Tokyo: Kaōsekken.

———. 1986. *Arau fūzokushi* (The history of washing). Tokyo: Miraisha.

Ogawa Eiji. 1993. "Korekara no tera to haka" (The future of temples and graves). *Sōgi* 3, no. 6: 39–42.

Ohnuki-Tierney, Emiko. 1993. *Rice as Self: Japanese Identities Through Time.* Princeton, N.J.: Princeton University Press.

Ooms, Herman. 1967. "The Religion of the Household: A Case Study of Ancestor Worship in Japan." *Contemporary Religions in Japan* 8, nos. 3 and 4: 201–333.

———. 1976. "A Structural Analysis of Japanese Ancestral Rites and Beliefs." In *Ancestors*, edited by William H. Newell. The Hague: Mouton.

Orikuchi Shinobu. 1955a. [1929] "Reikon no hanashi" (The story of the soul). In *Orikuchi Shinobu Zenshū* (Collected works of Orikuchi Shinobu), vol. 3: 260–76. Tokyo: Chūōkōronsha.

———. 1955b. [1952] "Minzoku shikan ni okeru takai kannen" (The cosmology of death in ethnohistory). In *Orikuchi Shinobu Zenshū* (Collected works of Orikuchi Shinobu), vol. 16: 309–66. Tokyo: Chuokoronsha.

Palgi, Phyllis, and Henry Abramovitch, eds. 1984. "Death: A Cross-Cultural Perspective." *Annual Review of Anthropology* no. 13: 385–417.

Palmore, Erdman. 1975. *The Honorable Elders*. Durham, N.C.: Duke University Press.

Parry, Jonathan. 1982. "Sacrificial Death and the Necrophagous Ascetic." In *Death and the Regeneration of Life*, edited by Maurice Bloch and Jonathan Parry, 74–110. New York: Cambridge University Press.

———. 1994. *Death in Banaras*. New York: Cambridge University Press.

Pine, V. R. 1975. *Caretaker of the Dead: The American Funeral Director*. New York: Wiley.

Plath, David W. 1964. "Where the Family of God Is the Family: The Role of the Dead in Japanese Households." *American Anthropologies* no. 66: 300–317.

Radcliffe-Brown, Alfred. 1965. [1952] *Structure and Function in Primitive Society*. New York: Free Press.

Reader, Ian. 1991. *Religion in Contemporary Japan*. Honolulu: University of Hawaii Press.

Rohlen, Thomas P. 1974. *For Harmony and Strength: Japanese White-Collar Organization in Anthropological Perspective*. Berkeley: University of California Press.

Sabata Toyoyuki. 1991. *Kasōno Bunka* (The culture of cremation). Tokyo: Shinchōsha.

Sahlins, Marshall. 1972. *Stone Age Economics*. New York: Aldine De Gruyter.

———. 1976. *Culture and Practical Reason*. Chicago: University of Chicago Press.

Saitō Tama. 1986. *Shito Mononoke* (Death and evil spirits). Tokyo: Shinjuku Shobō.

Sakai Toshihiko. 1933. [1903] *Sakai Toshihiko Zenshū* (Collected works of Sakai Toshihiko). Vol. 1. Tokyo: Chūōkōronsha.

Sakurai Tokutarō. 1968. *Nihonjin no sei to shi* (Life and death of the Japanese). Tokyo: Iwasaki Bijutsusha.

———. 1981. "Kesshū no genten: Minzokugaku kara tsuikyūshita shochiiki kyōdōtai kōsei no paradaimu" (The source of solidarity: A search for a paradigm for the structure of corporate groups). In *Shisō no bōken* (Explorations into thought structure), edited by Tsurumi Kazuko and Ichii Saburō, 187–234. Tokyo: Chikuma Shobō.

Sasaki Kōkan. 1993. *Hotoketo Tamano Jinruigaku* (The anthropology of the dead and the spirits). Tokyo: Shunjusha.

Sherry, John F., Jr. 1999. "Marketing and Consumer Behavior." In *Contemporary Marketing and Consumer Behavior*, edited by John F. Sherry Jr., 1–44. Thousand Oaks, Calif.: Sage Publications.

———, ed. 1995. *Contemporary Marketing and Consumer Behavior*. Thousand Oaks, Calif.: Sage Publications.

Shintani Takanori. 1985. "Ryōboseini tsuite" (About the double-grave system). *Nihon Mizokugaku* nos. 157–58: 28–38).

———. 1991. *Ryōbosei to takaikan* (Double-grave system and beliefs in the afterlife). Tokyo: Yoshikawa Kōbunkan.

———. 1992. *Nihonjin no Sōgi* (Death ceremonies of the Japanese). Tokyo: Kinokuniya Shoten.

Shizuoka Shimbun, ed. 1995. *Shizuoka ken no kankon sōsai* (Weddings and funerals in Shizuoka). Shizuoka: Shizuoka Shimbunsha.

Simmel, Georg. 1971. *On Individuality and Social Forms, Selected Writings*. Ed. Donald N. Levine. Chicago: University of Chicago Press.

———. 1990. [1978] *The Philosophy of Money*. Ed. David Frisby. Trans. Tom Bottomore and David Frisby. New York: Routledge.

Smith, Robert J. 1974. *Ancestor Worship in Contemporary Japan*. Stanford: Stanford University Press.

———. 1976. "Who Are the 'Ancestors' in Japan? A 1963 Census of Memorial Tablets." In *Ancestors*, edited by William H. Newell. The Hague: Mouton.

———. 1978. *Kurusu: The Price of Progress in a Japanese Village, 1951–1975*. Stanford: Stanford University Press.

———. 1987. "Gender Inequality in Contemporary Japan." *Journal of Japanese Studies* 13, no. 1: 1–25.

———. 1992. "The Living and the Dead in Japanese Popular Religion." Unpublished paper prepared for the Columbia University Modern Japan Seminar. 8 May 1992.

Smith, Thomas. 1977. *Nakahara: Family Farming and Population in a Japanese Village*. Stanford: Stanford University Press.

Sōgi. 1991. "Shinise tōjō: Hitoyanagi Sōgu Sōhonten" (The establishment of an old shop: Hitoyanagi Funeral Material Department). *Sōgi* 3, no. 3: 86–89.

———. 1993a. "Shinise tōjō: Kabushikigaisha Noiri." (The establishment of an old shop: Noiri Inc.). *Sōgi* 3, no. 4: 87–89.

———. 1993b. "Shinise tōjō: Itōtenreisha" (The establishment of an old shop: Itōtenrei company). *Sōgi* 3, no. 5: 81–84.

Sōsōbunka Kenkyūkai, ed. 1993. *Sōsō bunkaron* (Discussion of funeral culture). Tokyo: Kokin Shoin.

Strathern, Andrew. 1981. "Death Exchange: Two Melanesian Cases." In *Mortality and Immortality: The Anthropology and Archaeology of Death*, edited by S. C. Humphreys and Helen King, 205–23. New York: Academic Press.

Sudnow, David. 1967. *Passing On: The Social Organization of Dying*. Englewood Cliffs, N.J.: Prentice Hall.

Suenari Michio. 1992. "Higashi asia sanshakaino sōreini mirareru ishitsusei" (Different characteristics of funerals observed in three East Asian societies). In *Kanji bunkaken no rekishi to mirai* (The history and future of cultures based on characters), edited by Mizoguchi Yūzō et al. Tokyo: Taishū Shoten.

Suitō Makoto. 1991. *Chūsei no sōsō bosei* (The funerals and grave systems of the Middle Ages). Tokyo: Yoshikawa Kōbunkan.

Sullivan, Lawrence E. 1987. *Death, Afterlife, and the Soul*. New York: Macmillan.

Suzuki Hikaru. 1998. "Japanese Death Ritual in Transit: From Household Ancestors to Beloved Antecedents." *Journal of Contemporary Religion* 13, no. 2: 171–88.

Takahashi Shigeyuki. 1993. *Document: Gendai osōshikijijō* (The documentation of contemporary funerals). Tokyo: Rippu Shobō.

Takeda Chōshū. 1957. *Sosen Sūhai* (Ancestor worship). Kyoto: Heirakuji Shoten.

———. 1979. "Senzo kuyōno mondaishikaku" (Perspectives on the question of ancestor worship). In *Sōsōbosei Kenkyūshūsei*. Vol. 3: *Senzokuyō* (Research on funeral and burial traditions: Ancestor worship), edited by Takeda Chōshū, 11–42. Tokyo: Meicho Shuppan.

Takeda Katsuzō. 1967. *Furo to yuno hanashi* (Stories of the bath and bathing). Tokyo: Koshobō.

Takeuchi Yasuhiro. 1993. "Saishi shōkei ni okeru haka to hōritsu mondai" (Legal and grave problems in the inheritance of worship rights). In *Kazoku to haka* (Family and graves), edited by Fujii Masao, Yoshie Akio, and Komoto Mitsugi, 107–28. Tokyo: Waseda Shuppan.

Tamamuro Taijō. 1964. *Sōshiki Bukkyō* (Funeral Buddhism). Tokyo: Daihōrinkaku.

Tambiah, Stanley J. 1981. "A Performative Approach to Ritual." In *Proceedings of the British Academy 1979*, vol. 65: 113–69. London: Oxford University Press.

———. 1984. *The Buddhist Saints of the Forest and the Cult of Amulets*. New York: Cambridge University Press.

———. 1990. *Magic, Science, Religion, and the Scope of Rationality*. New York: Cambridge University Press.

Tanaka Hisao. 1979. *Sosen saishi no kenkyū* (A study of ancestral rituals). Tokyo: Kōbundo.

———. 1986. *Sosen saishi no rekishi to minzoku* (The history and folklore of ancestral rituals), edited by Tanaka Hisao. Tokyo: Kōbundo.

Taussig, T. Michael. 1980. *The Devil and Community Fetishism in South America*. Chapel Hill: University of North Carolina Press.

Thompson, Stuart F. 1988. "Death, Food, and Fertility." In *Death Ritual in Late Imperial and Modern China*, edited by James L. Watson and Evelyn S. Rawski, 71–108. Berkeley: University of California Press.

Traube, Elizabeth G. 1986. *Cosmology and Social Life: Ritual Exchange Among the Mambai of East Timor*. Chicago: University of Chicago Press.

Tsuboi Hirofumi. 1982. *Ine wo eranda nihonjin* (The Japanese who chose the rice plant). Tokyo: Miraisha.

———. 1983. "Nihonjin no saiseikan: inasaku nōmin to hatasaku nōmin no saiseigenri" (The concept of regeneration: The regeneration principles of the rice agriculture people and the field agriculture people). In *Nihon minzoku bunka taikei: Taiyō to tsuki, kodaijinno uchūkan to shiseikan* (Japanese folklore culture: The sun and the moon, the cosmology and the concept of afterlife among the ancient people). Vol. 2: 390–422. Tokyo Shōgakukan.

Turner, Victor. 1967. *The Forest of Symbols: Aspects of Ndembu Ritual.* Ithaca, N.Y.: Cornell University Press.

———. 1969. *The Ritual Process Structure and Anti-Structure.* Ithaca, N.Y.: Cornell University Press.

———. 1977. "Death and the Dead in the Pilgrimage Process." In *Religious Encounters with Death: Insights from the History and Anthropology of Religions,* edited by Frank E. Reynolds and Earle H. Waugh, 24–39. University Park: Pennsylvania State University Press.

Tylor, Edward Burnett. 1958. [1871] *The Origins of Culture.* New York: Harper & Row.

Urban, Glen L., and John R. Hauser. 1993. [1980] *Design and Marketing of New Products.* Englewood Cliffs, N.J.: Prentice Hall.

Van Gennep, Arnold. 1960. [1909] *The Rites of Passage.* Chicago: University of Chicago Press.

Vogel, F. Ezra. 1963. *Japan's New Middle Class: The Salary Man and His Family in a Tokyo Suburb.* Berkeley: University of California Press.

———. 1967. "Kinship Structure, Migration to the City, and Modernization." In *Aspects of Social Change in Modern Japan,* edited by Ronald Dore, 91–111. Princeton, N.J.: Princeton University Press.

Wakamori Tarō. 1981. "Nihon minzokugaku" (Japanese folklore). In *Wakamori Tarō chosakushū* (Collected works of Wakamori Tarō). Vol. 9: 199–255. Tokyo: Kōbundō.

Watson, James L. 1982. "Of Flesh and Bones: The Management of Death Pollution in Cantonese Society." In *Death and the Regeneration of Life,* edited by Maurice Bloch and Jonathan Parry, 155–86. New York: Cambridge University Press.

———. 1988. "Funeral Specialists in Cantonese Society: Pollution, Performance, and Social Hierarchy." In *Death Ritual in Late*

Imperial and Modern China, edited by James L. Watson and Evelyn S. Rawski, 109–34. Berkeley: University of California Press.

———. 1989. Class lecture in Anthropology 296, "Chinese Society." Harvard University, Cambridge, Mass.

———, and Evelyn S. Rawski, eds. 1988. *Death Ritual in Late Imperial and Modern China.* Berkeley: University of California Press.

Watson, Rubie S. 1988. "Remembering the Dead: Graves and Politics in Southeastern China." In *Death Ritual in Late Imperial and Modern China*, edited by James L. Watson and Evelyn S. Rawski, 203–27. Berkeley: University of California Press.

Weber, Max. 1958. *The Protestant Ethic and the Spirit of Capitalism.* New York: Charles Scribner's Sons.

Wilk, Richard. 1995. "Learning to Be Local in Belize: Global Systems of Common Difference." In *Worlds Apart: Modernity Through the Prism of the Local*, edited by Daniel Miller, 110–33. London: Routledge.

Wolf, Arthur P. 1970. "Chinese Kinship and Mourning Dress." In *Family and Kinship in Chinese Society*, edited by Maurice Freedman. Stanford: Stanford University Press.

———. 1974. "Gods, Ghosts, and Ancestors." In *Religion and Ritual in Chinese Society*, edited by Arthur P. Wolf. Stanford: Stanford University Press.

Yagisawa Sōichi. 1994. "Kasōgijutsuno hensento genjō" (The transformation and current practices of cremation). In *Hakakarano jiyū*, edited by Sōsōno jiyū wo susumerukai, 125–48. Tokyo: Shakai hyoronsha.

Yamamoto Yūzō. 1948. *Robōno Ishi* (Roadside stone). Tokyo: Shinchōsha.

Yan Yunxiang. 1996. *The Flow of Gifts: Reciprocity and Social Networks in a Chinese Village.* Stanford: Stanford University Press.

Yanagita Kunio. 1937. *Sōsō shūzoku goi* (A glossary of funeral conventions). Tokyo: Minkan Denshō no Kai.

———. 1962a. [1928] "Daijōsai to kokumin" (Daijōsai ritual and citizens). In *Yanagita Kunio Shū* (Collected works of Yanagita Kunio), vol. 31: 373–75. Tokyo: Tsukuma Shobō.

———. 1962b. [1940] "Komeno chikara" (The power of rice). In

Yanagita Kunio Shū (Collected works of Yanagita Kunio), vol. 14: 24–58. Tokyo: Tsukuma Shobō.

———. 1963a. [1953] "Ine no sanya" (Parturient hut for rice). In *Yanagita Kunio Shū* (Collected works of Yanagita Kunio), vol. 1: 178–209. Tokyo: Tsukuma Shobō.

———. 1963b. "Meiji Taishō-shi: Sesōhen" (The history of Meiji and Taisho: Their social conditions). In *Yanagita Kunio Shū* (Collected works of Yanagita Kunio), vol. 24: 127–414. Tokyo: Tsukuma Shobō.

———. 1975a. [1925] "Sōsei no enkaku ni tsuite" (The historical process of death ritual). In *Yanagita Kunio-Shū* (Collected works of Yanagita Kunio), vol. 14: 289–306. Tokyo: Tsukuma Shobō.

———. 1975b. [1946] "Senzo no hanashi" (The story about ancestors). In *Yanagita Kunio-Shū* (Collected works of Yanagita Kunio), vol. 14: 164–281. Tokyo: Tsukuma Shobō.

———. 1975c. [1949] "Tamashii no yukue" (Whereabouts of souls). In *Yanagita Kunio-Shū* (Collected works of Yanagita Kunio), vol. 14: 282–88. Tokyo: Tsukuma Shobō.

Zenkoku Kankon Sōsai Gojokai Renmei (National Wedding and Funeral Mutual-Aid Association), ed. 1974. Zenkoku Kankon Sōsai Gojokai Renmei 25 nenno daidō (The history of the National Wedding and Funeral Mutual-Aid Association: 25 Years of great principles). Tokyo: Zenkoku Kankon Sōsai Gojokai Renmei.

Adam's apple, 233n8
Advertising, 197, 208
Afterlife, 33–38, 40, 46, 116
Age: of deceased, 80–81; of funeral professionals, 123
Ahern, Emily Martin, 19, 20, 224n4
Akata Mitsuo, 31, 35, 36–37
Akita prefecture, 37
Akoya, 226–27n8. *See also* Box roofs
Alcoholic beverages, 88, 119, 148. *See also* Sake
Alms-giving, 184–85
Altars: Buddhist, 31; cost of rental, 71–73; funeral, 43; postfuneral, 119; selection, 218–19; shrine, 42; size and quality, 97 table
Ancestor worship, 22, 30–33, 35–38, 40, 48, 171–72
Anise plants, 107
Appreciation by customers, 131–33, 156
Ash collectors, 157–67, 177
Ashes, 91–92, 117. *See also* Corpses; Cremation
Authenticity, 186, 187, 200

Bara, 20–21
Bathing rituals, 12, 27, 43, 154–57, 236n1, 236n2; commoditization of, 195–97; in contemporary funeral ceremonies, 65–66, 75–83; devel-

opment of, 184–85; marketing of, 179–202; modernization of, 189–90; production of, 185–91; psychology and, 186, 199, 202; sales, 192 table, 195 table; significance of to bereaved, 188–89
Beads, 66, 67, 229n3. *See also* Clothing
Beer, 119. *See also* Alcoholic beverages
Bereaved: clothing of, 45; conductors' relationship to, 144–45; reactions toward bathing ceremonies, 80–82; service to, 122, 139–40. *See also* Chief mourners
"Black pollution," 42
"Black shadow," 42
Bloch, Maurice, 25, 27, 28, 29
Bon. See Festival of the Dead
Bond-breaking rites, 17, 40–48, 93
"Bone-biting," 207
Bones, 117–18, 164–65, 232–33nn7,8,9
Borneo, Indonesia, 15
Box roofs, 43, 226–27n8
Bright-Light altar, 71
Bubun-shūkotsu, 233n9
Buddhahood, 40, 43, 48, 87, 225n12; and bathing ritual, 76–77; and posthumous names, 169
Buddhist death rituals, 31, 49, 63, 66, 93, 116

Buddhist sects, 236n12
Bunke, 30, 38

Candles, 43, 44, 227n9
Cantonese culture, 23–24
Capitalism, 204–5
Cards, notification, 73
Cemeteries, 174–75. *See also* Graves
Ceremony Special Car Service (CSC),
    75, 76, 154–56, 180, 185–94, 197,
    200
Chief mourners, 84, 91, 99, 102, 104,
    110, 113–14, 115, 117, 198
Ch'inan people, rules for worship,
    224n4
Chinese funerals, 19–21, 23, 108, 109–
    11, 198
Chōji. See Memorial addresses
Chōnaikai, 215
Chopsticks for picking up bones,
    232–33n7
Chūmon-seisho, 71
Chūnichi-Yūkōkyōkai, 110
Clothing, 45, 66–67, 76, 95, 231n14
Coffins, 43, 50; closing of, 101–2,
    110–11; and community funeral rit-
    uals, 46–47; placement of corpses
    in, 67, 79–80; placement of flowers
    in, 101, 148; selection of, 63; treat-
    ment of, 230n7
Commercial funeral services, 3–5, 11,
    49, 61, 91–103, 207–10; and com-
    petition among funeral profession-
    als, 147; and concept of impurity,
    92–94; and interpersonal relations,
    210–12, 215–21; personalization of,
    119–20; and priests, 167, 170–76;
    purposes of, 177–78, 213–14; and
    standardization of ceremonies, 57–
    59. *See also* Modernization of
    funeral industry
Commoditization, 5–7, 11–13, 175–
    76, 181 fig., 183–202. *See also* Com-
    mercial funeral services

Community-based funerals, 4, 5, 8,
    11, 31; hierarchy in, 219; history of,
    38–59; interpersonal relations in,
    206–7, 210–12; shift away from,
    215–21; vigils, 89
Community cooperative. *See Kumi*
Company funerals, 103–6, 110, 142,
    209, 217, 232nn3,4
Competition among funeral conduc-
    tors, 143
Comprehensive services, 55, 56, 216
Conductors, 123, 138, 141–47, 150, 177
Consultation, 70–75
Consumers, 6, 7 fig., 12, 183
Consumption, 182, 191–202, 204–5,
    220
Contemporary funerals. *See*
    Commercial funeral services
Corpses: attitudes of living toward,
    16, 34–35, 38; handling and treat-
    ment of, 5, 10–11, 25, 55, 58, 60–
    90, 122, 127, 146, 150–52, 163, 216,
    228n19, 229–30n3, 233n3; picking
    up, 125–30; transportation of, 63–
    70, 102–3. *See also* Ashes; Bathing
    rituals; Cremation
Cosmology and Japanese death ritu-
    als, 27–30, 38
Cost of funerals, 57, 58, 70–75, 172–
    74, 216–19
Cremation, 4, 113–18, 153–54;
    attitudes toward, 11, 25–26, 61, 91–
    92; certificate for, 74, 113, 231n13;
    prohibition of, 228n20; rates, 235n5
Crematories and crematoriums, 52,
    53, 158–64, 234–35n2
Cremators, 157–67, 177
CSC. *See* Ceremony Special Car
    Service
Cultural values, 6, 7 fig., 12, 18–21;
    commoditization of, 181–83, 201–
    2, 205; in community funeral ritu-
    als, 206–7; homogenization, 219;
    interaction with producers and

DATE DUE